MW00914348

DAILY RECIPES for Simple Pleasures

DAILY RECIPES *for* Simple Pleasures

CORNERSTONE

239-9890 Fax 234-0381
8 Linsley St., North Haven, CT 06473

WORLD PUBLISHING

Grand Rapids, Michigan 49418 U.S.A.

Daily Recipe for Simple Pleasures

© 1996 by Dathene Stanley
Published by World Publishing, Inc.
Grand Rapids, MI 49418

All rights reserved. Except for brief quotations in printed reviews, no part of this publication may be reproduced, stored in a retrieval system or transmitted in any form or by any means (printed, written, photo-copying, visual, electronic, audio or otherwise), without the prior per-mission of the publisher.

Except where otherwise indicated, all Scripture quotations are from *God's Word*. *God's Word* is a trademark of God's Word to the Nations Bible Society and used by permission. *God's Word* is the name for **The Holy Bible: God's Word to the Nations** copyright © 1994 by God's Word to the Nations Bible Society. All rights reserved. Quotations from the New English Bible are followed by the designation *(NEB)*.

Permission granted for the use of "I, Too, Sing America" from *Selected Poems* by Langston Hughes. © 1926 by Alfred A. Knopf, Inc., and renewed 1954 by Langston Hughes. Reprinted by permission of the publisher.

Cover design by JMK & Associates, Grand Rapids, MI
Editing and interior design by Pinpoint Marketing, Kirkland, WA
Edited by Judy Bodmer. Designed by Scott Pinzon.
Drawings by Meg Hillary, Grand Rapids, MI

ISBN 0-529-10693-0

Library of Congress Catalog Card Number 96-60872

Printed in the United States of America

1 2 3 4 5 6 7   02 01 00 99 98 97 96

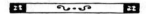

Dedication

To my loving and supportive family, and
to my mother, whose creativity
continues to inspire me.

Feed the Birds

SCRIPTURE: *Matthew 10: 29 – 31*
KEY VERSE: *Aren't two sparrows sold for a penny? Not one of them will fall to the ground without your Father's permission.*

A haunting scene in *Mary Poppins* shows pigeons crowding around an old woman in front of Saint Paul's Cathedral. "Feed the birds! Feed the birds!" The woman lifts her voice and holds out her bags of crumbs. "Only tuppence! Tuppence a bag!"

Long before the bird woman in *Mary Poppins* pled with strangers to take pity on the birds, Jesus said that the Heavenly Father intimately knows each one. As the fictional bird woman intuitively sensed, even a pigeon has value. Today imitate the Father by caring for his birds.

Pity a pair of cardinals who frequent the tall pine in front of the house and use your tuppence to buy birdseed. Throw sunflower seeds to purple finch gathered on the back yard fence, or scatter crumbs for a family of sparrows on the front sidewalk. Save leftover bread for the brave chickadees who spend the winter foraging through ice and snow. Give a handout to pigeons congregating in city streets.

Go a step further and attract birds all winter with a commercial or homemade bird feeder. Which birds frequent your neighborhood? Make or buy your feeder with their needs in mind. For an even better bird show this winter, provide several types of feeders.

 How does one become like God? Perhaps respect for all living creatures is high on the list of God-like attributes. The bird woman in front of Saint Paul's Cathedral had the right idea. Today spend your tuppence. Feed the birds.

Listen to the Wind

SCRIPTURE: *Psalm 18: 7 - 15*
KEY VERSE: *He rode on one of the angels as he flew, and he soared on the wings of the wind.*

> Who has seen the wind?
> Neither you nor I:
> But when the trees bow down their heads,
> The wind is passing by.

I n this poem, Christina Rossetti tells us what we already know; we do not see wind. We only see its effects. But we hear the wind, for it speaks. Sometimes it sings; sometimes it cries. There are times when it whispers and moments when it screams. It knows how to soothe and how to irritate.

What is the wind saying today? Listen to its voice as it rushes through the air and blows through the trees. Detect moaning or laughing, coaxing or nagging, hear animals or elves in the air. Hear your thoughts.

In your mind trace the path of the wind winding your thoughts back across seas and plains, over mountain peaks and down narrow valleys. Follow it from Asia to North America, from Mexico to Oklahoma, from Canada to Maine. Listen to it whistle over the Himalayas, roar through the crowded streets of Calcutta, flap a sail on the Gulf of Siam. Hear it sing to southern climes and menace northern ones.

Listen to God who began the winds, sends them, directs their course. Hear the music of creation, the sound of centuries, the pulse of eternity. For a moment creatively connect with God and his universe.

January 3

Happiness List

Scripture: *Psalm 23*
Key verse: *My cup overflows.*

When deafening thunder sent the baron's children scurrying to Maria's bedroom in *The Sound of Music*, she sang to them about her favorite things. Long ago the psalmist wrote about his cup running over. How full is your cup? Today measure your blessings by making a list of your favorite things.

Do whiskers on kittens give you pleasure, or do you delight in the eager lick of a frolicking puppy? Do your eyes light up when you see apple strudel, or does chocolate cake or steaming berry cobbler make the day sparkle? Does soft rain put you in a dreamy mood, or do fat flakes drifting from a white sky fill you with ecstasy? Whatever it is which fills your cup with happiness, name it.

Anything goes. The sound of wind in the trees. Working in the flower beds on a spring morning. Dinner out. Wading in the surf. Baking bread. Whatever it is that makes you happy is a blessing.

Very simple pleasures may fill your cup. The lace-edged half slip you like to wear. The small leather bound *Sonnets from the Portuguese* on your bedside table. A hot tub filled with bubble bath. The deep purple sweater which feels baby soft against your skin.

The contents of your cup is a portrait of who you are, for you are what you enjoy. Look into the cup and take pleasure in what you see. This image of yourself is more accurate than the one you see in the bathroom mirror, for this one reflects your inner qualities. Today appreciate both the special person you are and the special things which give you happiness.

Like the psalmist, give thanks for a cup full and running over.

January 4

Outing

Scripture: *Matthew 6: 25 – 34*
Key verse: *So I tell you to stop worrying about what you will eat, drink, or wear. Isn't life more than food and the body more than clothes?*

I n one of her poems, Elizabeth Barrett Browning describes a moment when life transcended daily demands:

> The little cares that fretted me,
> I lost them yesterday,
> Among the fields above the sea,
> Among the winds at play;...

Like her, today take an outing and find a larger world. Lose your own little cares, or even your big ones, among the fields and breezes or along country roads or even city streets.

Although most of us shed our belief in magic long ago, we tell ourselves someday we are going to do wonderful things, visit wonderful places, follow wonderful whims. Too often someday never arrives. It didn't happen yesterday, and as long as we continue waiting, it won't happen today, and it won't happen tomorrow.

Stop waiting. Make today that someday. Take that relaxing drive beside a stream in the countryside. Attend a special event advertised in the newspaper. Spend a few minutes in the local gallery you've recommended to others but haven't seen yourself. Attend a concert. Visit a village or neighborhood which has always sounded intriguing.

"Life is more than food and the body more than clothes," Jesus said. Today add that something more. Fall under the spell of a pristine, snow-filled meadow or the beauty of stained glass windows in an old church. Watch for the blue jay, listen to a brook gurgling beneath the ice.

Hear the sound of rain beating against the roof of the car. Lose your little cares today, and let a larger world fill you with larger thoughts. Make this a day of renewal.

January 5

Use Silver

SCRIPTURE: *2 Timothy 2: 20 - 21*
KEY VERSE: *In a large house there are not only objects made of gold and silver, but also those of wood and clay.*

> Bobby Shaftoe's gone to sea,
> Silver buckles on his knee,
> He'll come back and marry me,
> Pretty Bobby Shaftoe.

Four thousand years before Bobby Shaftoe wore silver on his knee, it accompanied kings to their tombs. It also lured explorers to the New World. When Francisco Pizarro captured Atahualpa, he set the Inca leader's ransom at 13,000 pounds of gold and 26,000 pounds of silver. Silver still remains precious enough to hand down, mother to daughter.

Today remind yourself of sterling qualities in your life by setting a table with your silver service. Most of the year we opt for the practical advantages of stainless steel, but today do not be practical. Be elegant. Make luxury and beauty a priority, and take time to dine rather than eat.

If you have pieces handed down by loved ones, picture a day when your once-young grandmother lined them up around your grandfather's plate. Feel a link with the past as you use pieces also treasured by generations before you.

If silver appears on your table daily, use stainless steel today. Although some of God's gifts appear sterling, others seem so ordinary we underestimate their value. Remind yourself these humbler gifts are equally valuable in God's kingdom.

New Bread Recipe

SCRIPTURE: *Matthew 6: 9 – 13*
KEY VERSE: *Give us our daily bread today.*

> Hot cross buns!
> Hot cross buns!
> One a penny, two a penny,
> Hot cross buns!

D id the call or the smell send English housewives running to the baker's cart? Bakeries have an advantage over other shops, for their aroma draws us. Since the dawn of history, that smell has satisfied some inner need of man. When early Egyptians discovered they could produce light, high loaves by fermenting the dough, they unlocked wonderful aromas. When they constructed ovens to bake the bread, they intensified the smells.

Our daily bread fills more than our stomachs. Its aroma fills our senses, comforting and exciting us. The hearth which emits that aroma is a happy, inviting hearth, especially in these dark winter months when bitter winds drive us indoors. Today fill the house with the smell of freshly baked bread.

Immigrants who populated this nation brought bread recipes from all over the world. These recipes, handed down from mother to daughter, eventually made their way into cookbooks. Today draw from this multi-ethnic heritage. Make German rye or Swedish cardamom bread, a crusty Italian or a Czechoslovakian caraway loaf, a Greek Easter bread or even a Middle Eastern flatbread.

Jesus grew up in a culture different from our own, and the bread his mother made was not like the white loaves familiar to us. Draw closer to the Jesus who walked the roads of Palestine by making the bread of another culture. Connect with the "us" in "Give us our daily bread."

January 7

Behold the Stars

SCRIPTURE: *Psalm 8*
KEY VERSE: *When I look at your heavens, the creation of your fingers, the moon and the stars that you have set in place...*

S ince 1806, every generation of children has loved and memorized these lines from Jane Taylor's poem published in that year:

> Twinkle, twinkle, little star,
> How I wonder what you are!
> Up above the world so high,
> Like a diamond in the sky.

Our fascination with the stars is much older. Many of the psalms reflect the awe of the shepherd boy so familiar with the heavens that he knew the place of each star. Two thousand years ago, he put his thoughts into the words of a psalm: "When I look at your heavens, the creation of your fingers, the moon and the stars that you have set in place— what is a mortal that you remember him?..."

Although we remain earthbound, gazing into a heaven filled with stars gives us a sense of eternity. We need this perspective, for so much of our lives is spent with the small details of living that we ignore the grand scale of life. The heavens connect us to infinity.

Tonight go out and gaze at a million stars twinkling over the iced world, and let them speak their message to you. Feel the presence and love of the Creator God who fashioned both you and the stars.

January 8

Clean Out a Drawer

SCRIPTURE: *Philippians 3: 7 - 11*
KEY VERSE: *These things that I once considered valuable, I now consider worthless for Christ.*

M any pioneers who settled the West left behind every thing which did not fit into their covered wagons. In one of her books, Laura Ingalls Wilder describes a Christmas when a new cup was enough to make the holiday wonderful.

John Wesley is one who found a heavenly treasure which far outweighed early possessions. It is said that when he died, his possessions consisted of a change of linen, a knife and a spoon.

In contrast to the simple lifestyles of past generations, clutter is an outstanding characteristic of today's society. Few of us are immune to its attraction, and we find ourselves in a love/hate relationship with things. On one hand, we profess a desire for a simple lifestyle, and on the other hand, we continue to buy and accumulate. Our compulsion to possess absorbs both our time and our energy, distracting us from heavenly values.

Today take one minuscule step towards a simpler lifestyle. Clean out a drawer. Throw away what should be thrown away, give away what can be used by someone else. Or begin a collection for the next yard sale.

One drawer will not rid us of clutter, but it may be enough to open our eyes to the truth of Paul's statement. Like him, we may decide to eagerly let go of even more clutter to make room for the treasure within our reach. Renewal could begin with one drawer.

January 9

Hot Bath

SCRIPTURE: *Isaiah 43: 18 – 21*
KEY VERSE: *Forget what happened in the past, and do not dwell on events from long ago.*

B y my troth, Nerissa, my little body is a-weary of this great world."Although we do not use the language of Shakespeare, we may echo the words of Portia in *The Merchant of Venice*. We, too, grow weary of this great world. We grow weary of routine and sameness, and we long for something new.

Routine is important; it creates order out of chaos. God began creating by establishing a routine of night and day. But God cannot be called a routine God. He is neither bored nor boring. He is constantly making all things new.

Boredom signals a need for change, and Isaiah tells us that God is trying to bring about the change in us. We often resist change because it produces stress. While complaining of boredom, we hold on to comfortable, predictable patterns which offer security. Ideally, we want things to change while they remain the same. Isaiah says that is not the way God works. We must let go of one thing to receive another.

Since small changes are less threatening, they are more comfortable and easier to make than big ones. Yet, even the smallest change pierces the concrete patterns of the past and sets in motion the process of renewal.

Today make a small break with the past by changing your bathing routine. Rather than jump into the shower, soak in a tub of hot water. Or if you are a bath person, today experience the stimulation of a shower. Make a change by doing the opposite of what you usually do.

Take Isaiah's words to heart. For a day make a symbolic break with the past and let go of a small fraction of routine. Prepare to receive the something new God has for you.

January 10

Nursing Home

SCRIPTURE: *Matthew 25: 31 – 46*
KEY VERSE: *"The king will answer them, 'I can guarantee this truth: Whatever you did for one of my brothers or sisters, no matter how unimportant they seemed, you did for me.'"*

I f God cares, why do vacant-eyed men and women sit strapped to wheelchairs in hallways of nursing homes? We neither know nor understand. However, Jesus tells us that God himself feels the pain and the alienation of those vacant-eyed ones. When we reach out to them, we reach out to him.

Today reach out with a visit to a nursing home or a shut-in. Take something with you, even if it is only the picture of a blue elephant your four-year-old painted yesterday. A touch of youth is a welcome addition to a nursing home, and an elephant with two legs is almost guaranteed to elicit smiles from those who have little reason to smile. Make the visit even more memorable by taking the four-year-old who did the painting.

If you lack a four-year-old, find another way to carry cheer. Become popular on an entire ward by taking a double batch of chocolate chip cookies. Soften institutional rooms with cheerful yellow daisies. Add new thoughts to old routines with the stack of magazines which has been piling up in your house.

As a boy, Jesus may have carried loaves of freshly baked bread to an elderly neighbor. But as a man he carried the gift of a listening ear. Today also carry that gift. Let a ninety-five-year-old man tell about the days when he walked fifteen miles to see a movie. Hear the story of the twelve-year-old whose mother died leaving her in charge of the household. Draw out treasures tucked away in the memories of gray haired men and women.

Take a gift to the elderly, and walk away with a gift from the King.

January 11

Letter to a Child

SCRIPTURE: *Matthew 18: 1 - 7*
KEY VERSE: *Then he said to them, "I can guarantee this truth: Unless you change and become like little children, you will never enter the kingdom of heaven.*

> The friendly cow all red and white,
> I love with all my heart:
> She gives me cream with all her might,
> To eat with apple-tart.

Like Robert Louis Stevenson, can you remember the things you loved in childhood? Water was for splashing and smooth stones for collecting. Bubbles brought joy, rainbows held magic, and pretend food tasted as good as real food.

Jesus said unless we become as little children, we will not enter the kingdom of heaven. Today re-enter the world of childhood long enough to write a letter to a child.

Write like a child. Use the concrete and be specific. As you describe a day at the beach, tell how cold the waves felt, how high they splashed, how noisy were the gulls, and how many sand castles you counted. Mention the white-sailed boats bobbing on the water and the hermit crabs scurrying over the sand.

When learning to talk, toddlers don't waste time on adjectives, adverbs, or prepositions. They concentrate on action. Daddy work. Baby cry. Lady sweep. Like these verb-centered toddlers, keep the focus on action. Make your sea gulls skim the water or steal the bread or stare at the waves.

If a child cannot himself touch, smell, or hear, he loses

17

interest. Therefore, allow your child to hear waves crashing on the rocks. Make traffic beep and airplanes roar on your page. Capture the smell of chocolate chip cookies on your stationery.

Today turn around, become like a child, and take a small step into the kingdom of heaven.

January 12

Hang Laundry Outdoors

SCRIPTURE: *Psalm 74: 12 - 17*
KEY VERSE: *You created summer and winter.*

> O, wert thou in the cauld blast,
> On yonder lea, on yonder lea;
> My plaidie to the angry airt,
> I'd shelter thee, I'd shelter thee.

Like Robert Burns, when we think of the cauld blast, we think of shelter. Avoiding raw winds and piercing cold outdoors, we gratefully toss wet laundry into clothes dryers instead of drying it outside. Yet, we ski in winter, and we shop in inclement weather. We take the dog out for his walk. So why not hang clothes outside on the line?

Poets praise the golden days of summer. But winter is an equally beautiful gift from the Creator, and cabin fever is the price we pay for ignoring his gift of cold. Today embrace the gift. As you admire the winter world, pin wet laundry to the outside clothes line. Delight in crystal clear skies and a docile sun. Thrill to pewter clouds announcing another storm. Through bare branches, scan the landscape and detect treasures hidden in summer by foliage. Breathe deeply and fill your lungs with oxygen.

When you fold the line-dried laundry, press it to your cheek, and once again breathe the outdoor air still clinging to the clothes. Put line-dried sheets on your bed and tuck

18

the fragrance of outdoors into your dreams. Wrap yourself in winter's gift, then gratefully whisper with the psalmist, "You determined all the boundaries of the earth. You created summer and winter."

January 13

Use a Foreign Language

SCRIPTURE: *Acts 2: 1 - 12*
KEY VERSE: *All the believers were filled with the Holy Spirit and began to speak in other languages as the Spirit gave them the ability to speak.*

The streets of Los Angeles, New York, or any of our big cities today resemble the streets of Jerusalem at the time of Pentecost, for in them the languages of the world can be heard. In Los Angeles over one hundred-forty languages are spoken daily. In even the most remote hamlet of our country, there is usually at least one recent immigrant who still speaks the language of his native country.

At Pentecost the apostles had a message to share. Through the Holy Spirit, God empowered them to communicate it in the native languages of the assembled crowd. Too often we insist that foreigners learn English in order to communicate with us. But we have a story of love to share, and we can hasten communication by learning their language.

Avez-vous oubli, tout le français que vous avez appris? Se le olvidó hablar en español? Have you forgotten all your high school French or Spanish? Today retrieve a fraction of it by reading something in a language you once learned.

If you have never studied a foreign language, begin today. With a library book, learn to say, "Guten Morgen, Fräulein. Ist hier das Postamt?" or "Sognefijorden er den lengste av Norges fjorder." Or learn a few phrases of Italian or Portuguese or Japanese or whatever language has long intrigued you.

The world, in all of its great diversity, has come to our land. Today better prepare yourself to communicate the wonderful message of God's love.

January 14

New Dinner Guest

SCRIPTURE: *Roman 12: 9 – 16*
KEY VERSE: *Share what you have with God's people who are in need. Be hospitable.*

> Polly, put the kettle on,
> Polly, put the kettle on,
> Polly, put the kettle on,
> And we'll all have tea.

In New Testament days it was juice, water, or wine, but the ritual of entertaining was important enough that Paul urged the early Christians to practice hospitality.

Many of us want to offer the world our theology when what it wants is our friendship. Without the friendship, the theology often has a hollow ring. Sharing a meal together is the time-honored way of developing and nurturing friendship. Hospitality opens wide the windows of friendship. Today look through a new window by inviting a new dinner guest into your home. Let your theology live in your deeds as powerfully as it lives on your tongue.

Sometimes we associate entertaining with elaborate meals accompanied by the best china, crystal, and linens. Whether we serve Chicken Cordon Bleu on Royal Doulton or dish up another plate of spaghetti on plastic plates, the dinner is a success when we graciously share ourselves and allow our guests to share themselves.

Jesus redefined wealth as participation in a Kingdom

characterized by love. Friends are a major source of wealth. The wider the circle of friends, the greater is our wealth.

By sharing a meal with someone who has not yet eaten in your home, today enlarge your friendship circle and increase your wealth. Benefit from a new exchange of thoughts and insights. Let God speak through your hospitality.

January 15

Use a Globe or Map

SCRIPTURE: *John 3: 16 – 21*
KEY VERSE: *God loved the world this way: He gave his only Son so that everyone who believes in him will not die but will have eternal life.*

It's a "Small World, After All." Disneyland delightfully proclaims what Christians should already know. Begotten by one Father, we are all brothers and sisters in one small world.

Since the world is so small, after all, it is surprising that we know so few of our global neighbors. Although more or less familiar with countries often mentioned in the evening news, most of us have little knowledge of the rest of the two hundred countries in our global community which never make the news.

Using a globe, locate Togo, Central African Republic, or Malawi which you hear mentioned in the news. Unfold the large world map and identify Guatemala where immigrants in your neighborhood once lived. Discover small countries like Croatia, Laos, and Armenia which have sent refugees to our land. As you study the globe or map, envision the billions of people who share life on this earth. For a moment picture yourself as one of five billion people and the United States as one of almost two hundred countries. The message of

the New Testament is that regardless of our cultural, geographic, or political environment, we are equally important to God.

Forgetting this message, we easily become self-centered and nationalistic to the point where we become blind to the value of diversity. Today appreciate the marvelous diversity of God's world. Enjoy being a global citizen.

January 16

Photo Composition

SCRIPTURE: *Matthew 11:2 - 6*
KEY VERSE: *Blind people see again,...*

Surrounded by beauty every instant of our lives, we often are oblivious to it. Having 20/20 vision is no guarantee that we will see the magnificence of a sunrise or the breathtaking spectacle of a sunset. Regardless of physical sight, we are spiritually blind when we miss the beauty around us, whether it is the gleam of sunlight on dried grasses or the golden hue of long evening rays. To eat bananas, oranges, and apples without seeing color and texture is to be vision impaired.

However, we often see secondhand what we fail to see first hand. We fail to watch the full moons rise over the place where we are, but we stand in awe before an Ansel Adams photograph of a moonlit night. Although we did not explore the meadows in springtime, we pause before the picture of poppies in the window of the photography shop.

It is easy to depend on the eyes of others who capture and record beauty for us. But today do your own seeing.

Take a photo of at least one beautiful thing which has captured your eye. Seen through the eyes of an artist, the basket of onions and potatoes on the kitchen counter may suddenly strike you as beautiful. The icicle hanging from a bush outside the kitchen window may be enough to forever remind you of the beauty of the winter world. Whatever you photograph, let your heart tell your eye what is good.

Today acknowledge your own blindness and your need of healing. Recover some of your lost sight, and capture it in a photograph.

Read an Old Testament Book

SCRIPTURE: *Psalm 119: 97 – 105*
KEY VERSE: *Your word is a lamp for my feet and a light for my path.*

> There was a Young Woman named Bright,
> Whose speed was much faster than light.
> She set out one day
> In a relative way,
> And returned on the previous night.

Perhaps we can't quite manage that one. But if we used more of our light, we would undoubtedly go faster—and perhaps even further. Today set out—in a relative way—and reach a previous night. Explore one ray of light held in a book of the Old Testament.

The books of the Old Testament once held all the available light for those seeking God. Nahum, Habakkuk, or Zephaniah can still throw light on today's different, but paradoxically, similar world. Today use one of these less familiar lamps.

After a lifetime of Bible reading, some of us have yet to discover and use the light available in many of the once-upon-a-time stories of the Old Testament. Most of us have a few favorite Bible passages which we shine on our paths like flashlights in the night. But by clinging to those trusted passages, we may miss the rays of light caught between other pages.

Like all great literature, the Bible mirrors the human situation. The Bible does more than articulate the human dilemma; it points to a way out of it. Although the specifics have changed over the centuries, mankind has not changed, nor has God changed. Today apply old words to a new setting. Once-upon-a-time often sounds strangely like today.

January 18

Visit a Cemetery

SCRIPTURE: *Hebrews 12: 1 - 2*
KEY VERSE: *Since we are surrounded by so many examples of faith, we must get rid of everything that slows us down, especially sin that distracts us. We must run the race that lies ahead of us and never give up.*

Me *toca a mi. C'est mon tour.* It's my turn. Whether the words are Spanish, French, or English; Swahili, Chinese, or Russian, the meaning is the same. Living involves taking turns.

Today wander through an old graveyard, read faded names on leaning tombstones, and remember that we even take turns inhabiting this spinning planet we call earth. Momentarily connect with Elisas, Jasons, and Elizabeths who have already had their turn.

January's frigid temperatures recall the world of past generations. These men and women braved winter with no central heat, indoor plumbing, or plush cars to insulate them from wind, rain, and storm. Many of them died young. Count the years between their birth and death, and feel the pain of losing infants, the grief of motherless families left behind, the struggles of fatherless ones.

Connect the dates on the tombstones with the social and political events of that time. If history is not your strong point, do some research. What epidemics decimated the people of this village? What famines abroad motivated families to cross an ocean and forge a new life in the wilderness? Was the nation immersed in civil war, fighting for independence, or struggling to reconstruct? How did this affect those who once walked where you walk?

Today is our turn. Yesterday it was their turn. Appreciate the sacrifices and endeavors of those now gone, and recognize soon we too will be gone. Ask yourself what you are leaving for those whose turn is next.

January 19

New Song

SCRIPTURE: *Psalm 40: 1 - 5*
KEY VERSE: *He placed a new song in my mouth, a song of praise to our God.*

> Sing a song of sixpence,
> A pocket full of rye,
> Four-and-twenty blackbirds
> Baked in a pie.

Have you ever held a sixpence, had a pocket full of rye, or seen a blackbird baked in a pie? Probably not. Nor has your mother or grandmother. But we still chant the song to our infants and toddlers.

Yesterday's songs expressed yesterday's experiences. But why continue to sing about blackbirds in a pie when new things are happening in our lives? Today is a new day, so celebrate it with a new song.

What do you catch yourself humming? It may depend on your generation. "Sweet Hour of Prayer" and "Shine, Jesus, Shine" come out of different generations and often date our entry into faith. But whatever automatically comes to mind may be so familiar we sing it without thinking about the message. Sometimes, it takes new words to communicate the old message of God's wonderful love. Today step out of your generational slot, move forward or move backward, and find a new song to sing.

Or play it. Retrieve the old flute or clarinet from the attic closet and brush up on your rusty skills. If you have no instrument to dig out of the cobwebs, listen to a new recording.

Today worship creatively. Sing a new song to the Lord and freshen your vision and commitment.

January 20

Recognition

Scripture: *Philippians 1: 3 - 11*
Key verse: *I thank my God for all the memories I have of you. Every time I pray for all of you, I do it with joy.*

H ow interconnected we are." What labor went into our ability to grasp those words! Like most words we use, they trace one path of human history. Ancient Phoenicians developed the alphabet which gave them meaning. In China, Ts'ai Lun created a sheet of paper, and someone else discovered ink. Gutenberg invented a printing press, and Webster facilitated spelling.

More recently, a first grade teacher taught us to decipher the mystery of how, we, and are. Perhaps a sixth grade teacher introduced the word interconnected, and an eighth grade teacher put it in a context we could understand.

The Gospel puts the word into still another context. One Father created us all, loves us all equally, and continually works to redeem all of us. The Bible tells us God is love. His inclusive love binds us together in both joy and pain. Any time we work for the good of another, we benefit ourselves. When we hurt another, we hurt ourselves.

Paul recognized both the debt of love he owed others and the one they owed him. Today acknowledge how indebted you are to others, and like Paul, articulate it. Say thank you to someone whose labors enrich your life.

Tell the mechanic who worked late Friday night repairing your car engine how much you appreciate his sacrifice of family time. Comment on the charming bulletin boards your child's teacher creates. Let city officials know how much you enjoy the new park facility. Write a note of appreciation to a store manager who sells only wholesome magazines.

Today enhance some blessing by thanking the one who made it possible.

January 21

Pray for the World's Children

Scripture: *Matthew 18: 10 – 14*
Key verse: *In the same way, your Father in heaven does not want one of these little ones to be lost.*

> Mother's arms under you,
> Her eyes above you;
> Sing it high, sing it low,
> Love me—I love you.

The state of our world's children is not always as Christina Rossetti pictures, or as our Heavenly Father wills. Every day almost 40,000 children under the age of five die. As many as ten million children are caught up in the sex industry, and in the United States alone there are an estimated 150,000 child prostitutes.

Today pray for these innocent victims of our troubled world. Let your mind dwell on the ones living in Africa, in India, in China, in all the continents and countries of the world. Think of the starving ones, the disturbed ones, the gifted ones. Think of the love and the pain which Jesus feels as he tenderly holds the hand of each child.

Recall the children you know personally, the ones in

your family, neighborhood, and church. Cry over the ones who come from dysfunctional families and the ones whose lives are already marked by neglect or abuse. Give thanks for those blessed with good families and secure homes, and pray that they will somehow be a blessing to the other ones.

Today hold up to God both the blessed and the un-blessed children of the world, and feel his compassion and his pain. Ask him what he wants you to do for the children of the world; the ones you know and the ones you don't know.

Today create a bigger place for compassion in your life.

January 22

Speak to a Foreigner

SCRIPTURE: *Ephesians 2: 11 - 19*
KEY VERSE: *That is why you are no longer foreigners and outsiders but citizens together with God's people and members of God's family.*

> Father, Mother, and Me,
> Sister and Auntie say
> All the people like us are We
> And everyone else is They ...

As this verse written by Rudyard Kipling describes, the secular world divides people geographically and cul-turally. To those who belong to the kingdom of God all people are "part of the family." Today do something to make someone feel like "one of the family."

Does your community sponsor a Hmong refugee or a Russian immigrant family? Almost every community has at least one immigrant in its midst. Today befriend one of these new arrivals you meet in the grocery store, on the sidewalk, or in your child's classroom. God's love knows no national boundaries. Let his love shine through your acceptance of those who came to this land seeking a better life.

A smile is universal in meaning. Even the non-English speaking immigrant understands the words, "Hello. How are you?" Any friendly gesture eases the alienation and loneliness which usually follow immigration.

Most of us come from immigrant stock. This blending of cultures and experience has enriched our nation. Each new immigrant has a special gift to add to our individual and collective lives, but only open hands and open hearts know how to receive the gift.

Since being creative is being different, every immigrant to this country increases our potential for diverse, creative living. He or she also opens a new window into the kingdom of God.

January 23

ℛesearch

Scripture: *Proverbs 1: 29 - 32*
Key verse: *Fools destroy themselves because of their indifference.*

> "The time has come," the Walrus said,
> "To talk of many things:
> Of shoes—and ships—and sealing wax—
> Of cabbages—and kings—
> Of why the sea is boiling hot—
> And whether pigs have wings."

What did Lewis Carroll know that we don't know? Most of us would be at a disadvantage in such a conversation. Perhaps we would have to keep steering the talk back to shoes, for there we have a little expertise.

Or we could do a little research. But then, who cares about cabbages and kings or whether pigs have wings? Obviously the walrus—and perhaps a child, but the rest of us are rather indifferent.

Jesus said that in order to enter the kingdom of heaven we must all be childlike. Children's questions go on non-stop as they discover the world and their place in it. But many of us stopped asking questions when we stepped out of childhood. In their place, we substituted faith in experts and opted for living vicariously on second hand knowledge.

Questions open the door of creativity at any age. Today, like a child, begin wondering about the world, and then follow through with research. What about cabbages? How many countries have kings? What is the name of the mountain peak you see from your kitchen window? What is the diameter of the sun? Why are some children more violent than others? Does spanking really help?

Today live more fully by replacing indifference with healthy curiosity.

January 24

Potpourri

Scripture: *1 Chronicles 9: 25 – 32*
Key verse: *Some of the priests' sons prepared the mixture of spices.*

E arly people worked hard to make the house of God as pleasant as they could. We think of the church as God's house, and we continue to make it as pleasant as we can. However, when Christ dwells in us, even the house where we live becomes God's house. Today do something to make your own little House of God more pleasant.

Like the priests of old, blend spices. Potpourri, a French word, means a blending of fragrant flowers and spices. Commercial potpourri mixes have four basic ingredients: dried flowers and/or herbs, spices, essential oils, and a fixative. If you are a gardener, you may already have bags of dried rose petals, lavender stems, and rosemary, thyme, and mint leaves. If not, browse through the shelves of a specialty store to find scents which intrigue you.

Begin by combining a fixative such as orris root powder with an essential oil such as vanilla or lavender. Add this to the dried flowers or herbs, cover, and let set for several days. Then add the spices, cover again, and leave undisturbed for another week or two.

Winter's long dark days have special need of cheer, and the fragrance of cranberry or sandalwood throughout the house dispels some of the gloom of dark days. A lingering scent of lavender, rose, or lilac preserves a touch of summer regardless of how low the thermometer falls.

Dark days need not be gloomy ones. Add a pleasant aroma to your own house of God.

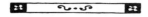

January 25

Write the President

SCRIPTURE: *Jeremiah 8: 9 - 12*
KEY VERSE: *All of them, from the least important to the most important, are eager to make money dishonestly.*

It is said that evil conquers when good men do nothing. Although most of us regret the world's injustice, we feel powerless to change it. We are not policy makers, we do not control the national purse strings, and we have no inside influence. As a result, we often tolerate the intolerable.

Today refuse to tolerate injustice. Like Jeremiah, make your voice heard. The opinions of voters make a difference, for most elected officials make decisions which will get them reelected. Not only the president's office, but each congressman keeps a tally of the number of people who write or call to support or oppose an issue.

Jeremiah was not popular with those who wielded power because he accused them of using their power for their own gain. More than two thousand years later, we still label prophets of doom as Jeremiahs. But without contemporary Jeremiahs, whitewashed injustice will continue to rob the poor, create a climate of violence, and breed war.

The squeaky wheel gets the oil. Too often that wheel is special interest groups who, like those of Jeremiah's day, have an eye out for their own profit. Today be a Jeremiah and speak on behalf of the have-nots of our world.

What policies are contributing to injustice, poverty and corruption? What bills are now on the President's desk? Address these issues. The biggest oak began as a little acorn. Today plant a seed of justice by writing the President.

January 26

A Visit

SCRIPTURE: *Philippians 2: 1 - 4*
KEY VERSE: *Don't be concerned only about your own interests, but also be concerned about the interests of others.*

In "A Time to Talk," Robert Frost tells about putting aside his hoe for a friendly visit when a friend calls out to him. In contrast, many of us frantically hoe our plots day after day as the world passes unnoticed. Meant to be a tool, the hoe has become a master.

Paul tells us to look to others' interest and not merely to our own. Often we do not even know who those others are. We are engrossed with our hoe, our neighbors are engrossed with theirs, and we remain strangers to one another. However, life is more fun among friends than among strangers. Today begin following Paul's advice by turning the face of one stranger into a friend.

Our mobile society produces millions of unconnected people, and while we hoe our plots, they experience one lonely day after another. Connect with even one of these millions and break one chain of loneliness.

There was an old woman
  who lived in a shoe;
She had so many children,
  she didn't know what to do.
She gave them some broth
  without any bread
And whipped them all soundly
  and put them to bed.

In a society where dysfunctional homes are becoming the norm, friendship may achieve what condemnation can never do. Reach out to a struggling young mother whose hoe is too short and too dull.

Today leave your fields long enough to have a good visit with someone. Look to the interest of another person.

January 27

ℒ𝒾ght a ℱire

SCRIPTURE: *Psalms 107: 10 - 14*
KEY VERSE: *Those who lived in the dark, in death's shadow were prisoners in misery.*

Turn up the lights,
I don't want to go home in the dark.

L ike the man in O. Henry's "The Unprofitable Servant," most living things seek light. When long winter evenings imprison us in darkness, our spirits rebel and become more vulnerable to depression. One of man's greatest gifts is his ability to make fire.

"Fire! Give me fire, man cub!" Louis, King of the Gorillas, pleads with Mowgli in Disney's version of *Jungle Book*.

From the earliest times, man has found emotional comfort in a fire which provides warmth and light. For centuries it was a campfire; then it was a fireplace. Tonight chase darkness and depression with a fire in the fireplace.

Draw a chair close to the hearth, and watch flames leap and curl. Open fires have ignited the thoughts and dreams of great men like David who tended his father's sheep, Socrates who pondered the universe, and Abraham Lincoln who deciphered the words in a book. Perhaps we too have thoughts and dreams waiting to be ignited.

We may sometimes feel ourselves prisoners of circumstances, background, or failure. Tonight let dancing flames create light in your darkness and fire in your soul. Let God set your spirit free.

If you do not have a fireplace, light a candle. Is it not better to light one candle than to curse the darkness?

January 28

Identify a New Constellation

SCRIPTURE: *Job 9: 5 - 10*
KEY VERSE: *He made the constellations Ursa Major, Orion, and the Pleiades, and the clusters of stars in the south.*

> Star light, star bright,
> First star I see tonight;
> Wish I may, wish I might
> Have the wish I wish tonight.

Most of us have a name for that first star. We call it Venus. God created and man named. One of the first acts of man was to name the animals. Early man also named the stars in the night sky. As he looked up, his creativity took over, and his eye grouped the stars to form pictures. Then he made up stories to go along with the pictures.

The need to name the world is one of the marks of man. Consider the delight of a small child in naming familiar objects and learning names of unfamiliar ones. Pooh Bear may be the all-time favorite bear of children, perhaps because he has a name. Naming our world puts us into an intimate relationship with it. We care about what we name.

Like the psalmist, Job saw God's hand in the night sky. He too called the stars by name as he worshiped the Creator who set them in place. From the beginning of time, the night sky has inspired wonder and awe in man. We enhance the awe and wonder when we name the stars.

Tonight claim more of the starry heavens by giving names to what you see. Before entering the frigid night, study a star chart and locate new constellations in relationship to star groups which you can already identify.

Once having identified a constellation, forever afterwards it is a friend. Like early man, feel closer to the Creator by naming his stars.

January 29

Character Sketch

Scripture: *Psalm 139: 13 – 17*
Key verse: *I will give thanks to you because I have been so amazingly and miraculously made.*

> Jenny kissed me when we met,
>   Jumping from the chair she sat in;
> Time, you thief, who love to get
>   Sweets into your list, put that in!
> Say I'm weary, say I'm sad,
>   Say that health and wealth have missed me,
> Say I'm growing old, but add,
>   Jenny kissed me.

People are people. But James Henry Leigh Hunt's Jenny is no Tom Sawyer, and in *Little Women* Jo is very different from Beth. Jane Eyre does not have the same personality as Anne of Green Gables or Victor Hugo's Cosette.

Like our fingerprints—and perhaps our kisses—we

come one of a kind, each of us expressing God's creativity. Our wealth lies in the value we give each other.

Today increase your own wealth by appreciating more deeply the gift of life in another person. Try to capture that gift on paper. Physical appearance gives clues to identity, for we are flesh as well as spirit. As with Jenny's kiss, our actions and reactions reveal our real identities, for behind them lie our values, hopes, or fears.

There is a direct relationship between appreciating ourselves and appreciating others. As we learn to accept others, we begin accepting ourselves. The reverse is also true. Once we accept our mixture of strengths and weaknesses, we become more tolerant of others.

Grow closer to God by greater appreciation of one of the greatest miracles of creation: man made in his likeness.

January 30

Memorize a Psalm

Scripture: *Colossians 3: 12 – 17*
Key verse: *Use psalms, hymns, and spiritual songs to teach and instruct yourselves about God's kindness. Sing to God in your hearts.*

> The Lord is my shepherd.
> I am never in need.
> He makes me lie down in green pastures....

A child runs away. A husband is unfaithful. A daughter is raped. We feel rejected by one we had felt to be a friend. There are times when anguish is so intense we have no words to express the pain.

At other moments joy defies expression. How does one put a sunset or a love into words? The first time a baby is held in her mother's arms? Feeling the presence of the Creator as one stands beneath the stars?

Words often elude us. However, in these moments the psalms have articulated both the agony and the ecstasy for countless people throughout the centuries. On the cross, the most painful moment the world has ever known, Jesus expressed inexpressible anguish in the words of a psalm.

Psalm 23 may be the most quoted Bible passage. However, all the psalms are wonderful affirmations of trust in a God who is both powerful and caring. Today memorize one of these great affirmations of faith.

Our creativity is a reflection of God's image. But too often we are out of touch with that reflection. Because they articulate our feelings, the psalms free up creativity by putting us more in touch with both ourselves and the power of the universe. Contact with that power always increases our own power and creativity.

Today become more creative by praising God with words written almost three thousand years ago.

January 31

Telephone Call

SCRIPTURE: *Colossians 4: 5 - 6*
KEY VERSE: *Everything you say should be kind and well thought out so that you know how to answer everyone.*

> Freeze, freeze, thou bitter sky,
> That dost not bite so nigh
> As benefits forgot;
> Though thou the waters warp,
> Thy sting is not so sharp
> As friend rememb'red not.

Our friends need not experience the tragedy of Shakespeare's words in *As You Like It*. With a dial of the phone, we can let friends in Hawaii, Kansas, or Maine know we remember them. We can instantly touch base with loved ones in Ecuador, India, or Zaire.

Since most of the earth lies only a telephone call away, why do we so easily lose touch with the important people in our lives? Sometimes telemarketers claim more phone time than a best friend from high school days. It is not that we prefer to talk to telemarketers. But we usually take the time to answer a ringing phone, while we wait for a convenient moment to make our calls.

Today make the time rather than wait for it. Ring someone important in your life, whether a friend from church or a sibling who lives on the other side of the country. For five minutes, or twenty-five minutes, forget that you are running behind schedule. Be present with the one you call and make stronger the ties which bind you.

One of the most creative ways to handle a hectic schedule is to step out of it for a few minutes. Today restore your poise with time out to graciously remember a valued friend or loved one.

February 1

Spiced Coffee or Tea

SCRIPTURE: *1 Kings 10: 10 - 13*
KEY VERSE: *Never again was such a large quantity of spices brought into Israel as those that the queen of Sheba gave King Solomon.*

When the Queen of Sheba planned her visit to wealthy King Solomon, she chose her gifts carefully. Among precious stones and talents of gold was a quantity of spices which impressed even the king who seemed to have everything.

Three thousand years later, spices still have their allure. Even before we understood what spice was, we paid it tribute by chanting, "What are little girls made of? Sugar and spice, and everything nice."

Throughout history, the allure of spices has led men over land and sea in search of cinnamon and cloves, cardamom and ginger, nutmeg and cloves. For these Bartholomeu Dias rounded the Cape of Good Hope and Columbus set sail across the Atlantic. The Spice Islands beckoned, and one explorer followed another: da Gama, Cabral, Cabot, Magellan, Sir Frances Drake. Most of them never saw the elusive islands, but they opened up the seas to new worlds, and the coveted spices eventually followed.

Long ago we gave up the little girls' chant, but we need not give up the allure. Today treat yourself to a cup of spiced tea or coffee. Enjoy flavors and aromas once reserved for royalty such as King Solomon and the Queen of Sheba.

Spices stimulate the taste buds, imbue the ordinary with zest, and bring cheer to winter's dark days. Imitate the Queen of Sheba and add spice to your life. Be queen for a day.

February 2

Picture Albums

SCRIPTURE: *Romans 16: 1 – 15*
KEY VERSE: *Greet my dear friend Epaenetus. He was the first person in the province of Asia to become a believer in Christ.*

> I thank all who have loved me in their hearts,
> With thanks and love from mine. Deep thanks to all
> Who paused a little near the prison-wall
> To hear my music in its louder parts
> Ere they went onward...

In this verse from her *Sonnets from the Portuguese*, Elizabeth Barrett Browning warmly remembers those who have loved her deeply.

Likewise, the faces which passed through Paul's mind

brought warm memories and deep encouragement. They recalled shared meals, labor, and worship. One was so dear he called her Mother.

We have an advantage Paul did not have, for cameras record the faces of those we love. We forfeit some of our advantage when we bury the faces in closed albums. Today leaf through old picture albums, and relive some of those moments which inspired the photographs.

Count your wealth as you examine once-upon-a-time little girls, once youthful parents, and old boyfriends who bring a smile to your face. Like Paul, give thanks for the people who have enriched your life.

Photo albums trace the stages of our lives. Be grateful for all stages, painful as well as joyous, for each made its contribution to growth and maturity. We learn from the heartaches as well as the joys.

Whatever your present situation, make it a happier one by remembering the good times of the past. Give thanks for friends—the ones you once had, the ones you still have, and the ones yet to come.

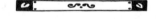

February 3

Browse in a Bookstore

SCRIPTURE: *Jeremiah 45: 1 – 5*
KEY VERSE: *This is the message that the prophet Jeremiah spoke to Baruch, son of Neriah. Baruch wrote these things on a scroll as Jeremiah dictated them during the fourth year that Jehoiakim, son of Josiah, was king of Judah.*

The Lord spoke not only to Baruch, but to millions of others who have read Jeremiah's words. We too have felt the power of the written word.

Do you remember a childhood Christmas when you crept down the stairs before anyone else was awake, found Johanna Spyri's *Heidi* under the Christmas tree, and immediately began reading? Perhaps you finished the tale of the little mountain girl before you went to bed that night. Or it may have been *Lassie* or *Little Women* that you found under the tree that morning.

How looked-forward-to was weekly library day at school when row after row of intriguing titles beckoned. The favorite hour of every day may have been the one after lunch when the teacher read aloud Kenneth Grahame's *Wind in the Willows* and Laura Ingalls Wilder's *Little House on the Prairie.*

What happened to this passion for books? It may be waiting to be rekindled. Within that dormant spore still lies the capacity to cry for a Lassie or to laugh uncontrollably at a Pippi Longstocking.

Engrossed in a good book, the here and now no longer poses limits. Words set in lines transport us to any world at any moment. Now, while evening is almost as long as day, rediscover this passion. Visit a book store, and find titles to turn dark hours into light ones.

The Lord continually sends us messages, many of them captured in words penned by others. We often see more clearly when looking at our own experiences through others' eyes. Today seek a message from the Lord.

Expectantly, even reverently, browse through the aisles of a bookstore.

February 4

High Tea

SCRIPTURE: *Mark 14: 22 – 25*
KEY VERSE: *"Take this; this is my body."*

W hen we share our food, we share ourselves. Early humans instinctively knew this; their bread represented their life. Their own hands tilled the soil, scattered the seed, cultivated, harvested, separated the wheat from the chaff, and ground the kernels into flour. Woman kneaded the dough, once again putting herself into the loaves which fed those she loved. When Jesus used the image of bread, his disciples understood the intimacy of his words.

As this winter evening encroaches on a short February day, share your food and yourself in a delightful British tradition called high tea. The venerable tea tradition in Britain is illustrated by the lady who sat under the table holding her cup of tea during a bombing raid in World War II.

Queen Victoria turned tea time into an elaborate affair and called it high tea. The rest of her kingdom soon followed. A light meal, high tea replaces supper or appeases the appetite when the dinner hour is a late one. In the English country side, thick slices of bread and cheese or a steak and kidney pie may make the tea a high one. A tray of sandwiches accompanied by tea and followed by dessert can also do it.

This afternoon or evening, create your own version. Bring out the fine china tea pot or silver tea service. Add elegance with cloth napkins. Whether you offer a tray of open face sandwiches, a thick piece of hot apple pie, or croissants, serve it with grace and warmth. Treat your family or friends to a touch of elegance introduced by one of Britain's remarkable queens.

Turn a dark February evening into a gracious and intimate sharing of yourself. Make it a small token of the meal Christ shared with his disciples and the life he continues to share with each of us. Be like him; offer yourself to another.

February 5

Exercise

SCRIPTURE: *Romans 6: 12 - 14*
KEY VERSE: *Offer all the parts of your body to God. Use them to do everything that God approves of.*

Little Boy Blue, come blow your horn;
The sheep's in the meadow, the cow's in the corn.
Where's the little boy that looks after the sheep?
He's under the haystack, fast asleep.

M any of us are Little Boy Blues. God's sheep wander over the meadow, but like Little Boy Blue, we are too tired to go find them.

Winter is the sitting time of the year. It should come as no surprise that it is also the tired time of the year. The more we sit, the less we feel like doing. But when we are too tired to do any more than we have to, life loses its creative edge. Tiredness drains the fun out of the hours.

Paul tells us to put our bodies at the disposal of God. Sedentary lifestyles easily turn our bodies into liabilities rather than assets for the Kingdom. Some of us need to stand up and begin moving.

Today chase fatigue by adding oxygen to the bloodstream. If you have long avoided any form of exercise, ease into it. A few toe touches, four or five sit-ups, and a dozen jumping jacks may be all flabby muscles and a lazy heart will tolerate.

If exercise is a regular part of your life, add something new. Work on tummy control or back strengthening exercises or weight lifting. Make your body an even greater asset to the kingdom.

Resist the extra cup of coffee when energy flags. Instead, do deep breathing exercises, run in place, or do a few jumping jacks. Chase fatigue, increase stamina, and turn your body into an asset.

We need to get in shape. The sheep have wandered so far into the meadow that we have a long way to run.

Clothing Inventory

SCRIPTURE: *1 Timothy 6: 5 - 8*
KEY VERSE: *As long as we have food and clothes, we should be satisfied.*

I n the famous fairy tale, a wave of a fairy godmother's wand changed Cinderella's rags into a gown so stunning that the prince fell for the girl who wore it. We may fantasize that our next purchase, like Cinderella's gown at the ball, will cause heads to turn when we enter a room.

Paul puts clothing in another light. The purpose of the gown is not to make heads turn, but to cover the body. However, we often fall prey to the fallacy that beautiful clothes make beautiful people. Hoping to impress, we spend and overspend, filling our closets rather than our souls.

Sometimes our efforts seem only to produce more rags—albeit expensive ones, for we still complain of having "nothing to wear." Although Cinderella had a fairy godmother, we do not, and no one is going to wave a magic wand over our rags—the ones that are too little or too big, too dressy or too gaudy, or too whatever.

Today turn a full closet into a useful one. Simplify by getting rid of the clothes you never wear and the ones that make you feel dowdy when you do wear them. Then make a list of the clothes you need to go with what is left. Plan mileage out of future purchases with a coordinated wardrobe.

Jesus said there is more to life than clothing. Even the fairy tales recognize that truth. Cinderella's sweet disposition brought a fairy godmother to her rescue, but the latest fashions wrought no miracle for the stepsisters with nasty dispositions.

Begin putting clothing into proper perspective; dress to meet needs rather than fantasies. Wear what you have handsomely.

February 7

Play Chess or Checkers

SCRIPTURE: *Proverbs 27: 17*
KEY VERSE: *As iron sharpens iron, so one person sharpens the wits of another.*

I t was no accident Solomon carved a kingdom in the ancient world or that Paul spread the news of the kingdom of God throughout the Roman world. Just as the well-prepared ground yields a greater harvest than the unprepared one, God can use a prepared mind better than a dull one. Thinkers like Solomon and Paul have a special place in God's plan.

The pharaohs of ancient Egypt sharpened their minds by playing checkers, and other thinkers in history have followed their lead. By the time the Pilgrims came to America, enough people in Europe played checkers that a book had been written on the subject.

Another mind-sharpening game, chess, began in another part of the world. Developed in China or India, it also found its way to Europe and became as popular as checkers. Over the centuries, both games have gained popularity, and today the maneuvers of world tournaments make the evening news.

Unlike children who sharpen their minds at school, adults must find or make their own opportunities. In automobiles, automatic gear shifts run efficiently, but minds set on automatic begin to atrophy. Creativity and growth evolve only out of change, so today shift gears, and like the ancient pharaohs, play a game of chess or checkers to sharpen the tool of your mind.

Solomon knew that victory depended upon wise strategy and planning. We often pray for victory, but expect God to drop seed into unprepared soil. Today bring out the kings and queens, and turn the soil of your thoughts a bit deeper. Line up knights and rooks, and till your mind with wise strategy and planning. Like wise men in all ages and like all wise teachers everywhere, turn work into play. Make a game of tilling the soil.

February 8

Fresh Flowers

SCRIPTURE: *Luke 12: 27 -31*
KEY VERSE: *Think of the lilies: they neither spin nor weave; yet I tell you, even Solomon in all his splendour was not attired like one of these. (NEB)*

> Daffodils,
> That come before the swallow dares, and take
> The winds of March with beauty;…

Who among us, like Perdita in Shakespeare's *Winter Tale*, has not dreamed of flowers while winter clings to the earth?

Spring parades pastels, summer splashes brilliant hues, and autumn sets fire to its colors. In contrast, winter offers a dull, impoverished landscape. Bare trees and empty fields greet us outdoors, and colorless living rooms greet us indoors. Problems which appear manageable among sun-splashed peony beds often take on the weight of slate skies in the colorless season.

When life seems overly complicated and frantic, we would do well to follow the advice of Jesus: consider the lilies. Recall a day in May when lemon lilies lit up a spring day or an afternoon in July when tiger lilies captured the rays of a generous sun. Extend your vision beyond passing gray skies and see the loving hand of a Father who provides in every season of life.

Go one step further. Not only consider the lilies, but bring them into your living room for a tangible reminder of Jesus' words. When the sun hides behind low gray clouds,

46

turn your eyes to the rays stored in yellow chrysanthemums, red carnations, or blooming narcissus.

Midwinter melancholy intensifies problems, but consider the lilies. In all seasons and in all circumstances, God is good.

February 9

Old Letters

SCRIPTURE: *Colossians 4: 10 – 18*
KEY VERSE: *After you have read this letter, read it in the church at Laodicea. Make sure that you also read the letter from Laodicea.*

E ven in prison, Paul was not passive. He spent his time writing letters which his friends read and reread before passing them on. Nineteen centuries later, we still read and reread them, finding fresh insight and new application to our situation with each reading.

In moments of need, we count on Paul's prison letters to encourage, strengthen, and instruct. But what about other letters, the personal ones written by the "Pauls" we have known? We may be overlooking their potential to also bring encouragement, strength, and wisdom.

Today forage through the old trunk in the attic and retrieve a bundle of old letters. While snow falls and winds howl, settle into a comfortable chair and re-read words once written just for you.

From a more distant perspective, appreciate the heartache and suffering which carved character out of those you love. Between the lines, see God's hand gently leading even through dark valleys. Appreciate warm thoughts and generous deeds of past years.

Epaphras, Aristarchus, Demas, and most of the people Paul mentioned are unknown to us. But they shaped the early church. The people mentioned in your bundle of letters made no headlines or history books, but they have influenced your life. Rereading their words may deepen that influence.

Every saved bundle is a witness of love. Today draw strength and encouragement from that love.

February 10

Seashells

SCRIPTURE: *Genesis 1: 20 – 23*
KEY VERSE: *So God created the large sea creatures, every type of creature that swims around in the water and every type of flying bird. God saw that they were good.*

> When I went down beside the sea
> A wooden spade they gave to me
> To dig the sandy shore.

We have dug our holes and built our castles beside the sea. And, as Robert Louis Stevenson experienced, the tide undid what we did. It did not rob us, for in exchange it left its shells.

Today spend a few minutes looking at these shells once found along a sandy shore. Hold a murex or a moon shell in your hand. Recall that once a living creature formed it in the depths of the great ocean. With your fingers trace the pattern of a conch or a sundial shell, and praise the Creator for the incredibly intricate world he has fashioned.

Consider the great ocean which cradled these shells. Envision the vast expanse of water stretching from shore to shore. Picture the swelling of the waves, and listen until you hear them crashing upon the shore. Reflect on how many of these small living creatures exist in all the oceans.

Like the sight of a night sky filled with myriads of stars, the thought of great oceans filled with these shelled creatures deepens our sense of who God is and of how incomprehensibly majestic he is. To examine a small shell is to remember all of life is a miracle.

It is also a reminder that God's creativity has no limits of size, shape, or color. Nor is he stingy with his gifts. On the contrary, he seems to delight in making all things new and different. As you examine shells, renew your own commitment to creativity and variety.

Breakfast Bread

SCRIPTURE: *Acts 27: 33 – 38*
KEY VERSE: *Just before daybreak Paul was encouraging everyone to have something to eat.*

By magnificently and brilliantly coloring the eastern sky, God begins each morning with celebration. Night has passed, once again day has broken, and the heavens shout with joy.

We do not always share God's enthusiasm. Our entrance into the day is more accurately characterized by a reluctant riser named Mary in this little nursery song:

> Lazy Mary, will you get up, will you get up,...
> Will you get up today?
> No, no, Mother, I won't get up, I won't get up,...
> I won't get up today.

Like the passengers on the ship adrift in the Sea of Adria, we sometimes awake panic-stricken by our troubles. All we can picture is our ship crashing upon the rocks.

Paul faced the same stormy sea, but he had a different picture. Putting his faith in God's protection, he urged his fellow passengers to eat so they would have strength to overcome the storm. Today imitate Paul. Believe that God will see you through any storm swelling the waves of your sea, and then celebrate the morning with a special break-fast bread.

Make a coffee cake and enjoy the aroma coming from the oven while you dress. Or plan to celebrate tomorrow morning with a yeast bread which takes more time. Today make a Bohemian braid, Swedish tea ring, or a Czechoslo-vakian vanocka filled with aniseeds, lemon, and almonds, or a prune filled kolache, and tomorrow morning reheat it for a special treat.

As God enthusiastically welcomes you to another day, respond with equal enthusiasm. Prove your faith by your celebration, and walk into the new day with joy.

February 12

£ine Drawings

SCRIPTURE: *Exodus 31: 1 - 11*
KEY VERSE: *I have filled him with divine spirit, making him skilful and ingenious, expert in every craft, and a master of design. (NEB)*

M oses connects the divine spirit with the artist Bezalel, but the same Divine Spirit has made an artist of each of us. The Creator of the universe has stamped beauty into every atom of the universe. Our love of beauty is simply a reflection of his image in us.

While other seasons express beauty in color, winter expresses it in simplicity. Never are nature's lines so obvious as in winter. In this month bare trees, denuded hills, and empty fields reveal the beauty of those lines.

Observe the simple lines of February's uncluttered landscape. Notice the beauty of a single head of dried grass protruding out of the snow-covered field, or of one dried leaf caught in a snowbank. Watch snowflakes fall on a swing set. Follow the lines of clumped birch in the meadow. Note sycamore balls hanging from bare limbs. Appreciate the exquisite icicle hanging from the kitchen roof.

Like Bezalel, Aholiab, and other skilled artisans of old, express the innate love of beauty which is God's gift to each of us. Choose some design from the winter world around you, and draw it with simple lines.

Although we are not called to design arks or stitch sacred vestments, in some sense we are all artists simply because we are created in God's image. Today exercise this gift and gain new appreciation for the beauty expressed in winter's simplicity.

As Jesus hung on the cross, the curtain of the ark was rent. A new covenant creates temples of each believer. The purpose of a temple is to worship, so like Bezalel, enhance praise and worship by expressing your own love of beauty.

February 13

ℐffirm a Clerk

SCRIPTURE: *Ephesians 4: 29 - 32*
KEY VERSE: *Don't say anything that would hurt another person. Instead, speak only what is good so that you can give help wherever it is needed. That way, what you say will help those who hear you.*

> Sticks and stones may break my bones,
> but little names can't hurt me.

We once delighted in chanting this little ditty to those who treaded on our dignity. But the chant is not entirely true, for the names others call us often shape our personalities. Likewise, the names we call others carry a blessing or a curse. Today accept that power and take Paul's words seriously.

"Clumsy ... Incompetent ... Why can't stores hire good clerks?" Does this sound vaguely familiar? Shopping seems to erode the gracious side of us, and checkout counters often breed less-than-Christian remarks.

Today dust off your checkout counter etiquette. When Paul urged his readers to utter only words good and helpful to the occasion, he probably meant in the market places of the Greek and Roman world as well as in the meeting houses of the new Christian congregations.

Regardless of long lines, mistakes in the transaction, or personal frustrations, affirm whatever clerk waits on you. Find something helpful to say as you wait for the store manager to correct a mistake on the cash register. Lighten the situation by being chatty and friendly. Ask if it has been a busy day, comment on the weather, or tell the clerk you like her loop earrings.

Often self-centered while shopping, we view clerks as part of the environment rather than as people like ourselves. Take Paul's words literally. At the cash register see a person whose feet ache, who dreads difficult customers, and who would love to be home taking care of the baby.

Take the Holy Spirit shopping with you. Graciously make the day better for at least one clerk today.

February 14

Write a Relative

SCRIPTURE: *Romans 1: 8 – 12*
KEY VERSE: *I long to see you to share a spiritual blessing with you so that you will be strengthened.*

I n Shakespeare's *Winter's Tale*, Camillo, a Sicilian Lord, speaks these words:

> They were trained together in their childhoods...
> That they have seemed to be together,
>   though absent;
> shook hands, as over a vast; and embraced, as it
> were, from the ends of opposed winds.
> The heavens continue their loves!

We too have childhood roots. But keeping in touch with one grandmother in Boston and another in Nebraska, an aunt in San Francisco, and cousins in Denmark, Japan, and Iowa challenges even the most family oriented among us. In an increasingly mobile society, sooner or later most of us lose contact with some of these relatives.

Paul had come to love his co-workers in the new congregations as dearly as if they were his own family. He often had to leave friends almost as soon as he grew to love them, and he deeply felt the pain of separation. However, he worked hard to keep mutual love intact through letters.

Almost forgotten strands of the past are woven into the fabric of our lives. If we lose touch with them, we lose touch with part of ourselves. Today rekindle affection by writing to a cousin who used to play kick-the-can with you. In a letter, remind your ninety-year-old grandmother of the paper dolls she once cut out of a catalogue for you. Send a card to a distant uncle who has just had a heart attack.

Like Paul, let loved ones know how much they mean to you.

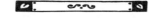

February 15

Handwork

SCRIPTURE: *Ephesians 2: 4 – 10*
KEY VERSE: *For we are God's handiwork, created in Christ Jesus to devote ourselves to the good deeds for which God has designed us. (NEB)*

When Eve stitched leaves together to make a garment, she introduced a new art. In the thousands of years since, women have expressed themselves by working with their hands. We honor these creative expressions, passing handwork down from generation to generation. However threadbare Grandmother's double wedding ring quilt may be, we still count the work of her hands among our treasures.

Likewise, God values his handiwork, and he counts us among his treasures. As the moon and the stars, the bee and the bird, the sea and the creatures of the sea, we too were fashioned by his hand. However, we have been given the gift of choice, even when our choices damage his handiwork. As we treasure a threadbare quilt, he continues to treasure us. Lovingly, he mends the torn edges, removes the stains, smooths out the wrinkles, and holds us to his cheek.

Our urge to create is simply a mark of his image. While February still keeps us inside much of the time, take advantage of housebound hours to create something with your hands. Bring out knitting needles or crochet hook, embroidery thread or a needlepoint pattern. Perhaps you have always wanted to know how to knit socks, crochet, or make dolls. Most knowledge is only one instruction book away, or possibly one neighbor away.

As you treasure what you create, think of how treasured each of us is by the hands which fashioned us.

February 16

Change Shelf Paper

SCRIPTURE: *2 Corinthians 5: 14 - 17*
KEY VERSE: *Whoever is a believer in Christ is a new creation. The old way of living has disappeared. A new way of living has come into existence.*

> None are so surely caught, when they are catch'd
> As wit turn'd fool...

When Shakespeare penned these thoughts in *Love's Labour's Lost*, he drew from real life. The most clever among us easily turns fool.

Likewise, the most devout easily turns shallow. Just as spring's intense green dulls with summer and disappears with fall, new life in Christ easily fades to the dull hues we see all around us. Nature does what we often fail to do— begin the cycle again.

Spring will not make its appearance for another month, but sap already stirs in the trees. While winter continues to send storms, nature anticipates new life. Today imitate nature. Examine the faded traces of new life in Christ and commit yourself to renewal. As a symbolic re-beginning, give your kitchen a cosmetic face-lift by lining old cupboards with new shelf paper.

Usher a touch of spring into the kitchen with dainty flowers on a soft background. Or add excitement with a bright, wild design. Give yourself a smile when you open the cupboards by lining them with a nursery print. Use new shelf paper to create any kind of mood which you would like to imitate in the inner room of your spirit.

Winter may still wrap the world in ice, but anticipate spring in your spirit. Make a simple change in your environment and dedicate yourself to deeper changes in your life.

February 17

Read a Children's Book

SCRIPTURE: *Luke 8: 49 – 56*
KEY VERSE: *But Jesus took her hand and called out, "Child, get up!"*

> When at home alone I sit
> And am very tired of it,
> I have just to shut my eyes
> To go sailing through the skies—
> To go sailing far away
> To the pleasant Land of Play.

Like Robert Louis Stevenson, perhaps long ago children in Palestine dreamed of the far away when the close at hand ceased to interest. And perhaps Jesus understood the thoughts and dreams of little ones. He often urged adults to become like them.

However, some of us have so lost touch with the child within that we no longer remember how to become like a child. Preoccupied by so much, we sometimes miss clues of the three-year-olds and ten-year-olds in our homes and neighborhoods. We need help to once again see life through a child's eyes, hear it through her ears, and ponder it through her mind.

As Jesus called the child back to life so long ago, today call the child within you back to life. Nourish your neglected child with some forgotten story from childhood and remember things you long ago forgot. Spend an enchanted hour re-reading *The Five Little Peppers* or *Little Women*. You may have discarded your own *Winnie-the-Pooh*, but find a copy in the library, and learn something from the bear of little brain who sees things we miss.

One feeding did not keep alive the child which Jesus called back to life. Nor will it be enough to keep alive the child within us. But it will remind us that there still is a child within us to feed.

February 18

Complaint-Free Day

SCRIPTURE: *Philippians 2: 14 – 18*
KEY VERSE: *Do everything without complaining or arguing.*

> Here's Sulky Sue;
> What shall we do?
> Turn her head to the wall
> Till she comes to.

P aul urges us to do all we have to do without complaint or wrangling so that we may shine like stars in a dark world. However, many of us resemble Sulky Sue in the familiar nursery rhyme more than we do the victorious Christian Paul describes. Some of us have never quite "come to," and we remain in the nursery with our faces to the wall.

With its inclement weather, winter offers a generous supply of complaint material. It also offers unique and exquisite gifts which we often ignore. Each time we choose to complain, we focus on the negative. Today make a conscious choice to concentrate on all that is positive. One thing after another may go wrong, but respond graciously.

God sometimes wraps his gift of children in muddy shoes, and we can focus on the mud or the gift. Even the fever which sends us to bed is God's gift to fight off a virus which has invaded our body. The toddler who spills the jug of milk while trying to pour herself a glassful is gaining the independence necessary for healthy living. Every gift is two-sided. We choose which side to hold face up.

Our complaints add no light to winter's darkness nor to humanity's darkness. Our thanksgivings shine like stars in a dark world. Take Paul's words to heart and sulk no longer.

February 19

Early Morning Walk

SCRIPTURE: *Psalm 92: 1 - 5*
KEY VERSE: *It is good to announce your mercy in the morning and your faithfulness in the evening.*

> Do you fear the force of the wind,
> The slash of the rain?
> Go face them and fight them,
> Be savage again...
> You'll grow ragged and weary and swarthy,
> But you'll walk like a man!

Hamlin Garland's challenge applies to women as well as men. By facing the elements and fighting them, we can begin walking like a woman.

This morning courageously face winter by taking an early morning walk. Put on enough clothing to maintain a comfortable body temperature and eagerly step into the cold. Feel the wind whip redness into your cheeks and push oxygen into your lungs.

Let a foggy dawn wrap you in softness, or thrill to the bright blue sky of a clear day. If still another February storm piles snow on tree and meadow, delight in exquisite thick flakes and ecstatically explore a fairylike world.

Hold hands with winter and enjoy the intimacy. As you walk across crusted fields, listen to the sound of boots crunching through ice. If rain falls, listen to tapping drops. Watch water trickle down the walk and enjoy the freshness of cold drops blowing in your face.

Declare God's love this morning by entering into the world he created. Then find yourself better prepared to proclaim his constancy this night.

February 20

Seed Catalogue

SCRIPTURE: *Galatians 6: 7 - 10*
KEY VERSE: *Make no mistake about this: You can never make a fool out of God. Whatever you plant is what you'll harvest.*

> When daffodils begin to peer,
> With heigh! the doxy over the dale
> Why, then comes in the sweet o' the year;
> For the red blood reigns in the winter's pale.

As in these words of Shakespeare's *Winter's Tale*, we associate flowers with the sweet of the year. This month we long for the first daffodil, and check for the first crocus.

But the crocus and the daffodil appear only if they have been planted. Paul tells us what we all know, but so easily forget: we reap what we sow. Most personal unhappiness announces we have sown the wrong kind of seed.

Seed catalogues not only set us dreaming over tulips, delphinium, and peonies, but they remind us we must plant if we want to reap. Today open up a catalogue or gardening book and dream away. Dreams planted in February have a good chance of taking root in May and June.

All beautiful gardens are not the same. One is wildly splashed with color; another is tidy and formal. There are romantic gardens and practical no-fuss ones. One holds a rose trellis, another a grape arbor, and some consist of petunia-filled window boxes.

Our lives are God's flower gardens. We are the gardeners who choose the seed which gives character to our garden. Before choosing which kind of garden you want, dream of flowers—flowers in the yard and flowers in the soul. Make the sweet of the year even sweeter by planning now.

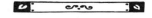

February 21

Memorize a Poem

Scripture: *Philippians 4: 6 - 8*
Key verse: *Finally, brothers and sisters, keep your thoughts on whatever is right or deserves praise: things that are true, honorable, fair, pure, acceptable, or commendable.*

> Sweet and low, sweet and low,
> Wind of the western sea,
> Low, low, breathe and blow,
> Wind of the western sea!

When winds howl in a black night, different people respond in different ways. While one person cringes, another listens enraptured. Those who cringe conjure up the ghosts and monsters, thieves and kidnappers of child-hood tales. The enraptured ones recall gentler scenes, perhaps ones like the wind picture given by Alfred, Lord Tennyson in "Sweet and Low."

Whatever we see and hear, we filter through our pool of memory. Paul knew that we become like what we think about, and we can only think about what has gone into the mind. Thus, he urged the Christians of Philippi to fill their minds with the excellent and the admirable.

The childhood poems we memorized and the stories we read give shadows friendly faces or frightening ones, turn the night gentle or menacing, and paint day as opportunity or drudgery. Although we have long ago forgotten the words of these poems and stories, their power over us lingers.

Today add something beautiful and admirable to your pool of memory. Turn to Robert Frost or Emily Dickinson, Helen Steiner Rice or Isaac Newton, Carl Sandburg or William Wordsworth and memorize something that is lovely and gracious. Put poetry back into your life and turn your ghosts into friendly ones.

February 22

Pray for the United States

SCRIPTURE: *Jeremiah 22: 13 - 17*
KEY VERSE: *But your eyes and your mind are set on nothing but dishonest profits.*

From the empire of Alexander the Great, the largest empire of the ancient world, to the Soviet Union, the largest of the modern world, empires rise and fall. An outside enemy seldom causes the collapse of an empire or great power. Rather it is the final result of a growing inner rot. No nation, including our own, has any special immunity against corruption.

One of the first symptoms of inner rot has been a great disparity between the rich and the poor. By entertaining the increasingly impoverished masses with lavish circuses, Roman politicians tried to appease the poor. But discontented people want reform, not appeasement. Healthy nations take care of their poor while sick nations try to ignore or appease them.

In this month when we celebrate the birth of George Washington, think about the course our nation has taken in its two hundred years of democracy. Where have we succeeded? Where have we failed? What is the challenge we face at this point in our history?

Turn to prayer for ideas and power. Pray for our nation and its leaders. Pray for the wealthy and those who exploit, and for the poor and those who are exploited. Pray that those who care may be empowered with wisdom and knowledge. Pray that those who no longer care about anything may be redeemed by some action of love.

Today take a first step towards creative change by creatively praying.

February 23

$Best$ China

SCRIPTURE: *Nehemiah 8: 9 - 12*
KEY VERSE: *Then all the people went to eat and drink and to send portions. They had a big, joyful celebration because they understood the words that had been explained to them.*

"D on't be sad because the joy you have in the Lord is your strength," Nehemiah the governor, Ezra the priest and scribe, and the Levites instructed the people who wept while hearing the reading of the law.

Even on the eve of his death, Jesus did not leave his disciples in a mourning state. "Be of good cheer," he told them, "for I have overcome the world."

Today, regardless of conditions which elicit sorrow, find joy in the Lord's strength rather than in an ideal world. Like the ancient Jewish people who heard the word of the Lord and celebrated that word by feasting, turn this day into celebration. Use your best china and bring out the lace tablecloth, the crystal candle holders, and the cloth napkins.

Those ancient women celebrated with tables loaded with rich food. If your idea of celebration includes French soup, steak and lobster, and cherry cheese cake, this is the day for it. But if meat loaf or tuna casserole is tonight's fare, give it the same first class elegance by serving it on elegant table service.

Birthdays and anniversaries fill too few days with celebration, but the joy of the Lord turns even nonevents into celebration. Like the characters in *Alice in Wonderland* who celebrated a very merry unbirthday, today celebrate life. Celebrate family and friends, food and shelter, sun and rain. Celebrate winter. Celebrate laughter and tears. Celebrate every gift from a loving Father and Lord.

While most people celebrate special occasions, *Alice in Wonderland* characters have more fun because they celebrate anything. Today creatively celebrate an ordinary day made extraordinary by joy in the Lord.

February 24

Give Away

SCRIPTURE: *2 Corinthians 9: 10 – 15*
KEY VERSE: *And you will always be rich enough to be generous. (NEB)*

> Old Mother Hubbard went to the cupboard
> To get her small dog a bone,
> But when she got there, the cupboard was bare
> And so the poor doggie had none.

In real life, people rather than animals face bare cupboards. UNICEF estimates that between 30 million and 100 million children from impoverished families live on the streets of our world. We do not lack resources; we lack a willingness to distribute them evenly.

In the Old Testament, the Lord commanded the Israelites to redistribute property every fifty years. In the Year of Jubilee they were to free slaves and return alienated property to its original owners. Thus the rich did not continually get richer and the poor continually get poorer. In a twist of modern history, we have legally ended human slavery but emotionally enslaved ourselves to possessions. We fashion twentieth century idols out of clutter.

We have no Year of Jubilee to inspire the redistribution of wealth. However, today make a change in your attitude toward possessions. View them as resources for creating a more equitable world for all people, and in that spirit, give something away. Your gift will not take a homeless child off the streets or suddenly create a just world. But it will stimulate new thoughts about what you own, and new thoughts, watered and tended, may one day blossom into creative action.

Today think new thoughts, and do a new thing for God.

February 25

Jigsaw Puzzle

SCRIPTURE: *Romans 12: 3 - 5*
KEY VERSE: *Our bodies have many parts, but these parts don't all do the same thing.*

A single piece of a jigsaw puzzle is useless unless other pieces go with it. Yet many of us frame our own small puzzle piece as if we were complete within ourselves.

Remembering Paul's words about fitting into the body of Christ, spend an evening, or many evenings, fitting the

500 or 1000 pieces of a puzzle together. From a box of seemingly unrelated pieces, make a Vermont covered bridge, a Navajo family, a Rubens canvas, or an English garden.

Life continually falls apart on us. Getting it all together is an ongoing challenge. When we put together the pieces of a puzzle, for once all the pieces fit neatly together and form a whole.

Those who work with emotionally damaged people use handwork to help heal wounded spirits. To some extent, each of us is emotionally damaged; none of us is immune from life's bruises. Today busy your fingers putting pieces first here and then there, laying them down, picking them up again, and finally fitting each into the one correct space. Imagine yourself as one small piece in the kingdom of God. Mentally fit your life here and there, trying to find the perfect match.

Paul admonishes the Roman Christians not to think too highly of themselves, but to envision themselves as limbs and organs of one body. While winter winds whip snow across the fields and low temperatures form jagged icicles along the porch roof, fit your life into God's big picture.

February 26

Mexican Dinner

SCRIPTURE: *Romans 15: 22 - 29*
KEY VERSE: *I will visit you on my way to Spain.*

N o one knows if Paul ever fulfilled his dream of visiting Spain. But he longed to win his world for Christ, and Spain was on the edge of that world.

Today Spain's descendants are not only on the edge of our world, but play in our own yard. Begin taking more interest in this neighbor.

¿Te gusta la comida mexicana? Do you like Mexican food? Fast food restaurants have turned tacos and burritos

into household words for most Americans, and most supermarkets stock tortilla shells and taco sauce, even in places where no one of Mexican heritage lives. Our neighbor to the south has added a touch of adventure to our dinner tables.

Tonight remember Paul's dream by preparing Mexican food. If tacos on the dinner table are as common as hamburgers, this evening try something new. Burritos come in enough varieties to make a new kind every day of the month. Tonight try a chicken guacamole one. Or make a chicken enchilada casserole, a sopa, or chicken fajitas

¿Te gustan las fiestas? Do you like parties? Creatively turn this winter day into a fiesta occasion with fajitas or enchiladas, tortilla chips and guacamole, green chili sauce or red chili sauce. Add a piñata, a sombrero, and a poncho to the room. Put a bit of *musica* in the cassette player, and the party is complete.

Keep alive Paul's dream to win the world to Christ. Appreciate and take more interest in the descendants of Spain.

February 27

Borrow a Painting

SCRIPTURE: *Genesis 29: 15 – 28*
KEY VERSE: *Jacob loved Rachel. So he offered, "I'll work seven years in return for your younger daughter Rachel."*

Jacob's eye found Rachel beautiful. In order to have her he agreed to work seven years for her father. He rose early each morning for seven years to plow, sow, and reap another man's fields. The image of the beautiful girl made his burden light. However, on the longed-for-night, he found he had been given Leah, not Rachel, as a wife. Once again, the beautiful Rachel was promised him if he would serve another seven years. Once again, the image of the beautiful girl carried him through years of labor.

Like Jacob, we need vision to carry us through the demands of each day. The need to find meaning in life distinguishes humans from the rest of the animal world.

Good art expresses meaning and even glory in ordinary moments which we so easily miss when we are caught up in them. Under the brush of a Rembrandt or a Vermeer, a woman peeling potatoes, a young girl beside a cradle, a child at play become sacred acts.

For five hundred years, Leonardo de Vinci's Mona Lisa has captivated the imagination of the world, but few of us could explain its appeal. The language of art is deeper than words. Rock paintings predate written history in all civilizations, and cuneiform, the writing system invented by the Sumerians, began as picture writing.

Most libraries lend paintings. Today check out a print. Even if like Jacob you toil another man's soil, or like Rachel you wait forever for your day, let a work of art lift the ordinary moments of each day to beautiful or even sacred ones. For a few weeks, let Renoir, Whistler, or another of the great masters remind you of the glory of life.

February 28

Silent Time

Scripture: *Isaiah 30: 15 – 18*
Key verse: *In stillness and in staying quiet, there lies your strength. (NEB)*

Winter is the season of quiet, when earth rests. Without a season of quiet, we too become spent, burned out. Even pleasant activities become burdensome.

Yet, like the ancient Israelites, we often pursue an activity rather than let go of it. We fall asleep thinking about things we have to do, we wake up thinking about them, and they pursue us through the day. In spite of this preoccupation, we seldom get it all done.

The word of the Lord commanded the Israelites to be still, to stay quiet in order to find strength. We too seek strength to cope and to overcome. Today find strength in quietness. For thirty minutes be still. Have no agenda, no goal or expectation. Simply be silent.

God often waits until we are silent to begin speaking. Some things are heard only in silence, and amid frantic activity we miss them. For this half-hour, let God speak to you, for you, about you. When we fail to listen to God, we lose touch even with ourselves. Today get back in touch with hopes and fears which are too deep for words.

Hear the scraping of boughs against the house, the ticking of the clock, the call of a bird flying overhead. Then gradually hear other sounds of heart and soul. Unbidden thoughts will begin to break through, some with surprise, some with urgency.

Isaiah told his people the Lord was waiting to show them favor. For thirty minutes today creatively listen to silence and hear God speak his word of love to you.

February 29

Dictionary

SCRIPTURE: *Proverbs 9: 7 - 9*
KEY VERSE: *Teach a righteous person, and he will learn more.*

I will show myself highly fed and lowly taught." At times, many of us resemble the Clown in Shakespeare's *All's Well That Ends Well*. Not only our manners, but our speech becomes sloppy.

When we think of the classroom, we think of children. Yet the writer of Proverbs observed that even the wisest people become still wiser when they are taught. We often reserve the study of vocabulary for the classroom, but the wise adult described in Proverbs makes it a lifelong practice. Language creates tools for thinking. The richer our language, the richer our thoughts.

If nothing we read or hear contains a word we do not fully understand, we are limiting both our world and our ability to express ourselves. Today increase your vocabulary, and take one small step towards better thinking and understanding. Look up at least one unfamiliar word in a dictionary, and be wiser today than you were yesterday.

If the evening news brings word of a Sikh uprising in India, ask yourself what a Sikh is. With the help of a dictionary, shed more light on the news story. Look up the meaning of any unfamiliar word you hear today, whether coming from the lips of a friend, the page of a book, or the evening news.

Use the new word immediately. Repeat it in the context in which you read or heard it, and then put it into another context. Try it out on family or friends around the dinner table. Turn the new word into a tool to help you better express your thoughts.

Clowns can afford to show themselves lowly taught or highly funny. But the wise woman learns to express herself clearly. The right word is one key to that expression.

March 1

Darn a Sock

Scripture: *Psalm 128*
Key verse: *Your wife will be like a fruitful vine inside your home.*

> The mother, wi' her needle and her shears,
> Gars auld claes look amaist as weel's the new.

The mother described by Robert Burns came from a past generation when thrift was a way of life. These women patched clothes until fibers were too weak to hold more thread. Then they put them into the rag bag. Bits of old dresses reappeared in cloth dolls, patchwork quilts, and strips for curling hair on Saturday night.

In many countries, women's creativity still keeps possessions in service long after we would have cast them off. A gray patch may replace most of the original blue cloth in the crotch, but in Thailand, Zaire, or Venezuela, a pair of pants is still worn with pride if the mending is neat.

We long ago abandoned such thrift. Why patch an old dress when new styles are available? Why darn socks when new ones cost so little? Few of us want to return to the curling-hair-with-strips-of-cloth days.

Yet, many of us are having second thoughts about the decreasing ozone layer, polluted air, and contaminated soil. Some old-fashioned virtues begin to make sense even in a technological world.

Perhaps we remember watching our grandmother darn a sock. As her needle carried thread first one way, and then another, we saw the hole magically disappear. We may even have tried it ourselves. However, after a few tries, some of us lost any desire to ever do it again.

Today give it another try. Darn a sock, even if you must seek help to do it. The psalmist pictures a wife as a fruitful vine in the heart of the house. Enrich the vine with a touch of almost forgotten ingenuity.

March 2

Watch the Wind

SCRIPTURE: *Psalm 104: 1 - 5*
KEY VERSE: *You use the clouds for your chariot. You move on the wings of the wind.*

Rock-a-bye baby on the tree top,
When the wind blows the cradle will rock;
When the bough breaks the cradle will fall,
Down will come baby, cradle and all.

Words were nothing more than pleasant sounds to our ears when our mothers first sang this nursery song to us. But wind was a fun word, and we soon learned that the wind made fun sounds. Puffing faces in story books gave the wind personality, adding to the fun. At some point on the way to adulthood, wind simply became wind.

Wind was never simply wind for the writer of the psalms. Wind spoke of the supernatural, and looking into the sky, the psalmist sensed the presence of the Almighty.

Let wind once again become more than wind in your life. Lying in the soft green grass, perhaps you once imagined animals and people in the clouds sweeping across the sky. Today gaze heavenward again, and follow the arrangements and rearrangements of these puffy travelers. Follow the flight of a hawk gliding so effortlessly on the currents of the wind. Watch a young sapling bend under its force. Thrill at giant pine boughs performing a ballet in the breeze. The heavens dance on the wings of the wind.

Give the wind a chance to whip life into your face and lungs, your thoughts and dreams. Sense the presence of the Almighty. Perceive the hand of the supernatural in the forces of the universe and rejoice. At the beginning of this month which comes in like a lion and goes out like a lamb, creatively befriend the lion. Like the psalmist, praise the creator of winds.

Cook for Fun

SCRIPTURE: *Luke 13: 20 - 21*

KEY VERSE: *It's like yeast that a woman mixed into a large amount of flour until the yeast worked its way through all the dough.*

When God seems remote, we may be looking for him in the wrong places. To explain a heavenly kingdom, Jesus drew images from daily life. What could be more common than a woman sweeping a floor, a lost lamb, a lamp without oil, or as in this passage, a woman mixing yeast into flour? Even in the kitchen, Jesus found reminders of his Heavenly Father.

The kitchen is woman's inescapable domain. We hold spatula-shaped scepters in kingdoms bordered by cupboards, sink, refrigerator, and range. If we feel more like a galley girl than a queen in this little castle, it is probably because we see spatulas instead of scepters.

Today rule over pots and pans, flour and salt, stove and refrigerator, and create something wonderful and fun. Make pizza and begin with dough you knead yourself. Stir up a batch of English muffins, shape them, let them rise, and then grill them until they are ready to pop into the mouth. Serve Yorkshire pudding with roast beef, lobster with steak, or ice cream with chocolate waffles.

Yeast changes flour, and as you change ordinary ingredients into special dishes, think about how the yeast of the kingdom changes us into special people. God's spirit permeates our lives with his goodness and love so that we rise above all that is not good and loving.

In his childhood, Jesus must have often watched his mother knead bread, and in this common experience he gained understanding of God. Today meet God in your kitchen, and like Jesus, let an ordinary experience speak to you about the presence and power of God.

Practice the Presence of God

SCRIPTURE: *Psalm 73: 21 - 28*
KEY VERSE: *Yet, I am always with you.*

O n hearing that God lived everywhere, a little city girl visiting relatives in the country responded, "Well, he certainly doesn't live in New York!"

Although most of us believe God lives even in New York, it is harder to picture him living in our homes. Perhaps this is why we find it so hard to dwell in his presence.

Each day we juggle a thousand details of running a household, managing a family and/or a job, and smoothing muddy waters of relationships. When we go to bed at night, an uncomfortable number of details still hang somewhere up in the air. Most of us are mothers, not saints, and we find it difficult to keep our thoughts focused on God when so many voices call from so many directions.

How much richer life would be if we could! Long ago, in his little book *Practicing the Presence of God*, Brother Lawrence describes how he managed an awareness of the presence of God at all times, whether he was washing pots and pans in the kitchen or kneeling in prayer in the chapel. In fact, both were one and the same to him.

Today imitate Brother Lawrence and try to practice the presence of God even in the kitchen. Be aware of God's presence in the same way you are aware of the presence of other people in the house. Jesus was called Emmanuel or God-With-Us. Acknowledge the intimacy of God-With-You. Rather than measure success by the number of minutes you spend thinking about God, measure it by the blessings coming out of an awareness of his presence.

If you live in your kitchen, find God in your kitchen. If you spend the day in an office, find him among colleagues and stacks of paper. If you live in New York, discover that God also lives in New York.

March 5

Calligraphy

SCRIPTURE: *Galatians 6: 11 - 14*
KEY VERSE: *Look at how large the letters in these words are because I'm writing this myself.*

P aul not only preached the good news, but he kept in touch with those who responded to it. Even after he had left them, he continued to teach and encourage new Christian communities through letters. He apparently did not have 20/20 vision, but he often concluded his dictated messages by adding a few lines written in his own hand.

The words we speak have lost much of their value. Carelessly we utter them, write them, and listen to them. At times, they seem to lack a message. Today use words to convey a message. Like Paul, emphasize the message by writing a few lines in your own hand.

For centuries calligraphy embellished letters, documents, and books and turned the written message into an art form. Then came the printing press, and gradually the art of calligraphy almost died out. However, in the late 1800s when artists revolted against the mechanization of the industrial revolution, calligraphy, among other arts, revived.

Even in today's computer world, calligraphy still holds the power to highlight the important words. We pen wedding invitations in calligraphy, we expect it on diplomas, and we hang it on our walls. A wedding, graduation, or birth calls for special recognition, and the beautifully penned words communicate that message. Use this art form to emphasize a message of love, encouragement, or faith which you wish to send.

All art forms, including calligraphy, must be practiced for beautiful results. Today learn the simple basics and write a message to a special person. Like Paul, emphasize the sincerity of your words with your own hand.

$\mathcal{L}unch$ Out

SCRIPTURE: *Matthew 12: 1 - 7*

KEY VERSE: *Then on a day of worship Jesus walked through the grainfields. His disciples were hungry and began to pick the heads of grain to eat.*

I n Shakespeare's *Merchant of Venice*, Portia utters these famous words:

> The quality of mercy is not strain'd,
> It droppeth as the gentle rain from heaven...
> It becomes the throned monarch
>   better than his crown...
> It is an attribute to God himself,...

Jesus was the incarnation of mercy. Recognizing physical hunger as well as spiritual hunger, he himself ate and drank as he spoke of heavenly kingdoms. When his disciples found themselves hungry on the Sabbath, he allowed them to pluck grain and eat it even though he knew it would anger the Pharisees. He seemed to enjoy moments he spent eating with his friends.

Recognizing that food is a gift from God, today take special joy in the gift by eating out. Have you long admired the charming little cafe on Main Street where small round tables overlook the sidewalk? Or do the wonderful smells of the bakery tantalize you every time you pass? Have you always been intrigued by the artistically designed sign hanging over the door of the Good Earth Cafe? Today stop and refresh yourself as you walk through the grainfields of life.

Like Jesus, share this impulsive, fun moment with others and strengthen the bonds of love. Or, as he did at other times, go off alone and renew the inner springs which nourish your soul.

Jesus enjoyed life, and whether you go alone or with

a friend, make your outing fun. Enjoy lunch out and feel winter's hand relax her grip.

March 7

Russian Alphabet

SCRIPTURE: *Psalm 95*
KEY VERSE: *The farthest places of the earth are in his hands, and the folds of the hills are his. (NEB)*

Learn the Russian alphabet? Why not? The psalmist says the farthest places of the earth are in God's hands. Thus, wherever we are, we are bound to all others in all places by the common thread of God's love.

Russian history has shaped much of the world's history. Its rich culture has added to ours through its literature and music. Many of us have fallen under the spell of Leo Tolstoy's *Anna Karenina* and Sergey Rachmaninoff's Symphony No. 2 in E Minor. Some of us learned to play "Volga Boat Song" before our toes could touch the floor, but we still do not know where the Volga River runs.

The former Soviet Union, which blended Russian culture with other cultures, covered twelve time zones, half the width of the globe. Such rich culture deserves exposure and appreciation. One aspect of that culture, the alphabet, is especially interesting because it combines Roman, Greek, and Hebrew letters.

"Everything that I understand, I understand because I love." Leo Tolstoy wrote the words in *War and Peace*, but they also hold true for us. The more we know of each other, the more we know of the love of the One who brought us into being.

One day you may be a tourist in Russia. Or you may never go. But take a few moments to examine and practice a different alphabet, and enlarge your capacity to appreciate the collective richness of our world.

Today sing an expanded song of praise to the Lord who is present in even the folds of the most remote hills. Learn another alphabet and envision other sheep in other hills listening to the voice of the same Shepherd.

March 8

Discuss the News

SCRIPTURE: *Proverbs 14: 15 - 18*
KEY VERSE: *A gullible person believes anything.*

I n *Hamlet, Prince of Denmark* by Shakespeare, the main character utters these words: "Ay, sire; to be honest, as this world goes, is to be one man picked out of ten thousand."

With details of individual and collective sins, each morning's newspaper reinforces Hamlet's words. The evening news carries more examples of government scandal, domestic violence, and inner city crime. We begin to wonder if even one honest man out of ten thousand can be found.

Yet, the fault is not all in the news reports. Sometimes we listen poorly, draw opinions from sketchy reports, or twist what we hear to fit our own needs. In another scene from *Hamlet*, Horatio speaks to the queen in Elsinore Castle:

> Her speech is nothing,
> Yet the unshaped use of it doth move
> The hearers to collection; they aim at it,
> And botch the words up fit to their own thoughts ...

Three thousand years ago, the writer of Proverbs contrasts the simple man with the wise one. The first, he told us, believes everything he hears. The second demands proof.

Today be wise as you listen to the news. What are the roots of the problem? What special interest groups influence policy and even control the media? Discuss the news with an informed person whose opinion you respect. Reserve judgment until you are better informed. Take the advice of the writer of Proverbs and ask questions about what you hear.

March 9

Praise Music

Scripture: *Psalm 150*
Key verse: *Praise him with sounds from horns. Praise him with harps and lyres.*

W hen Saul of the Old Testament felt an evil spirit come over him, he called for David to play the harp until the spirit went away. Three thousand years later, music still affects our moods.

Countless mothers have lulled fretful infants to sleep with these words from "Brahms' Lullaby:"

> Guten Abend, gut' Nacht,
> Mit Rosen bedacht...

Music speaks to us, and it speaks for us. It carries us both inside ourselves and outside ourselves, putting us in touch with who we are and where we are. But until we know God, we cannot really know who we are or where we are. Perhaps Saul's evil spirit went away because the harp reconnected him to God. Whether she is aware of it or not, the loving mother singing "Brahms' Lullaby" reflects a greater love originating in the heart of God.

The psalmist urges his people to praise the Lord with trumpet, lute, harp, tambourine, flute, strings, cymbals. He says to praise him with dancing. "Let everything that breathes praise the Lord," he adds.

Today use music as a vehicle of praise. Take out the Canon in D Major by Johann Pachelbel, "Listen" by the

Monks of the Weston Priory, or whatever has been gathering dust, and like Saul or the infant in a mother's arms, find comfort. Find in music expression for the inexpressible. Praise the One who created, the One who is present, and the One who continues to re-create and redeem.

Expand your soul with praise.

March 10

Dreams

SCRIPTURE: *Psalm 37: 1 - 7*
KEY VERSE: *Be happy with the Lord, and he will give you the desires of your heart.*

Was mankind first conceived in a dream of the Eternal? Perhaps our own dreams simply reflect the image of a God who dreams. The psalmist indicates that God understands the dreams and deep yearnings of the human heart and participates in their fulfillment.

Victor Hugo wrote:

> Be like the bird, who
> Halting in his flight
> On limb too slight
> Feels it give way beneath him,
> Yet sings
> Knowing he hath wings.

Those wings often take the shape of dreams. Martin Luther King's "I have a dream!" has lifted the wings of people around the world. Gandhi had a dream, Alexander the Great had a dream, and Billy Graham had a dream. Few things hold as much power as a dream. Those who dream change the course of history.

When Jesus told us he came that we might have life and have it more abundantly, he implied that God has dreams for us. We too have dreams for ourselves. Some of them were born out of his dreams for us. Today take a look at these dreams. Dust them, polish them, list them, and ask God what he thinks of them. God's dreams for us are bold, so we need to learn to make our own dreams bold. Timid dreams make timid people.

Like stars, dreams light the night. The darker the night, the more important our dreams. When the limb beneath you gives way, sing, knowing you have wings.

March 11

Soup Kitchen

SCRIPTURE: *Acts 4: 32 - 35*
KEY VERSE: *The whole group of believers lived in harmony. No one called any of his possessions his own. Instead, they shared everything.*

> There was an Old Man who said, "Do
> Tell me how I should add two and two?
> I think more and more
> That it makes about four—
> But I fear that is almost too few.

Even in the early church, many new Christians found it too few. But they came up with a solution: "No one called any of his possessions his own. Instead, they shared everything." Perhaps we too would turn the world upside down if we solved our math problems that way.

Today peer into the world of those who always find four too few. Visit a soup kitchen or a shelter. Talk to those who have few possessions to call their own.

Media stories of poverty have ceased to shock us, but when poverty has a face it is harder to ignore. The engaging, or perhaps withdrawn, five-year-old across the table nags our hearts longer than television images of starving people in Ethiopia. The empty-eyed man who has been without work for two years puts a new face on unemployment. The homeless man helping wait on tables robs our stereotypes of some of their power.

The power of the early church was its openness to the Holy Spirit even when it cost early Christians their possessions. Before his death, Jesus cried over Jerusalem. Today perhaps he cries over his people who make possessions their idols. Today see your possessions through the eyes of those who have none.

<hr>

March 12

Be Innovative

SCRIPTURE: *Acts 9: 20 – 25*
KEY VERSE: *However, Saul's disciples lowered him in a large basket through an opening in the wall one night.*

P aul was not the only person to escape in a basket. Falstaff in Shakespeare's *Merry Wives of Windsor* also made an escape in a basket, but with disagreeable results.

In many parts of Europe, baskets carry home yogurt, bread, and endive from the market. The people of Thailand steam rice in baskets. South American mothers cradle newborns in baskets, and in Africa baskets often replace suitcases. In the United States they may decorate the beams of country kitchens.

Survival often depends on our ability to be innovative. Hiding in a basket, Paul, the great missionary, shed pride, dignity, and comfort. But he refused to shed the compelling mission of evangelization, and he did whatever he had to do to carry it out.

God is a God of innovation. From the anteater to the giraffe and from the Red Sea to the cross, God uses all things for his purposes. Perhaps we too would be more fit for his purposes if we became more innovative.

Today put your innovative powers to work. You may have no need to escape in a basket, but consider using one for the baby's toys. Or put scarves, mittens, and hats in a basket near the back door. Decorate a wall with a stenciled tablecloth from Mexico. Put wooden spoons in your ceramic flower pot or hang a pretty place mat above the breakfast table. Put a bouquet of roses in a silver tea pot or arrange them in a lined basket.

Be open to anything, and like Paul, circumstances will never block your ability to function.

March 13

Phone Etiquette

SCRIPTURE: *Proverbs 25: 8 – 11*
KEY VERSE: *Like golden apples in silver settings, so is a word spoken at the right time.*

Some of us can relate to Laura Richards' thoughts about telephones:

> Once there was an elephant
>   who tried to use the telephant.
> No! No! I mean an elephone
>   who tried to use the telephone.
> Dear me, I am not certain quite
>   that even now I've got it right.
> Howe'er it was, he got his trunk
>   entangled in the telephunk.
> The more he tried to get it free
>   the louder buzzed the telephee.
> I fear I'd better drop the song
>   of elephok and telephong.

The first commercial telephone switchboard was installed in New Haven, Connecticut in 1878. The jangling instrument carried both fearsome, awful news and town gossip along its party lines. For years calls were placed to San Francisco's China Town by giving the operator the name instead of the number of the person. A ring of the phone once had importance.

Today the ring awakening the baby may only be another offer to receive the *Daily News* all week for the price of Sunday's edition. The call in the middle of the night, once foreboding awful news of accident or death, now may be only a wrong number. The dinner hour may be interrupted by people returning messages left on their answering machines.

Regardless of what the ring of the phone brings, answer graciously. Even unsolicited telephone calls offer opportunities to bless those we will never meet in another way. Our voice may stand out among a host of irritable responses.

The writer of Proverbs compares a fitting word to apples of gold set in silver filigree. Today turn clanging metal into apples of gold, and make the day a more beautiful one for someone on the other end of the telephone.

March 14

Befriend a Teenager

SCRIPTURE: *1 Timothy 4: 11 - 14*
KEY VERSE: *Don't let anyone look down on you for being young.*

Timothy was still a young man when the elders of the church laid their hands on him. When he was twelve, Alexander the Great inherited his father's kingdom. John Quincy Adams, fourth President of the United States, was fourteen when he went to Russia as secretary to the ambassador. Like other new mothers of her time, Mary, the mother of Jesus, was a teenager.

How well adolescents shoulder tomorrow's responsibilities largely depends on what direction their teen years take. Belonging neither to childhood nor adulthood, today's teen years are often empty, holding neither purpose nor direction. Gangs often try to fill the gap by providing a semblance of identity to searching youth.

The strange clothes and weird behavior of some of today's Timothys, Alexanders, John Quincys, and Marys scare us, and we respond by looking the other way. But the more we distance ourselves, the more we sharpen an already wide gap between generations. Looking the other way contributes to the polarization rather than the healing of an ailing society.

Today make a bridge, or perhaps a footpath, between generations. Become acquainted with a teenager. Speak to the many ear-ringed young man who lives next door. Befriend the girl who has a cigarette dangling from her lips as she passes your house after school every day. Listen to rather than lecture the long-haired, tattooed teenagers you wish would move out of the neighborhood. Hear what your own teenagers wish they could tell you.

In some defiant face, see the potential of an Alexander the Great. See a Timothy in the neighborhood troublemaker, a John Quincy in the young man writing graffiti on the wall, and a Mary of Nazareth in the bewildered face of a pregnant teenager. Lovingly respond to the fears and hopes of today's youth. Encourage some beautiful person hiding behind a sullen face.

March 15

Shakespeare Play

SCRIPTURE: *Proverbs 15: 12 – 14*
KEY VERSE: *The mind of a person who has understanding searches for knowledge.*

A famous line from Shakespeare's *All's Well That Ends Well* says, "The web of our life is of a mingled yarn,

good and ill together." To live is to know the truth of that line.

The Saul who terrorized the early church later wrote the most beautiful love passage in the Bible. The David who called God his shepherd so coveted another man's wife that he arranged the man's murder. The Peter who denied Christ also died for his Lord.

Although the Pharisees preceded Shakespeare by fifteen centuries, Shakespeare described them well in *Twelfth Night* when he wrote, "Since you make pleasure of your pains...." or in *Two Gentlemen of Verona* when he wrote, "For truth hath better deeds than words to grace it."

The writer of Proverbs said a discerning mind seeks knowledge and a stupid one feeds on folly. Shakespeare, in *The Taming of the Shrew*, echoed his words: "He that is giddy thinks the world turns round."

Ben Jonson described Shakespeare as a man not of an age, but for all time. As we read Shakespeare's work, most of us find ourselves nodding or smiling as we recognize ourselves and our acquaintances in his words. Like the writer of Proverbs, Shakespeare was a master observer. When he cast his characters, he put each of us into them.

Today seek knowledge by turning to a Shakespeare play. Whether you read an entire play or only a scene, gather insight into how ridiculous and how tragic our world is. Apply the words of Proverbs by learning something from Shakespeare's discerning mind.

March 16

Neighborhood Walk

Scripture: *Luke 17: 11 – 19*
Key verse: *As he was went into a village, ten men with a skin disease met him.*

B ecause Jesus traveled by foot, ten lepers were healed. Entering a village on the borderlands of Samaria and Galilee, he met, interacted with, and healed these untouchables. Most of Jesus' ministry was on-the-spot ministry, taking place along the road, beside the sea, in the village streets. Jesus met people because he went where they were.

Like Jesus, today spend some time on foot. Take a neighborhood walk and discover more of the world around you.

The sun has now turned companionable, and earth is responding to its frequent visits. Trickling water sings beneath ice, red buds swell on maples, and crocus peer above the crusty snow. With the sun's gentle encouragement, the earth is coming alive again.

Neighbors are also responding to warmer air with more frequents forays into the thawing world. Make this a day to reconnect with some of them, by thought if not by word. Remind yourself that even though winter sometimes inters whole neighborhoods, we still live in community.

Winter has taken its toll on many around us, handing some unemployment, others illness, and still others loneliness. As you walk today, wonder about these people, ask about them, speak to them. As trickling streams and cold winds stimulate your senses, let the renewed awareness of community stimulate your care and concern for those who live around you.

One of those you meet today may be a leper. Friendship may begin a healing process.

Entertaining Ideas

SCRIPTURE: *1 Peter 4: 7 – 11*
KEY VERSE: *Welcome each other as guests without complaining.*

> Do not save your loving speeches
> For your friends till they are dead;
> Do not write them on their tombstones,
> Speak them rather now instead.

As Anna Cummins suggested, do not wait to let your friends know how much you appreciate them. Today consider Peter's words about entertaining as one way to speak your love. We often have wonderful intentions to be hospitable, have people over for dinner, and host parties.

But like kites yanked out of our hands, we see our intentions entangled in telephone wires and tree branches or sailing off across a tossing, restless ocean. Some of our intentions never make it as far as our hands.

Hospitality runs through the Bible like a thread. Abraham entertained strangers; a penniless woman fed Elijah; Mary and Martha opened their home to Jesus. Today make hospitality more than a fantasy. Turn it into reality by depending on creativity rather than perfection for fulfillment.

If meetings clutter evening skies, find another time to entertain. Consider a Saturday picnic in the back yard or a morning coffee after the children have left for school. Make a list of comfortable menus which carry you effortlessly through the skies. If your lasagna is mouth-watering good, make that your speciality. If your pancakes are so light your family can never get enough of them, treat your friends to a pancake supper. If you make a great meat loaf, feature it often.

Create and list ideas which will fly in the free spaces of your life.

March 18

Baked Blessing

SCRIPTURE: *James 2: 14 - 17*

KEY VERSE: *Suppose a brother or a sister is in rags without enough food for the day, and one of you says, "Good luck to you, keep yourselves warm, and have plenty to eat," but does nothing to supply their bodily needs, what is the good of that? (NEB)*

I am: yet what I am who cares, or knows?

J ohn Clare wrote these words over a century ago, but they sound strangely modern. Who cares? We hear the words from the lips of a belligerent teenager, an embittered old man, or a mother on welfare. Sometimes we ask the same question ourselves.

We can endure almost anything if we believe someone cares. Without that assurance, a wall of isolation surrounds our emotional and physical suffering. Because our assurances of caring often sound hollow, today send the message in a more tangible way. Bless someone with a gift of food.

The smell of freshly baked bread or warm apple pie speaks to the subconscious as much as to the conscious. Our first bonding experience was with the one who relieved the painful stress of our hunger. For most of us food continues to meet a psychological as well as a physical need. At some subconscious level, food still represents caring.

Today take that gift to someone who needs a lift. Surprise the teenager next door with chocolate chip cookies still so warm that they melt in the mouth. Then make another batch for your family. Bake an angel food cake for someone going through chemotherapy treatments or take a casserole to the man down the street who just lost his wife. Treat an elderly neighbor to a homemade cherry pie.

Turn flour, baking powder, and spices in your cupboard into healing smells and soothing tastes, and give a lift to someone's day. Show you care with actions as well as words.

March 19

Sunset Discovery

SCRIPTURE: *Psalm 113*
KEY VERSE: *From the rising of the sun to its setting may the Lord's name be praised. (NEB)*

In *Le Petit Prince* by Antoine de Saint-Exupéry, a small boy fell from another planet and landed in the Sahara Desert where a pilot was repairing his plane.

"Allons voir un coucher de soleil..." Let's see a sunset, *le petit prince* told the pilot on the fourth morning.

The surprised pilot had to explain sunsets on earth to the foreign prince.

Then, nostalgically, the little prince spoke of watching sunsets on the miniature planet where he lived. One day, he watched forty-four of them by simply moving his chair forward a few steps at a time.

Although limited to one sunset per day, if we took time to watch it, we, like the Psalmist, would more often lift our voices in praise. This evening watch the glorious spectacle of the sunset, and catch a glimpse of the glory of the Creator of suns and sunsets, earth and sky, eye and soul. Write a poem expressing what you see or feel. The lines of poetry need not rhyme, for expression, rather than rhyme, converts words into poetry.

Praise transcends the world of ourselves, and by lifting our souls in awe we often discover an unsuspected poet within us. Make this an evening of discovery. Discover a sunset, discover an inner poet, and rediscover praise.

March 20

Popcorn

SCRIPTURE: *Luke 6: 1 - 5*
KEY VERSE: *One Sabbath he was going through the corn-fields, and his disciples were plucking the ears of corn, rubbing them in their hands, and eating them. (NEB)*

H ad Jesus and his disciples skipped dinner the day they helped themselves to corn in someone else's field? Or, knowing that the few kernels they ate would not affect the harvest, were they simply enjoying a crunchy treat? Apparently, even the disciples of Jesus appreciated an occasional snack.

The corn the disciples ate that day was not maize, for the grain we call corn was a gift of the New World. Half the Plymouth pilgrims had died from exposure and malnutrition in that New World when Squanto took gifts which would change the fate of the still living. However, neither the Indians nor the Pilgrims foresaw a day when one of those gifts, small puffs of corn, would be avidly consumed in theaters and fairs, malls and ball games, in front of fire-places and on city streets.

As Jesus and his disciples paused to pluck and savor kernels of wheat, rye, barley, or oats, tonight pause to enjoy the last hours of winter with a bowl of popcorn. Wrapped in an afghan, a book in your hand, and a bowl of popcorn at your side, relax while winds howl and night grows colder.

The Pharisees could not understand a teacher of the law who openly delighted in food. But Emmanuel, God-With-Us, pauses while we pluck and munch a few grains of corn. Tonight take childlike joy in hearing the swelling kernels finally pop. Enjoy Squanto's gift to the Old World. Enjoy God's gift of hunger and food to alleviate it. Enjoy sound and taste. Enjoy a Savior who gives his disciples permission to enjoy food.

ℱly a 𝒦ite

Scripture: *Psalm 19*
Key verse: *The heavens declare the glory of God, and the sky displays what his hands have made.*

> I saw you toss the kites on high
> And blow the birds about the sky …
> O wind, a-blowing all day long,
> O wind, that sings so loud a song.

Along with Robert Louis Stevenson, this month we hear the wind singing "so loud a song." We also see it tossing the kites on high, for in this month little boys and girls send many of them soaring into the sky.

But kite-flying need not be limited to childhood. In the last scene of *Mary Poppins*, new spirits broke through old bodies when the Banks family and the staid bankers flew kites in the park. Imitate them and send your own kite into the blue.

The psalmist may not have flown a kite, but his thoughts played with the heavens. He always saw a glory in them and he knew it was the glory of the one who had created them.

Like the stuffy bankers in *Mary Poppins*, too many of us have grown arthritic from lack of play. Today enjoy the wind with the abandon of a small child, or with the imagination of the psalmist. Thrill as the breezes lift your kite higher, carrying it the length of your string.

Raise your eyes to the canopy of sky, the sailing clouds, the magnificent blue dome of God's heavens. Soar into a new season of the soul as well as a new season of the earth.

Budding Branch

SCRIPTURE: *Isaiah 61: 10 – 11*

KEY VERSE: *For as the earth puts forth her blossom or bushes in the garden burst into flower, so shall the Lord God make righteousness and praise blossom before all the nations. (NEB)*

B efore her wedding, the bride's jewels lay waiting on a shelf. Before the earth put forth her blossom, her branches lay bare. Thus, in one of the bleakest moments of Israel's history, Isaiah envisioned a day when righteousness and praise would blossom before all the nations.

Today envision the fulfillment of God's promise in your own life. While the bare March landscape still resembles winter more than spring, the tips of oak and maple, elm and plum begin to swell and redden. Carry one of these harbingers of spring into the living room. Then, while winter clings to a denuded earth, watch life emerge from a small knobby promise on a bare branch.

Although raw winds and icy nights intimidate these small buds outdoors, the warmth of the house forces earlier blossoming. Forsythia, one of the brightest flowers of the month, responds especially well to forcing. When set into a flower frog in a shallow vase, long arching branches of intense yellow blossoms shout hope on the darkest day.

Sometimes life's dark seasons seem unending. Rain follows rain, storm follows storm, and the rare blue skies in between are not enough to convince us winter has ended. Yet Isaiah rejoices because he knows God. He has seen Him turn bleak fields into green ones, slate skies into golden ones, frozen brooks into trickling ones. His God brings blossom out of a bare earth. That kind of God, he reasons, can also make bare souls blossom.

As you wait for the greening of an unhurried earth, live with the promise of things to come.

March 23

Take Ten

SCRIPTURE: *Luke 19: 11 - 26*
KEY VERSE: *"The first servant said, 'Sir, the coin you gave me has earned ten times as much.' The king said to him, 'Good job! You're a good servant. You proved that you could be trusted with a little money. Take charge of ten cities.'"*

> Little drops of water, little grains of sand,
> make the mighty ocean, and the pleasant land.
> So the little minutes, humble though they be,
> Make the mighty ages of eternity.

In theory, we recognize the truth in Julia Carney's verse. But in reality, we usually fail to take it seriously. Perhaps none of us really wants to make an ocean or even a pleasant land. Oceans, lands, and eternity are in God's hands.

But what do we hold in our hands? For some of us, it is a house so cluttered that we don't even know where to start working. Today take ten. Go through the house and pick up ten—just ten—items in each room. The house may not sparkle, but at least you can walk through it.

Some of us have laundry baskets full of wrinkled clothes. Today iron ten—only ten—garments. The basket may not be empty, but at least, it is less intimidating.

Others of us look forward to having the time to sort out recipe collections, make a quilt, write a book, learn to play the piano, or exercise. Today sort out ten recipes. Cut out ten quilt blocks. Spend ten minutes writing, practicing the piano, exercising—or whatever.

In the illustration Jesus used, a master entrusted three servants with one coin each. Perhaps feeling humiliated by its insignificance, one man lay his coin aside. But the other two took their coins seriously. They used what they had, to do what they could. Both men were rewarded for their efforts.

Today take the coin in your hand seriously. Turn it into ten coins.

March 24

Genealogy

SCRIPTURE: *Matthew 1: 1 - 17*
KEY VERSE: *So there were 14 generations from Abraham to David, 14 generations from David until the exile to Babylon, 14 generations from the exile until the Messiah.*

When Abraham was leaving the land of Ur, your pool of genes was in the making. Some contemporary of his was an ancestor of yours. When Moses led the children out of Egypt, your ancestors were baking bread and plowing fields in Egypt, Babylon, or some other part of the ancient world. Your ancestors were there when Persia conquered Babylon, Greece conquered Persia, and Rome conquered Greece.

The genes we carry come from a unique blend of chromosomes passed through every generation of men and women from time's beginning. Any change in these combinations would have eliminated our existence, for exact combinations of genes create the individuals we are.

How much do you know about these combinations which created your genetic makeup? Genealogy was important to people of the ancient world; it defined who they were. Often their ancestry was their identity, and reciting their genealogy connected them to a God who began working before they were born and who continued working through them.

Today make a family tree which traces your ancestry as far back as records allow. If you have already done this, see how much of it you can produce from memory. Then go a step further. Research the political, economic, and social conditions surrounding the life of one of your ancestors. Learn something about shelter, food, disease, and inventions of that time. Step in the shoes of those men and women whose genes still live in you.

Because there is only one God, whether our ancestors acknowledged him or not, their God was also our God. Today see God through the telescope of time.

March 25

Small Treat

SCRIPTURE: *Matthew 22:34 - 40*
KEY VERSE: *The second is like it: 'Love your neighbor as you love yourself.'*

> Three plum buns
> To eat here at the stile
> In the clover meadow,
> For we have walked a mile.

W hether you have walked Christina Rossetti's mile or not, today treat yourself to three plum buns. Or an ice cream cone, or a long soak in the bathtub. Have your hair done, buy yourself a new book, or go to a movie. Before the day is over, take time out to do something loving for yourself.

In Frogner Park in Oslo, Norway, a 60 foot granite monolith by Gustav Vigeland depicts 121 figures struggling with each other to reach the top. Many Christians see self-love in this light. They are afraid to really love themselves because they believe it means selfishly pushing themselves ahead of others. This is not healthy theology.

It is not loving ourselves which makes us selfish, but gratifying our desires at someone else's expense. Failure to take into account the needs of others results in the terrible struggle which Vigeland so graphically depicted and which so many people experience. However, healthy self-love, which extends to consideration for others, is simply a celebration of the life which God has given us.

Paradoxically, those who find it difficult to love themselves also find it difficult to love others. When we love ourselves, we affirm our value, and this, in turn, helps us recognize the value of others. So, today give yourself a small treat, and enjoy the life God has given you. Perhaps the highest form of gratitude we can offer our Creator is to daily celebrate life.

March 26

Reassess Budget

SCRIPTURE: *1 Timothy 6: 17 - 19*
KEY VERSE: *Tell them to do good, to do a lot of good things, to be generous, and to share.*

> If there were dreams to sell,
> What would you buy?
> Some cost a passing bell;
> Some a light sigh,
> That shakes from Life's fresh crown
> Only a roseleaf down.

How would you answer the question asked in T. L. Beddoes' poem? No, of course, there are no dreams for sale. But the fulfillment of our dreams carries a cost. There are dreams we can buy.

What are your dreams, and how much are you willing to pay for them? Today look at your spending patterns and determine if they are giving you the things you really want out of life.

Money is one of the tools we hold in our hands, but tools have many uses. A hammer can build a casket or a cradle. Our dollars can put a piano in our living room, supply a child in India with food, or send us on the vacation of our dreams. A hammer drives the nails into the places we put them.

Paul advises Timothy to encourage the wealthier Christians of his congregation to reevaluate their attitude towards money and to seek wealth in noble actions. Every investment reflects our values. Today look at your budget and determine what changes are needed to give first place to your priorities.

If dreams were for sale, what would you buy? Creatively use your money to serve your needs and the needs of others rather than the needs of advertisers who manipulate us for their own profit.

Count your wealth through God's eyes and use it for his glory.

March 27

Remove Cobwebs

SCRIPTURE: *1 Corinthians 13: 1 - 7*
KEY VERSE: *It isn't rude. It doesn't think about itself. It isn't irritable. It doesn't keep track of wrongs.*

The itsy bitsy spider went up the water spout,
Down came the rain and washed the spider out,
Up came the sun and dried out all the rain,
So the itsy bitsy spider went up the spout again.

I n early childhood, our chubby fingers acted out the little spider's adventure, each time rejoicing in his victory over the rain. Later we taught our children and nieces and nephews to be glad because the itsy bitsy spider went up the spout again.

However, all does not seem quite as well when the itsy bitsy spider begins spinning its wonderful silk net across our ceilings. The adhesive property of those silken strands not only captures the spider's prey, but it captures the dingy grime and dirt in the air and then displays it for all the world to see.

All the world often notices our webs before we do. Although we continually look their way, in our preoccupation we easily miss them.

Today lift your eyes to your ceilings, and see them from the fresh perspective of guests who enter the house. Give the itsy bitsy spider a message that it is time to return outside to the water spout.

As you clean ceilings and corners, think about other, less visible cobwebs in your life. Cobwebs of the soul need to be seen and removed as much as cobwebs on the ceiling. Paul's description of love is one of the best mirrors we have for seeing those internal cobwebs. Today take a swipe at some of those soul-webs as well as the ceiling webs.

Put all the spiders in your life back outside where they belong.

March 28

Reconnect

SCRIPTURE: *1 Thessalonians 2: 17 - 19*

KEY VERSE: *Brothers and sisters, we have been separated from you for a little while. Although we may not be able to see you, you're always in our thoughts. We have made every possible effort to fulfill our desire to see you.*

> Reuben, Reuben, I've been thinking
> What a grand world this would be
> If the men were all transported
> Far beyond the shining sea.

B ecause, at times, we've all been fed up with people, we laughingly sing these words with Rachel. But deep inside we know the truth: relationships give life its meaning.

Calling the Thessalonians his joy and glory, Paul chafed at circumstances which separated him from them. However, he assured them by letter that even though they were lost to sight, they were not lost to heart.

Today follow the example of Paul and assure someone of his or her place in your heart. Just as bright orange impatiens turn anemically pale without regular feedings, bright and beautiful relationships also become anemic when neglected. Like Paul, restore or maintain some friendship, especially one suffering from lack of contact.

Surprise a neglected friend with an invitation for lunch, then linger long enough to hear the heart as well as the tongue. Touch base with someone by phone. Write a letter to a faraway friend in some Thessalonica. Let someone who has missed several church services know how much you miss her by taking her a box of homemade cookies.

Paul talked a lot about love, but it was the way he lived it which made an impact on the new Christian communities. Today put love into action and discover its power to usher in the kingdom of God.

March 29

𝒟ecorate

Scripture: *Isaiah 45: 11 - 13*
Key verse: *I made the earth and created humans on it. I stretched out the heavens with my own hands.*

> A thing of beauty is a joy forever:
> Its loveliness increases; it will never
> Pass into nothingness.

John Keats articulated what we have all felt. The night skies, the surging sea, the springtime blossom have filled man with joy from the beginning of time. The flaming sunset, the nesting sparrow, the hanging icicle not only gladden the hearts of humans, but reflect the joy of the Creator.

We find a star-filled night sky beautiful because God first found it beautiful. The patterns of the Milky Way, the Big Dipper, and Orion please us because they pleased God when he created them. Beauty attracts us because God himself loved beauty and filled the universe with it.

The beauty around us is God's gift to us, but our ability to create beauty is another gift from his hand. When we are like God, we are also making our world beautiful. Today be more God-like by making something more beautiful.

As the heavens and earth are the domain of God, our homes are our domain. Here beauty depends on our touch. A carefully arranged bouquet of flowers on the coffee table transforms even the most ordinary room. A bowl of apples, oranges and lemons on the dining room table delights the eye. A child's toy beside the sofa, an afghan thrown over a chair, or a basket of teddy bears in the hallway lend charm to the small world of our home.

God wove beauty into everything he created. Imitate him, and weave beauty into the small world you create within the walls of your home.

March 30

Body Care

Scripture: *1 Corinthians 6:12 – 20*
Key verse: *Don't you know that your body is a temple that belongs to the Holy Spirit?*

> Mirror, mirror on the wall,
> Who is the fairest one of all?

The wicked queen in the fairy tale daily sought assurance that she was the most beautiful lady in the land. The day the mirror spoke Snow White's name, the heart of the jealous queen burned within her. She could not tolerate a rival, and she made plans to have Snow White killed.

The fabric of the fairy tale is truth, for at times, most of us have compared ourselves to others and grieved when we found the other more beautiful. But the Christian gospel carries a greater truth. Our bodies are shrines of the indwelling Holy Spirit. The Lord of our soul is also the Lord of our body.

Today make the bodily shrine of the Holy Spirit more beautiful. Although most of us long ago abandoned our dream of being the fairest one of all, a chance glance in the mirror may, nevertheless, bring a sigh. Work on one area of dissatisfaction, not to impress others with our physical beauty, but to honor the Holy Spirit who dwells within us.

If your hair brings the sigh, have it cut, permed, or conditioned. If winter has been harsh to your skin, take a long soak in a tub filled with bath oils, and then add more moisture with lotion. If you have neglected your nails, clip them and push back the cuticles. Shave your legs. Give yourself a facial. Take care of any area of your body which detracts from the beauty of God's shrine.

Glorify God in your body as well as your soul. Create a shrine worthy of the Holy Spirit.

March 31

Family Quiz

SCRIPTURE: *1 Kings 10: 1 - 9*
KEY VERSE: *The Queen of Sheba heard about Solomon's reputation. (He owed his reputation to the name of the Lord.) So she came to test him with riddles.*

M ost of us choose a well-sharpened knife over a dull one. God also seems to prefer well-sharpened knives. The wisdom he gave Solomon made the surrounding world take notice, and one queen of a neighboring country made a special trip to investigate the rumors she had heard about this king. The writer of Kings says that she asked every question in her heart and was satisfied by every answer Solomon gave.

Unlike Winnie-the-Pooh, a stuffed bear of little brain, we have all the brain power we need. Like Pooh Bear, many of us have to force ourselves to think, think, think, not because we are of little brain, but because we have become sloppy thinkers. Although created in God's divine image, sometimes our speech and behavior more closely resemble the little bear stuffed with fluff.

Today sharpen your mind on a quiz you find in a book, or have fun creating your own quiz. Whether a family trivia quiz, including an aunt who once hiked the Appalachian Trail and an uncle who spent time in jail for stealing chickens, or a geography quiz recalling details of family travels, quizzes add laughter to learning. Exercise some of your "much brain" with a musical quiz, a history quiz, or a literature quiz.

All God's gifts are meant to be used. We may never become Solomons whose fame made queens take notice, but we can more accurately reflect God's image by using more of our brain power. When God asks for a knife, offer him a sharp one.

April 1

Buying Alternative

SCRIPTURE: *Mark 6: 35 – 44*
KEY VERSE: *They said to him, "Should we go and spend about a year's wages on bread to feed them?"*

Astrid Lindgren's Pippi Longstocking once came across a rusty can. Picking it up, she thought it might make a cookie jar. Then putting it on her head, she decided it might make a hat. If she just thought long enough, it might be anything.

We can learn a lot from Pippi Longstocking, one of

the most delightful little girls in the pages of children's literature. For Pippi, the world is one big adventure where something exciting or wonderful might happen at any moment.

When did we adults lose this delightful way of looking at life? Was it when we began assuming any problem could be solved with enough money? Even the disciples of Jesus made that assumption.

Today return to a Pippi Longstocking world. A rusty can may not be something you want to add to your life, but substitute imagination for some purchase. Lacking dates, use raisins in a recipe. Rather than buy a birthday card, use an old one. Cross out the sender's name, and write in your own. Then add recycled and a smiling face. If a four year old pleads for Pocahontas paper dolls, make them yourself.

The disciples found that in Jesus' hands their resources could stretch to meet any need. Today reclaim God's gift of creativity in a moment of need.

April 2

Public Radio

SCRIPTURE: *Ephesians 4:14 - 16*
KEY VERSE: *Then we will no longer be little children, tossed and carried about by all kinds of teachings that change like the wind. We will no longer be influenced by people who use cunning and clever strategies to lead us astray.*

Although the term "sound bite" is only a few years old, we have rapidly become accustomed to simplified messages which train us to react rather than think. However, life is not as simple as this. Paul urges us to think rather than react to simplified, but distorted messages. We see clearly only when we concentrate on the whole picture.

In an age of compressed and often sensational news treatment, public radio still takes times to examine people and issues behind the headlines. Today listen to a public radio commentary and draw your opinions from a larger pool of information. Hear about people who have not made headlines but who are quietly making a difference. The story of a welfare grandmother who tutors high school dropouts may give you another perspective on welfare recipients, rebellious teens, or education. Her story may prod you to tutor a learning disabled child, write your congressman, or befriend a teenager in your neighborhood.

Whether you listen to an in-depth analysis of the headlines or the story of a private agency's work with pregnant teens, the larger context will make you less vulnerable to those who try to manipulate you. If you are already a public radio listener, stretch your horizons by tuning in at a different hour.

Enlarge the frame your opinions hang upon.

April 3

ℒisten

Scripture: *Proverbs 18: 13 - 15*
Key verse: *Whoever gives an answer before he listens is stupid and shameful.*

> Listen, my children, and you shall hear
> Of the midnight ride of Paul Revere...

W as it one lantern in the church belfry or two which indicated the British were coming? Some of us no longer remember. Although Henry Wadsworth Longfellow pointedly cautioned us, we heard his story without listening to it.

Listening is not the forte of all of us. Nor, perhaps, has it ever been the forte of very many. Apparently, some people failed to pay attention even when a king known for his wisdom spoke. Calling them stupid, Solomon pointed out that the wise ear listens to get knowledge.

We miss much because we do not listen. A bird's song fills the air, but we remain oblivious. Beside us, the heart of another may bubble with joy, rage in pain, or shrink from shame. But as we easily miss a bird's song, we easily miss a soul's song because we're not really listening.

The careless listener of three thousand years ago may or may not have repented. But today repent of your own inattentiveness, and begin listening. Listen to birds outside the window and to wind in the trees. Most of all, listen to those speaking on the other end of the phone, on the television set, or around the dining room table.

Rather than hear a friend complain, a gang scream, or a child whine, listen to frustration and feelings of helplessness. Listen to the repeated rejection of one who corners you with a detailed description of her fortunes or misfortunes. Hear the fear and frustration, happiness and excitement, deep pain and fragile hope others are trying to communicate. Hear more than words; hear the heartbeat of the one who speaks the words.

Today gain wisdom by listening rather than speaking.

April 4

Clean Copper

SCRIPTURE: *Ezekiel 24: 11 - 13*
KEY VERSE: *Then set the empty pot on the coals so that it gets hot and its copper glows. Its impurities will melt away, and its tarnish will burn off.*

> To market, to market,
> To buy a fat pig,
> Home again, home again,
> Jiggety-jig.

Perhaps, six thousand years ago, some young Egyptian set off to market to buy a fat pig, but first his eyes caught the gleam of metal in the next stall. Fascinated by the shining pot, he carried it home to his bride.

Since Egyptians began smelting copper, brides throughout history have basked in the warm light of copper cookware. Even in an aluminum-and-stainless-steel age, we treasure copper-bottomed pans for their conductive property.

We also treasure them for their beauty—at least, we treasure them for the potential. As the first Egyptian bride who put her new pan on an outdoor fire discovered, copper quickly tarnishes.

Ezekiel may have once cleaned his mother's corroded pots, for he used the image to describe the rebellious and unfaithful Israelites. What had once been shining and beautiful had become first tarnished and then deeply corroded. Every man and woman had seen corrosion removed by placing copper pots on red-hot coals, and each person understood Ezekiel's reference.

Today restore the beauty of a tarnished copper-bottom pan, and then display it in your kitchen. At the same time, clean off a bit of tarnish spoiling the beauty of your life. God not only creates, but redeems. Imitate him by restoring lost beauty to both your pans and your heart.

April 5

Walk in the Rain

SCRIPTURE: *Joel 2: 21 - 26*
KEY VERSE: *People of Zion, be glad and find joy in the Lord your God ... He has sent the autumn rain and the spring rain as before.*

> Rain, rain, go away,
> Come again another day.
> Little Betty wants to play.

J oel told the people of Zion to rejoice and be glad in their Lord who had once again sent down rain. If Joel were in our midst, he might be disappointed to hear us begging the rain to go away.

Spring beckons, and just as we head for an open door, rain often seems to shut it. Thursday we plan Saturday's outing, Friday we shop for it, and Saturday we watch raindrops collect on the windowpane while the empty picnic basket sits idle on the shelf.

Chanting "rain, rain, go away" may move us to tears, but it has no power to move clouds anywhere. Rather than bemoan the rain, today accept it as God's gift, open up an umbrella, and go out and enjoy it.

Wrapping itself around us like a cocoon, rain insulates us from the world. In the dim light of dark skies, we see no dust on furniture or smudges on windows. However urgently yard work calls, it must wait. Rain invites us to shed Martha-like obsessions and enjoy being Mary-for-a-day.

Letting the distant world remain distant, today contentedly embrace the here-and-now. Go out into the misted fairylike world, and let its softness penetrate you. Listen to raindrops fall onto the softened earth, tap leaf-carpeted woods, or splash in widening puddles on the sidewalk. While rain freshens the earth, feel its drops freshen all that has become stale in you.

April 6

Photo Change

Scripture: *Ephesians 1: 15 – 19*
Key verse: *I never stop thanking God for you. I always remember you in my prayers.*

> Sur le pont d'Avignon
> On y danse, on y danse,
> Sur le pont d'Avignon,
> On y danse tout en rond.

O nce we danced on the bridge of Avignon or around the school May Pole, or we wore an exquisite peach dress to the prom. Only once, but the images captured by our mothers' Brownie cameras fix the time and place forever afterwards.

Like a camera, Paul pictured loved ones scattered across Asia Minor. He saw them as they were and gave thanks for them. He also saw them as they could be, and he continually prayed that they might know even more of God's presence and power in their lives.

Although photos bridge time and space, they may become so familiar that we no longer see the persons behind the faces. Today refresh affections with fresh pictures. Old photos remind us who our loved ones once were, but with the help of updated photos, begin seeing them as they are today.

Replace the smiling third grader in the picture on your desk with a current sixth grade one, and like Paul, pray that she may know the wealth and glory of God's kingdom. Giving thanks for his unique gifts, grant Johnny the privileged place on the mantle. Replace your wedding picture with a photo of your husband trimming roses, and pray that God will fill your marriage with his own love and glory.

By replacing a too-familiar picture with a new one which draws attention, today restore sight to a blind spot. Then, like Paul, keep the loved one in your prayers as well as in your mind.

April 7

Three Course Meal

SCRIPTURE: *Psalm 63*
KEY VERSE: *I am satisfied as with a rich and sumptuous feast and wake the echoes with thy praise. (NEB)*

Salt-sparkled Tomato Juice
Assorted Crackers
Hard Rolls
Tenderloin of Beef Wellington
Whipped Potatoes
Broccoli with Hollandaise
Spinach-Apple Toss
Lime Parfait Pie
Demitasse

P ut on your hat. Put on your gloves. Whatever the occasion, we know this is no jeans-and-sweatshirt supper. Nor is it simply a combed-hair occasion. Daily routines do not call for this kind of elegant dining around a candle-lit table in an expensive restaurant.

Apparently, the psalmist was no stranger to rich and sumptuous food. Perhaps the weddings, births, and festivals of a large family filled the year with feasting occasions. As sumptuous course followed sumptuous course, he ate until his enormous appetite was fully satisfied. He also knew this feeling of total satisfaction in another context. In the presence of the Lord, his spiritual hunger was fully satisfied.

Today, with no occasion other than being in the Lord's presence, prepare a three course meal and feast. Experience the satisfaction of eating all you can until you want no more. Then, like the psalmist, wake the echoes with praise of a God who satisfies the deepest hungers of your life.

April 8

Museum

SCRIPTURE: *Jeremiah 52: 17 – 23*
KEY VERSE: *There were 96 pomegranates on the sides. The total number of pomegranates on the surrounding filigree was 100.*

F or a brief moment, Greece rose on history's stage, and artifacts give small hints of the drama. Examining one of them, John Keats shares his thoughts in "Ode on a Grecian Urn":

> What men or gods are these? What maidens loth?
> What mad pursuit? What struggle to escape?
> What pipes and timbrels? What wild ecstasy?

Reading Jeremiah's account of the plunder of the temple in Jerusalem, we ask similar questions. What faith, dreams, and visions lie behind ninety-six bronze pomegranates running around a pillar eighteen cubits high and twelve cubits in circumference? Whatever the answers, the devastated captives expressed their dashed hopes by hanging up their harps in a foreign land and refusing to sing.

The harps did not remain silent forever. The song goes on in foreign lands never imagined by those captives, and by generations who never laid eyes on the bronze pomegranates. How and why? Today visit a museum, peek through a small window into the past, and learn something about the struggles, dashed dreams, and new hopes which carried the song from one century to another, one land to another, and one person to another.

Examine churns, spinning wheels, and shaped-note songbooks in an 1839 schoolhouse, and mentally walk a few steps with those who used them. Go to a major museum, browse among Egyptian mummies, Roman busts, and Middle Age tapestries; then try to clothe named and unnamed people with flesh and blood.

Contemplate the rise and fall of cultures, and marvel at God's hand working his purposes into and through it all. Wonder about the story behind a bronze pomegranate or an old harp.

April 9

Reorganize a Cupboard

SCRIPTURE: *Leviticus 26: 10 - 13*
KEY VERSE: *You will clear out old food supplies to make room for new ones.*

T here is a time to keep and a time to throw away, the writer of Ecclesiastes wrote.

The book of Leviticus tells us the proper time to throw away. When the new comes into our lives, we must make room for it even if it means getting rid of the old. Last year's harvest was not intended to last forever.

Two thousand years later, Paul emphasized the need to clear out the old to make room for the new. The book of Revelation stresses the new heaven and new earth after the passing of the old one. Newness or renewal is a key word in the Bible, and we call the books written after the incarnation the New Testament.

However, afraid we might need it someday, many of us are reluctant to let go of anything. Sometimes we pass up the fruits of a new harvest because bits and pieces of the old one take up all the space in our lives. If you can't let go of all of them, today, at least, arrange them better. Create space by reorganizing a cupboard. Turn dead space into useful space, and useful space into more efficient space.

God's word to the Israelites was that he himself would walk among them and take care of them. Our God is forever bringing newness into our lives.

April 10

Volunteer

SCRIPTURE: *Matthew 9: 35 - 38*
KEY VERSE: *Then he said to his disciples, "The harvest is large, but the workers are few."*

I can easier teach twenty what were good to be done,
than be one of the twenty to follow mine own teaching.

C an't we all! Like Shakespeare's Portia in *The Merchant of Venice*, we find it easy to tell others what to do, but less easy do it ourselves.

With accounts of a speeding driver shooting a policeman, an enraged man murdering his wife's boyfriend, and a homeless child sleeping in a grocery cart, newspapers create Portias in many of us. We know what the White House, state legislature, and city council should do.

But few of us do anything. Jesus must have been surrounded by Portias, for he saw a heavy crop going to waste for lack of workers. The morning newspaper emphasizes his words, for the crop appears to be rapidly spoiling.

Today volunteer to save part of it. We cannot save the policeman who was shot. But by tutoring an adolescent with learning problems, we may replace frustration with coping power and root out some of tomorrow's violence. We can do nothing for the enraged husband, but by reading to children in an elementary classroom, we may help break the cycle of violence in dysfunctional homes.

Nor do we have answers for the homeless. But by becoming a Mentor-Mom to a pregnant teenager, giving English lessons to an immigrant, or teaching a junior high Sunday School class, we may equip future families with coping skills for difficult times.

Jesus told his disciples the crop was heavy, but the laborers were few. Today become a laborer and change at least one of tomorrow's headlines.

April 11

Hop, Skip, and Jump

Scripture: *Psalm 114*
Key verse: *The mountains jumped like rams. The hills jumped like lambs.*

> Spring, the sweet spring, is the year's pleasant king;
> Then blooms each thing, then maids dance in a ring,
> Cold doth not sting, the pretty birds do sing;
> Cuckoo, jug-jug, pu-we, to-witta-woo!

O ver five hundred years ago, the sweet spring gladdened the heart of Thomas Nashe. As earth awoke, each thing on it bloomed, sang, or danced, and he joined his own song to theirs.

The same sweet spring emerges before our marveling eyes. Baby bunnies appear beneath the roots of the maple tree in the yard. Robins pull long worms from the rain-softened ground. Phoebes nest in the porch eaves. Daffodils and tulips color the lawn, and hummingbirds dip long beaks into the bright blooms. Some trees wear pastel green organdy, and others don soft pink or white blossoms.

Earth sings. Bees buzz. In the meadow, lambs and kid goats skip and frolic. The whole earth rejoices in a new season, and all creation participates in a burst of enthusiasm. The psalmist says that the mountains jumped like rams, the hills like young sheep. Only man holds back, forgetting he too has the capacity for unrestrained joy.

When life fills up, small children let it spill over. They skip down the path or jump across the lawn just for the fun of it. They hop, turn somersaults, and swing high into the air. They blow bubbles and catch rainbows.

Why should we adults hold back joy? Today let it out by skipping, hopping, or jumping. Let the child in you out to play. Imitate bunnies and lambs, birds and butterflies. Play and praise in unrestrained joy.

April 12

$\mathcal{N}atural$ $\mathcal{F}ood$ $Store$

SCRIPTURE: *Jeremiah 5: 21 - 25*
KEY VERSE: *But your wrongdoing has upset nature's order, and your sins have kept from you her kindly gifts. (NEB)*

> Oats, peas, beans, and barley grow,
> Oats, peas, beans, and barley grow.
> Do you or I or anyone know
> How oats, peas, beans, and barley grow?

O f course, we know. They grow in fields. Taking a package of instant cinnamon-and-apple flavored oatmeal off the shelf, we empty it into a bowl, add boiling water, and begin stirring. Suddenly, our brows wrinkle. Barley? What's barley?

In our generation, we have lost touch with our grains. From farmers' hands to engineers' hands, oats, peas, beans, and barley exchange a field fragrance for an instant-cinnamon-and-apple flavor. Still, eating on the run, we may give thanks for progress which leaves the field fragrance in the fields. The instant flavor simplifies our rushed morning schedules.

Jeremiah may have been less enthusiastic about the exchange of flavors. Over two thousand years ago, he told Israelites they were upsetting nature's order and robbing themselves of her kindly gifts. Since dirty air hovers over our cities, filling our lungs and affecting every cell of our bodies, evidence indicates we are still robbing ourselves of nature's kindly gifts.

Today, like Jeremiah, give attention to nature's order. Get back to your grains by visiting a natural food store filled with non-processed foods low in cholesterol, high in fiber, and rich in natural sugars. Run fingers through bins of oats, peas, beans, and barley. Smell and enjoy the natural field fragrance. Discover the excitement of healthy eating in natural foods cookbooks.

Oats, peas, beans and barley still grow in the fields.
Today become better acquainted with their natural state.

April 13

Stimulating Guest

SCRIPTURE: *Luke 24: 28 - 32*
KEY VERSE: *They said to each other, "Weren't we excited when he talked with us on the road and opened up the meaning of the Scriptures for us?"*

Pussy cat, pussy cat, where have you been?
I've been up to London to look at the queen.
Pussy cat, pussy cat, what did you there?
I frightened a little mouse under the chair.

He could have seen lords and ladies, but he saw only a mouse. Like the little pussy, we often see no further than our own concerns.

Long ago, the risen Lord walked beside Cleopus and his companion on the road to Emmaus. But they did not recognize him. However, they were drawn to this stimulating man, and as they arrived home, they pressed the stranger to stay with them. He did, and their lives were never quite the same.

Like Cleopas, today share a meal in your home with some stimulating person. Invite the English teacher who introduces your daughter to the wonderful world of literature. Then over the dinner table, walk with her through English manor houses she explored last summer.

If you have always appreciated your dentist's interest in the world beyond his office, discover how big his world really is by asking him and his family to come for dinner. He may volunteer his services in a Latin American barrio every year, support an orphan in India, or bike through Europe, but you may never know unless you take the initiative to get better acquainted.

Rather than go to London to see the queen, invite another person to be royalty in your home tonight. Instead of the rustle of fine dresses, you will hear the thoughts and dreams of another human being. Like Cleopas, you may discover another dimension to life.

April 14

Sounds of Music

SCRIPTURE: *Psalm 65: 9 – 13*
KEY VERSE: *The pastures are covered with flocks. The valleys are carpeted with grain. All of them shout triumphantly. Indeed, they sing.*

> Farewell to the mountains, high-covered with snow!
> Farewell to the straths and green valleys below!
> Farewell to the forests and wild hanging woods!
> Farewell to the torrents and loud-pouring floods!

Before he wrote the words, how much time had Robert Burns spent listening to the song of the highlands? Hiking the mountains, looking down on the valleys, and listening to the torrents, he heard music which never left his soul.

Her beautiful voice swelling above the majestic mountains of Austria, Julie Andrews reminded us the hills are alive with the sound of music. Three thousand years earlier, the psalmist heard the same sound of music in hills, meadows, and valleys, and he too sang about it.

Today hear some of that music which the psalmist described, Robert Burns felt, and Julie Andrews brought to our attention. Listen to the music of earth, sky, and sea. Thrill to more than words; thrill to sounds which have no words.

Few of us recognize a bird by its call. However, rather than hearing birds, today hear robins, finches, and blue jays.

Hear mocking birds and woodpeckers, quail and doves.

Hear a symphony in falling rain or a concerto in a storm. Listen to the cantata of water rushing down the side of a mountain. Detect a melody in the gurgling sounds of the stream at the bottom of the hill.

Birds return, winds blow, bees explore. For a few minutes, be silent and hear the sounds of life. God raises a baton; sit still long enough to hear a few strains of his music.

April 15

Copy

SCRIPTURE: *Philippians 3: 15 - 17*

KEY VERSE: *Brothers and sisters, imitate me, and pay attention to those who live by the example we have given you.*

> Diddle diddle dumpling, my son John,
> He went to bed with his stockings on;
> One shoe off, one shoe on,
> Diddle diddle dumpling, my son John.

L ittle John will not always go to bed that way. He will soon notice his father, mother, and sisters remove both stockings and shoes before they climb into bed, and he will do the same.

Knowing how role models shape our lives, Paul begged the Philippians to adopt healthy ones. He offered himself as a model and urged new Christians to find other models whose life conformed to the teachings of the Lord.

We owe much of our faith, personality, and lifestyle to the role models we followed. We eat Rice Krispies® for breakfast, Chinese eat rice, and Thai eat soup because of the role models we each followed. The way we dress, decorate our house, and speak reflects the books we have read, the people we have watched, and the friends we have chosen.

Today change something you do not like about yourself by choosing a new role model. Whether improving social skills by watching a gracious hostess or adding charm to your home with ideas from *Country Journal,* copy the ways of those  who excel in an area where you feel deficient. As we learned behavior patterns from others, we can relearn them in the same way.

Rather than pouring his world in concrete or ceramic, God created living organisms which continually change. As Paul urged, today change some area of your life by changing role models.

April 16

Share Your Faith

SCRIPTURE: *Romans 1: 16 – 17*
KEY VERSE: *I'm not ashamed of the Good News. It is God's power to save everyone who believes, Jews first and Greeks as well.*

> Wee Willie Winkie runs through the town,
> Upstairs and downstairs, in his nightgown,
> Tirlin' at the window, cryin' at the lock,
> "Are the weans in their beds?
>   For it's now ten o'clock."

W as a ten o'clock bedtime really so crucial that Wee Willie Winkie had to warn everyone of the hour? Perhaps not. But what was important was that Willie believed it was.

Like Wee Willie Winkie, when we believe something is important, we let others know. Learning that the water will be turned off on Tuesday or the electricity on Thursday, we alert our neighbors. We notify acquaintances when a mutual friend dies. If we were to read about the recent discovery of a drug to prevent Alzheimer's disease, we would eagerly tell our friends.

Paul believed the Gospel was important, and he traveled from one end of Asia Minor to the other talking about it. Some disciples must have been reluctant to talk about their faith, for in his letter to the Romans, Paul emphasized he was not ashamed of the Gospel. He believed it had saving power for all who had faith, and he had to share it.

After 2000 years, the good news still transforms us from mere specks among the galaxies into children cradled, loved, and redeemed by the Creator. Today pass on the wonderful news.

Eagerly let someone know what God is doing in your life. Even in the blackest night, express your faith that God is working. However small your candle, today hold it high. Someone out there needs the light.

April 17

Creative Journal Entry

SCRIPTURE: *2 Timothy 4: 9 - 13*
KEY VERSE: *When you come, bring the cloak I left with Carpus at Troas, and the books, above all my notebooks. (NEB)*

In a Brazilian *favela* where people lived by begging, stealing, and scrounging, Carolina Maria de Jesus, a woman as poor as her neighbors, kept a diary. When it was discovered, sociology professors around the world referred to it.

A fourteen-year-old girl kept a private diary of her thoughts and the details of her life in hiding. Perhaps more than any statistics, *The Diary of Anne Frank* gives a face to the horror of Nazi persecution of Jews.

In *White House Diary*, Lady Bird Johnson recorded her private thoughts, fears, and reflections, adding a soul account to the media accounts of a presidency. But she also wrote about eating stuffed peppers and corn bread, something any of us could write about.

From a cardboard shack in one of the world's worst slums to the halls of one of the world's most privileged houses, women find healing by writing about their hopes, fears, and struggles. Paul may have also worked out his frustrations and developed his insights through writing in his journal. Giving Timothy a list of things to bring him, he wrote "above all, my notebooks."

Whether your day is filled with ordinary details like preparing stuffed peppers and corn bread for dinner, or whether it carries the trauma of being singled out for persecution, today write about it. Neither events or nonevents give a journal significance, for only our responses can do that. Creatively and honestly record what is going on inside you or around you.

Our journal probably won't be published. Like Paul, most of us will simply find more power in our lives by expressing what we feel and think.

April 18

National Geographic

SCRIPTURE: *Acts 17: 24 - 26*
KEY VERSE: *From one man he has made every nation of humanity to live all over the earth.*

> We are the music makers,
> And we are the dreamers of dreams,
> Wandering by lone sea-breakers,
> And sitting by desolate streams ...

In his poem "From Ode," Arthur O'Shaughnessy talks about the dreams of all men of all ages. Paul says in Him, the universal giver of life and breath, all of us live move, and have our being. Today learn more about some of those people to whom he gave life, breath, and above all, love.

Open the pages of *National Geographic* and peer inside an open door in Tibet, sit around a low table in Afghanistan, or attend an Easter festival in Poland. Look for the image of the divine in diverse ʹ ⸱ ⁻ᵗ⁻res and cultures where other people live, move, and have their being in their Creator.

Examine Cairo through the eyes of an Egyptian woman, climb the Andes with a Bolivian farmer, and weave your way through Mexico City with a street child. Hear raucous sounds of a Bombay street, smell fresh fish changing hands in a Bangkok market, or sniff the fragrance of cardamom on Stockholm streets. Climb a peak of the Himalayas, or sail the Mediterranean.

Since God transcends all boundaries, today step across one of your own, travel to a far away place, and take a short walk with him. See his love reflected in new faces and new places.

April 19

A Drive

SCRIPTURE: *Psalm 147: 1 - 11*
KEY VERSE: *He provides rain for the ground. He makes grass grow on the mountains.*

God clothes the mountains in green grass, and like a newly painted canvas, his handiwork begs admiration. When spring rains turned the hills of Palestine green, the psalmist must have often walked up into them to explore the miracle of returning life. Moved by what he saw, his soul lifted in praise, and he wrote songs of thanksgiving to the Lord.

Like him, today pause to admire this miracle of renewal. Drive into the fresh country side, meander along winding back roads, and for a few minutes stop beside a gushing waterfall. Pull over beside an old red barn where a week-old calf eagerly nurses. Walk across a covered bridge and listen to the rushing stream below. Watch hawks swoop over newly plowed fields.

Examine wild flowers in the grass. How many wild flowers does one spring contain? Thousands? Millions? But how many do we miss? We may be blessed with eighty springs, but unless we keep our eyes and ears open, we miss the miracle in all of them.

Since fickle memories so soon turn traitor, record the beauty of this day on film. Photograph pink blossoms against old gray barn boards and fix skipping lambs in your memory with a picture. One glorious field of dandelions captured by the camera can last a lifetime.

Spring has a hundred voices, or a thousand voices, and they all call. Newly dressed robins call, shy winds call, small pussy willows call. Today, answer. Take a drive and tuck a miracle into an hour of life. The earth was dead, and now it lives! Like the psalmist, lift your heart in thanksgiving and sing a song of praise to the Lord for his handiwork.

April 20

Langston Hughes Poem

SCRIPTURE: *Luke 16: 19 – 31*
KEY VERSE: *Lazarus would have eaten any scraps that fell from the rich man's table. Lazarus was covered with sores, and dogs would lick them.*

> I am the darker brother.
> They send me to eat in the kitchen
> When company comes,
> But I laugh
> And eat well
> And grow strong.*

* Excerpt from "I, Too, Sing America" by Langston Hughes, © 1926 by Alfred A. Knopf, Inc.

The beggar at the rich man's gate may not have shared the dreams of Langston Hughes who wrote "I, Too, Sing America." Like the lighter brother who sent the darker one to the kitchen, the rich man may never have given any thought to the familiar beggar at his gate.

What would it have taken to make him aware of the poor man? What would it take to awaken us to the plight of the poor in our midst? Today make yourself more sensitive by reading a Langston Hughes poem.

In disarmingly simple language, this African-American poet articulates the struggles of the disenfranchised as perhaps no other poet has done. He captures not only the plight of victims of injustice, but their soul as well.

Not many of us have our own lives totally together. While blaming others for their failures, we often justify our own. However, the poetry of minority poets often helps us realize how much others are trying in the face of great odds.

Because we all struggle with some character defect, unhealthy chapter of the past, or difficult circumstance, the poems of Langston Hughes do more than speak about the plight of others. They help us identify our own struggles.

But today let his poetry, or the poetry of another minority poet, awaken you to the presence of Lazarus the next time you pass him.

April 21

Serve Fish

SCRIPTURE: *Luke 24: 36 – 43*
KEY VERSE: *They gave him a piece of broiled fish. He took it and ate it while they watched him.*

Man told his first fish story the first time a fish eluded his spear. And he has told them ever since. For thousands of years, we have told and retold the story of Jonah, and new generations continue to read Herman Melville's

Moby Dick and Ernest Hemingway's *The Old Man and the Sea.* The sea with all its fish captures man's imagination.

And his appetite. Whether served dried in a Zairean open-air market, raw in a Tokyo restaurant, or floating in their shells in a Mediterranean soup, fish remains a favorite of people around the world. The gospels record few details of what Jesus and the disciples ate, but fish is mentioned several times. After the resurrection, Jesus proved his reality to skeptical disciples by eating fish in front of them.

Tonight connect to the living Jesus by eating fish. Like the disciples, when life falls apart, we often think of Jesus in the past tense, losing faith in the living Jesus in our midst. Eating lobster, stream trout, or canned mackerel, tonight acknowledge a living Jesus who ate fish after leaving the grave.

Low-cholesterol fish may have kept the disciples' arteries unclogged, but the outings which brought in their fish undoubtedly played their part. The storyteller Jesus must have often laughed with the disciples over their big fish stories, and their laughter probably also contributed to healthy hearts.

Through the centuries, how many million families have sat down to a fish dinner? How many billions of fish have all the waters of time produced? Today enjoy this miracle of the seas which even God-become-man enjoyed.

April 22

Turn a Day

SCRIPTURE: *Luke 11:33 – 36*
KEY VERSE: *Your eye is the lamp of your body. When your eye is unclouded, your whole body is full of light.*

There was a little girl, who had a little curl
Right in the middle of her forehead,
And when she was good, she was very, very good,
But when she was bad she was horrid.

Like Henry Wadsworth Longfellow's little girl, some of our days are very, very good. But when they are bad, they are horrid. If today is one of those horrid, dark days, work hard to reverse it.

Jesus said poor eyesight creates these dark days; for when our eyes are healthy, we dwell in the light. Therefore, change a bad day into a good one by healing your eyesight.

When friends gloss over difficulties, we call them Pollyannas. But Pollyanna simply saw sunlight behind every shadow. Paul also looked beyond negatives to a brighter side of life where a loving God worked good in any circumstance.

When the family antique breaks, discover for yourself that life is far more than any possession. If rain darkens the skies, see beyond the clouds to the blade and blossom they leave behind. Let a nasty mood alert you to something wrong below the surface. Rather than trying to force open the door which closes in your face, look around for a still-open or newly-opened one.

Polyanna's positive spirit influenced an entire community. Today unashamedly be a Pollyanna and see good wherever you look. Or be a Paul and believe that all things work together for good for those who love the Lord and live for him.

Bad days come, but they only stay when we make them feel welcome.

April 23

Freebie

Scripture: *1 Timothy 6: 9 – 12*
Key verse: *Certainly, the love of money is the root of all kinds of evil.*

> I love sixpence,
> Jolly little sixpence,
> I love sixpence
> Better than my life.

H anging on to our sixpence with one hand, we use the other to grab anything free. A car dealer on South Main is handing out free digital watches, a book club offers three free books, and a bank is giving away free calculators.

We love the feel of jolly little sixpence, and we eagerly run after freebies so we can hold on to our sixpence a little longer. However, some of us run after too many freebies. We end up with hands, arms, and houses full of clutter. Today, resist the temptation to accept anything which is free. Wisely accept only a free offer which meets a genuine need.

If you need a cheap digital watch, accept one from the car dealer on South Main. But if you already have too many cheap watches which don't keep proper time, spend your sixpence and buy a good one. If three free books or a first-one-free magazine would bring a breath of fresh air into your life, jump at the offer. But if magazine or book space already competes with people space, get rid of some rather than add more.

The wise woman uses rather than loves her jolly little sixpence, and she is not tempted to clutter her life with free offers. Wisely accept free offers which contribute to the quality of life rather than to the quantity of possessions.

April 24

Great Person

SCRIPTURE: *John 1: 6 - 18*
KEY VERSE: *Out of his full store we have all received grace upon grace. (NEB)*

S he was a small, wrinkled lady who wore neither jewelry nor makeup. She had no possessions, and she survived on scanty food rations. She wandered the streets and picked up friends who also wandered the streets.

Who was she? Mother Teresa, recognized by queens, statesmen, and journalists as one of greatest people of this century.

He was a small wizened man, and he wore a cloth that some Westerners called a diaper. He possessed a loom, for he liked to weave, and two books, the Koran and the Bible, which he read daily. He ate little, walked almost everywhere he went, and slept on a mat.

Who was he? Ghandi, the man acclaimed by history books for conquering an empire without a weapon.

Mother Teresa lived among the dying on the streets of India; Ghandi set India free from foreign control. Some great people wake up in the White House, and others wake up to the cry of an autistic child. Some work out peace accords with warring nations, and others carry soup to the bedside of an invalid. Neither bank account, newspaper coverage, nor citizenship determines greatness.

John tells us that out of Christ's full store of grace we have all received grace upon grace. Few of us were born with a silver spoon in our mouth, but with grace we do not need one. Great people use that grace to face life courageously and creatively. Rather than being overcome, they are overcomers.

Today think about the great people you know. Whether a Mother Teresa or an aunt who triumphed over great heartache, find inspiration in the way another person faces life's heartaches and traumas.

Accept more grace into your own life, calling out more of the greatness in yourself.

April 25

Pick Up Litter

SCRIPTURE: *Isaiah 24: 4 – 6*
KEY VERSE: *The earth is polluted by those who live on it.*

Rub-a-dub-dub,
Three men in a tub;
And who do you think they be?
The butcher, the baker,
The candlestick-maker;
And all of them gone to sea.

B ut what did they do with the tub when they finished using it? Some of us may have seen it on the beach, its rusted, bent shape half-buried in the sand.

The have-nots of the world suffer because of what they don't have. But we who have, suffer because of what we have left over. Like the inhabitants of ancient Israel, we behold the desecration of the earth simply by walking down the street. Litter here, there, and everywhere meets our eyes.

Whether it is the remains of the tub that went to sea or the leftover wrapper from someone's candy, today dispose of a piece of litter. Why should you pick it up?

Sometimes, we either haul away the rusting tub, or we walk around it every time we go to the beach. In today's world, we often choose between disposing of other people's litter or living with it. While most neighborhoods have many angry role models, many lack caring ones. Picking up one candy wrapper on the sidewalk and throwing it into a trash can may send a more powerful message than a lifetime of anger and condemnation.

Isaiah's words have become our words. Today look beyond Isaiah to the Savior. In Christ-like fashion, take the wages of sin on yourself.

April 26

Frisbee

Scripture: *Zechariah 8: 1 – 6*
Key verse: *The city will be filled with boys and girls playing in the streets.*

Some nights seem to last forever, and Israel's lasted so long that the Jewish exiles began to lose faith in the power of light. But in a moment of deep discouragement, the Lord spoke through Zechariah. The night of the exiled people would give way to the full light of day.

One day the Lord would return to Zion, and that day joy and gladness would also return. No longer would men and women of great age hide away because of darkness, but go outdoors to sit. When night passed, boys and girls would again play in the streets.

Five hundred years after Zechariah's vision, the Messiah brought the night to an end. Walking through the streets, he opened his arms to the boys and girls playing there. He touched the sick ones so they could again go outdoors and jump, climb, and play ball.

Have we forgotten? The Lord has come! Night has passed, and the day of joy and gladness has dawned! Jesus insisted that healthy adults in the kingdom of Heaven keep the inner child alive. Today express your joy and gladness the way a child does. Go outside and play.

While the spring breeze reddens your cheeks and puts a sparkle in your eyes, throw a Frisbee® back and forth with a friend or family member. Run as it sails past you, laugh as the wind carries it off course, and reach tall as it flies above you. Inhale deeply and welcome fresh air into your bloodstream.

Share Zechariah's vision. Be one of the playing children symbolizing the presence of the Lord in our world.

April 27

Illustrate

SCRIPTURE: *Galatians 3: 15 - 18*
KEY VERSE: *My brothers, let me give you an illustration. (NEB)*

I never saw a moor,
I never saw the sea;
Yet know I how the heather looks,
And what a wave must be.

Like Emily Dickinson, many of us who have never seen a moor can picture one. All the authors describing heather-filled moors have practically placed our feet in them.

Paul also makes his readers see things they have never laid eyes on. Like Jesus, he drew stories from everyday life to explain the Gospel. As he pictured the known, his listeners caught a glimpse of the unknown.

The more we illustrate, the more we communicate. Paul gave illustrations with words, and early Christians communicated their faith with the illustration of a fish. Today we use a cross to illustrate our faith. With both words and pictures, Beatrix Potter created such a convincing little character that her readers know a rabbit who exists only in their minds.

Today communicate through illustration. Announce the arrival of spring on the envelope of your letter by sketching a robin pulling a worm out of the lawn. Draw the purple crocus you saw in the flower beds yesterday afternoon. Leave a big happy face on the mirror of the clean bathroom or in a child's lunch pail.

Like Paul, illustrate with words. Give someone a chance to see the cute baby by describing how she dressed up in her father's hat and shoes. Make God's goodness tangible by sharing how he sent help when the car broke down on the freeway. Illustrate a good day by pointing out you made every green light on the way to the supermarket.

We all have good news to share. Today share yours so vividly others see what you are saying.

ℱresh Garment

SCRIPTURE: *Galatians 3: 26 - 29*
KEY VERSE: *Clearly, all of you who were baptized in Christ's name have clothed yourselves with Christ.*

Clothes make the man, it is said. Even if they don't make the woman, they play their part. Put us in beggar's clothes, and we feel a beggar. Deck us in exquisite attire, and we feel exquisite.

Paul says when we have been baptized in Christ's name, we have clothed ourselves with Christ. If exquisite attire makes us feel exquisite, how do we feel dressed in the majesty of the Lord of Lords and the glory of the King of Kings? In such garments we should walk tall, hold heads high, and face each day with confidence and joy.

Today clothe yourself with Christ, and as a symbolic gesture, wear a different outfit. If you automatically reach into the closet for jeans and knit shirt, pull out a skirt and blouse instead. Choose a dress you haven't worn all season, resurrect one of the sweaters in the bottom drawer, or wear a blouse still carrying the price tag on the sleeve.

Is the green corduroy skirt married to the white tailored blouse? Today break up the couple and wear a frilly blouse. Match the green skirt with a blue blouse or purple sweater. Create your own stunning color combination.

Bring out your finer qualities by wearing your best pearls. Or add color to the day with gaudy red and purple bracelets on your wrist. Pin your grandmother's antique brooch to your most elegant dress.

As a new creation in Christ, today dress the part. Look new and feel new. Be sophisticated or wonderfully casual. Be pretty. Be practical or impractical. Be different, and carry over the difference into the rest of the day.

April 29

Tourist Sight

SCRIPTURE: *Acts 17: 16 - 23*
KEY VERSE: *While Paul was waiting for Silas and Timothy in Athens, he saw that the city had statues of false gods everywhere. This upset him.*

A thens, Greece! What little boy of the Mediterranean world had not heard of the great city which turned out philosophers as easily as Rome turned out soldiers?

Since childhood, Paul had heard of Athens, and now he eagerly walked its streets. But he met disappointment, for the city was full of idols and men discussing them. At that point, he could have walked away in disgust. Always a thinker, Paul connected the clues to the Athenian mentality and began preaching at the point where they were.

Unlike Paul, we often try to share the good news at the point where we are rather than at the point where others are. Today gain some insight into where others are by visiting a tourist sight in your area. Use your mind as well as your eyes to better understand the hearts and minds of those around you.

Walk through a historic church where Puritans worshiped in closed pews, or one where Spaniards leafed frescoes in gold, and better understand the values of today's descendents of these long ago men and women. Wander through the birthplace of Robert Frost, then touch base with local Frost-lovers by brushing up on his poetry. Explore a cemetery holding the remains of massacred pioneers and see the footprints of these men in contemporary society.

Visit an old ghost town and see the shadows of their founders in the character of the area. Take a guided tour of an old mansion, a lumber mill, a coal mine, and learn something about men and women you pass each day on the street.

Like Paul, when you share the good news, connect it with the value of those needing the news.

April 30

Meal Plans

SCRIPTURE: *Proverbs 31: 15 – 18*

KEY VERSE: *She wakes up while it is still dark and gives food to her family.*

"Ay, when fowls have no feathers and fish have no fin." With these words in Shakespeare's *Comedy of Errors*, Dromio of Syracuse answers Dromio of Ephesus who begs admittance at the door.

Aha! When cooked, neither fowls have feathers nor fish have fins. But perhaps the thought never occurred to Dromio of Ephesus, for he did not gain entrance by delivering them to Dromio of Syracuse.

Nor does it always occur to us. Meetings run longer than anticipated, traffic jams tie us up, and three o'clock doctor's appointments turn into waiting sessions. Finally rushing home, many of us think macaroni rather than fowl, and hot dogs rather than fish.

How long has it been since you served barbecued chicken or stuffed baked potatoes? Too long? The writer of Proverbs described a capable wife in these words: "She puts on strength like a belt and goes to work with energy."

When we simply let things happen, they usually don't. Barbecued chicken and stuffed baked potatoes give way to packaged-something.

Like the well-organized wife in Proverbs, go to work with energy, and plan so well your meals go right. Today plan thirty-one dinners for May and tentatively arrange them on a calendar. Balance old favorites with new recipes, time-consuming meals with instant ones, and pricey dinners with low-cost options. Prepare for at least one company dinner.

Then, when traffic ties you up or a headache throbs, shift an instant-meal forward. When an unexpected guest arrives, graciously invite her to stay for dinner. This next month give your family the good food they deserve.

The Sea

SCRIPTURE: *Psalm 93*

KEY VERSE: *The Lord above is mighty—mightier than the sound of raging water, mightier than the foaming waves of the sea.*

> I must forth again tomorrow!
> With the sunset I must be
> Hull down on the trail of rapture
> In the wonder of the sea.

Although few of us dream of sailing, as did Richard Hovey in "The Sea Gypsy," the sea nevertheless enraptures us. Tired of the confines of life and land, we long to look past limits, to stand at the edge of the surging sea where infinity seems to swallow both small concerns and great aching chasms.

Like the psalmist so many centuries ago, standing beside the pounding waves we begin to comprehend the reality of the incomprehensible. From all eternity God is God, mightier far than the breakers of the sea, mightier far than any tangled threads in our own lives. With the psalmist, we bow our souls in adoration.

Today go to the sea, stand before the breakers, and worship the Lord. Or connect with the ocean through part of the network feeding into it. Sit beside a rushing stream, stand beneath a waterfall, or watch small waves lap a lake shore. In your mind, follow the creek, stream, or rushing river to its mouth where the great sea swallows it up.

Back away from problems, and let them fall into the context of eternity and infinity. Set free from nagging concerns, hear a few notes of the music of the universe and trace it to the Creator. Then return to your responsibilities praising the Eternal.

Encyclopedia

SCRIPTURE: *Proverbs 16: 16 – 18*
KEY VERSE: *How much better it is to gain wisdom than gold, and the gaining of understanding should be chosen over silver.*

> We are all in the dumps,
> For diamonds are trumps;
> The kittens are gone to St. Paul's.
> The babies are bit,
> The Moon's in a fit,
> And the houses are built without walls.

Perhaps, rather than a trump of diamonds, the nursery rhyme's sad victims needed a bit more knowledge to turn their fate around. Like them and the cripple seeking silver and gold, we often seek help in the wrong way.

Proverbs says that neither silver nor gold can compare with the value of knowledge. Therefore, whatever the trumps, today hold out your hand for knowledge. Turn to an encyclopedia, one of the all-time greatest collections of knowledge, and learn something from it.

When a porcupine nibbles the tips of the willow tree, do you wonder about his eating habits? Find out that and more in the entry about porcupines, and gain new insight into God's handiwork. If another major earthquake levels a city, read about this natural disaster, and learn more about the earth which sustains us. Discover something about an unfamiliar nation mentioned in the newscast, and enlarge your view of the world.

With the wealth of nature and human experience at our fingertips, some of us remain paupers. Today set aside the counting and recounting of coins. Catch a glimpse of the kingdom, the power, and the glory in our midst.

Gardening Start

SCRIPTURE: *Proverbs 24:30 – 34*
KEY VERSE: *I passed by a lazy person's field, the vineyard belonging to a person without sense.*

> Our remedies oft in ourselves do lie,
> Which we ascribe to heaven: the fated sky
> Gives us free scope...

L ike the writer of Proverbs, Helena in Shakespeare's *All's Well That Ends Well* knows we are responsible for our actions. Perhaps the idle man in Proverbs blamed fate for the condition of his fields. His soil was rockier than his neighbors', his oxen more clumsy, or his constitution weaker. The wise man knew that the man, not the conditions, determines the field.

Today wisely determine your own field, flower bed, or window box. Still soft from melting snow and spring rains, soil responds readily to spade and trowel, rake and hoe. Seize the moment of readiness to begin creating the beautiful garden of your dreams.

Borrow ideas from others to help create patches of paradise around you. Give color an early start with potted geraniums, impatiens, or petunias. Invite summer to fill your garden by planting seed now. If you expect another freeze, germinate seed indoors.

While the idle woman uses lack of space as an excuse, the wise one makes even limited space beautiful. Potted daffodils bring fields inside, window boxes lend charm to apartments, and hanging planters of fuchsia or pansies brighten the smallest room.

God has given us power over our environment. Today relinquish all excuses, and make the small patch of earth under your control more beautiful. Let those who pass your house observe occupants of good sense.

Care Package

SCRIPTURE: *1 John 3: 14 - 17*

KEY VERSE: *Now, suppose a person has enough to live on and notices another believer in need. How can God's love be in that person if he doesn't bother to help the other believer?*

> Who alone suffers most i' the mind,
> But then the mind much sufferance doth o'erskip
> When grief hath mates and bearing fellowship.

In Shakespeare's *King Lear*, Edmund expressed how most of us feel in hard times. But Cain expressed another side of human nature when he asked, "Am I my brother's keeper?"

Continually exposed to television's images of suffering people around the world, we shut out much of it in order to sleep at night. Perhaps God's kingdom would come more quickly if more of us tossed and turned.

Today look around and find someone in need. Whether he or she suffers in mind, body, or soul, relieve a little of it by bearing fellowship, as Shakespeare's Edmund suggested. With a care package, participate in another's suffering.

Ease a student's end-of-term stress with a box of peanut butter cookies. Send an anonymous gift to a family struggling financially, or buy bath oil for a single mother who has no money to spend on herself. If the suffering is emotional, pass along a book which helped you weather a dark hour.

If you do not see need nearby, look far away. Suffering comes through shame as well as grief, and the family of the criminal may need a care package as well as the family of the victim. The children's ward of the hospital may need toys, or the mission box going to Africa may still be missing a child's dress.

Through some tangible expression of care, today give divine love a larger room in your heart.

Wash Windows

SCRIPTURE: *Psalm 24*
KEY VERSE: *Who may go up the Lord's mountain?...The one who has clean hands and a pure heart...*

> Tell tale tit!
> Your tongue shall be split,
> And all the dogs in our town
> Shall have a bit.

T he author of the little nursery rhyme may or may not have dreamed of climbing the mountain of the Lord. If she did manage to climb it, she would have quickly slid back down when she sought revenge.

The psalmist says those with clean hands and a pure heart may go up the Lord's mountain. With smudged hands and stained hearts, many of us stand at the foot of his mountain and wistfully look up.

Even the Lord's mountain appears rather hazy through dirty windows. When cloudy days hid smudges and stains, we overlooked grime. Now sunshine reveals all. Today get rid of some of the smudges in your life by washing windows.

Wash more than the windows of your house. While applying ammonia to those panes of glass, examine the ones in your soul. We may not wish a tell tale's tongue split, but at times we have resented, and even misrepresented.

Traces appear on soul windows as well as house windows. Those streaks and smudges remain until we apply ammonia there too.

Rain and wind on the outside and little fingerprints on the inside accumulate so gradually that dirty windows can catch us by surprise. The same thing happens in our soul. Today give a sparkle to all the windows in your life— the inner ones as well as the outer ones. Step on the path leading to the Lord's mountain.

May 6

Pray for Understanding

SCRIPTURE: *Ephesians 5: 6 – 13*
KEY VERSE: *Light produces everything that is good, that has God's approval, and that is true.*

> I like little Pussy, her coat is so warm;
> And if I don't hurt her, she'll do me no harm.

U nless someone else has hurt her, Jane Taylor could have added. For once a pussy has been savagely hit, she may never trust anyone again. It may take a lot of gentle love to make her respond positively to a tender touch.

It has been said that God whispers in our pleasure, speaks in our silence, and shouts in our pain. However, many of us waste our prayers by asking God for relief rather than understanding.

Ask him to shed light on the pain in your life. Bring to mind annoying, embarrassing, or shameful behavior patterns, and try to determine when and why they started. Deep-rooted fears often dominate more of our lives than we suspect. As with physical pain, use inner pain as a clue to areas which need the healing touch of the Great Physician.

Next hold the irritating, disturbing, or distressing behavior of another person up to that same light. Few people want to be difficult, ugly, or immature, but inner pain drives them, as it does us, to lash out in hurting ways. Ask God to help you sympathize with another's pain even if you don't understand his or her behavior. Then, with God's help, today soothe even a little pain with compassion.

Paul told the Ephesians that where light is, all goodness springs up. When we take pain out of hiding and expose it to bright light, healing finally takes place. Today hold pain, both yours and another's, up to the Lord.

When healing occurs, inappropriate behavior takes care of itself.

May 7

Picnic Basket

SCRIPTURE: *John 6: 8 - 13*
KEY VERSE: *A boy who has five loaves of barley bread and two small fish is here. But they won't go very far for so many people.*

> Four ducks on a pond,
> A grass bank beyond,
> A blue sky of spring,
> White clouds on the wing;
> What a little thing
> To remember for years—
> To remember with tears!

Like William Allingham, perhaps a long ago little boy felt the call of blue sky, white clouds, and ducks on the pond, and he set off for the day with his picnic basket. Maybe on impulse he joined the crowd around the teacher.

He must have liked the sound of the man's voice, for he forgot to eat the bread and fish in his lap. When he heard the man's friends say they had no food, he offered his five loaves and two fish.

We don't know if a picnic actually led the little boy to Jesus. But it could have, for picnics have always invited surprises. Birds still sing the same songs they sang long ago in Palestine, meadows wear the same flowers, and white clouds still float across blue skies. The same teacher awaits us there where the brook sings and the violets bloom.

The meadows call and the hills urge more often than we are ready to listen. Today prepare for the next call by stocking a picnic basket. Fill it with staples such as dried fruits, nuts, crackers, and instant food. Add canned beverages, paper plates, and a table cloth.

Then, when ducks on a pond, blue skies, and white clouds beckon, grab the basket, a thermos of hot water or a bag of ice cubes, and take off. A little thing to remember. A big thing to remember.

May 8

Class

SCRIPTURE: *Matthew 13:47 - 52*
KEY VERSE: *So Jesus said to them, "That is why every scribe who has become a disciple of the kingdom of heaven is like a home owner. He brings new and old things out of his treasure chest."*

> A dillar, a dollar, a ten o'clock scholar,
> What makes you come so soon?
> You used to come at ten o'clock
> But now you come at noon.

Since the nursery rhyme leaves unfinished the story of the reluctant scholar, we do not know what became of the lazy little boy. However, we suspect that he never became a great success. When the final accounting of life sorts the good fish into pails and throws the worthless away, our ten o'clock scholar sounds like a candidate for the latter.

Perhaps, like most of the scribes, the little boy believed he already knew all he needed to know. But Jesus reminded his followers they never knew enough. He said that the learner in the kingdom of God, like a good householder, produces both the new and the old from his store.

Most of us shortchange ourselves. Not suspecting the countless possibilities tucked into our own genes, we wistfully eye the talents of others. However, we usually only lack their technique and practice.

The scribes may have known everything they needed to know for their lifestyle, but had they been open to something new they might have discovered life rather than a lifestyle. Instead of clinging to a lifestyle, today open yourself wider to life. Sign up for a class at a library, community college, or museum.

Whether you take a one hour lecture on mushroom identification, an all day workshop to refresh CPR skills, or a semester class on Byzantine art, today become an active learner in the kingdom of God. Uncover some sparkling gene tucked into one of your unseen chromosomes, and glorify God by using it.

May 9

Window Shop

SCRIPTURE: *Luke 12: 15 - 21*
KEY VERSE: *He told the people, "Be careful to guard yourselves from every kind of greed. Life is not about having a lot of material possessions."*

> Peter, Peter , pumpkin eater,
> Had a wife and couldn't keep her;
> He put her in a pumpkin shell,
> And there he kept her very well.

Apparently, Peter possessed a wife who did not appreciate being possessed. Keeping her must have cost him many an hour guarding the pumpkin shell. The nursery rhyme tells us his strategy succeeded, and he probably bragged about his cleverness. There is no indication Peter ever realized there is more to life than possessing.

Perhaps Jesus had such a person in mind when he told the story of the man who accumulated so many possessions he had to build a new barn. Calling the man a pauper, Jesus warned his followers about such greed. The more we possess, the more easily we lose sight of the kingdom of God. Today let go of a little of the desire to possess.

Begin by mentally picturing one day in the life of the world community. See five billion people expressing unique gifts in individual ways. Then go window shopping, and appreciate the creative expressions of some of those five billion individuals.

Admiring exquisite china, beautiful clothes, and charming figurines, focus on the gifts of the designers. In front of a bakery, count the shapes of bread and wonder how many more shapes are coming out of ovens around the world. Browsing in a bookstore, marvel at how many ways we reflect the unlimited creativity of our maker.

Today concentrate on appreciating rather than on possessing.

May 10

Creative Letter

SCRIPTURE: *2 Thessalonians 3: 16 – 18*
KEY VERSE: *I, Paul, am writing this greeting with my own hand. In every letter that I send, this is proof that I wrote it.*

> How do I love thee? Let me count the ways.
> To the depth and breadth and height
> My soul can reach, when feeling out of sight
> For the ends of Being and ideal Grace.

With these words, Elizabeth Barrett Browning expressed her love for a man she first met in a letter. When Robert Browning wrote the letter telling Elizabeth how much he admired her poetry, she caught a glimpse of the man who held the pen, and she liked what she saw. As letter followed letter, love grew and blossomed. In her *Sonnets from the Portuguese*, perhaps the most beautiful love poems written in the English language, Elizabeth left a rich legacy to all who love deeply.

Paul, too, wrote letters which inspired love and commitment. Many early Christians first knew the man through his letters, and twenty centuries later we still meet him there. He wrote so vividly that we know the man, and we know the Lord he loved.

We too have the power to move others with our letters. Today, like Paul, Elizabeth Barret Browning, and Robert Browning, touch someone's life with words you write from your heart.

Whether describing his vision for the church or his personal problems, Paul's passion for the gospel breathed life into the words he wrote. In *Sonnets from the Portuguese*, we can't miss the passion of Elizabeth's love.

Only passion breathes life into words on a sheet of paper, so light up your letter with the same passion which lights up your soul. Put your stamp on words about planting a garden, waiting at a bus stop, or crying in the wee hours of the night. Communicate the passion behind your heartbeat.

May 11

Papier-Maché

SCRIPTURE: *Acts 18: 1 - 4*
KEY VERSE: *And because they made tents for a living as he did, he stayed with them and they worked together.*

> One misty, moisty morning,
>   when cloudy was the weather,
> I chanced to meet an old man
>   clothed all in leather.
> He began to compliment and
>   I began to grin, "How-do-you-do?"
> And "how-do-you do?" and
>   "how do you do?" again!

The exchange related in the nursery rhyme appears to have ended the conversation. If we don't find some common interest to keep the talk going, most conversations would end at that point.

Paul seemed to approach everyone at the point of a common interest. Trying to persuade Pharisees of the power of the Gospel, he related his own experience as a Pharisee. With the philosophical Greeks, he pitted his sharp mind against theirs, using their own literature to illustrate his points. In Corinth, he approached Aquila and Priscilla as a fellow tent-maker.

For the sake of the Gospel, he drew from the depths his education, background, and experience to become all things to all men. Like Paul, we have many sides, or like a circle, we have unlimited points of contact.

Regardless of the form it takes, papier-maché remains papier-maché. Dipped in a flour-and-water paste, strips of newspaper can create any shape. Layered over a cardboard box, they may form a cat or a giraffe. Wrapped around a cardboard ring, they become a bracelet or a napkin ring.

In the same way, becoming all things to all people does not change our basic flour-and-water paste. We simply express ourselves in the most useful form of communication. Today make something in papier-maché, reminding yourself of the need to adapt to the situation.

Like Paul, find a way to get beyond, "How-do-you-do?"

May 12

Affirm

SCRIPTURE: *1 Thessalonians 5: 14 – 15*

KEY VERSE: *We encourage you, brothers and sisters, to instruct those who are not living right, cheer up those who are discouraged, help the weak, and be patient with everyone.*

> Tom, Tom, the piper's son
> Stole a pig, and away he run.
> The pig was eat
> And Tom was beat,
> And Tom went crying down the street.

L ike every other little boy, Tom found his stomach regularly demanding food. But, apparently, the piper had other things on his mind, and Tom sometimes had to find his own food. After being beat, perhaps he never stole another pig. But his harsh punishment may have planted the seeds of humiliation which eventually grew into an angry, revengeful adult.

Through criticism or affirmation, we plant the seeds of self-hate or self-love in children even before they begin walking and talking. Although merely reflections of caregivers, these early self-images become so imbedded they sometimes last a lifetime.

To some extent we are all victims of other people's insecurities, but some of us have had affirmation to balance the scale, and others have not. Affirmation works miracles at whatever point it comes. Paul may not have thought in terms of self-images, but he knew that some people need more encouragement and affirmation than others.

Today be affirming. Look people in the eye, genuinely listen, compliment sincerely. Encourage the fainthearted, support the weak, and be very patient with everyone. Help some little Tom know he is both loved and valued.

May 13

On Foot

SCRIPTURE: *Mark 4: 26 – 32*
KEY VERSE: *It's like a mustard seed planted in the ground. The mustard seed is one of the smallest seeds on earth.*

> Sound the flute!
> Now 'tis mute;
> Birds delight
> Day and night;
> Nightingale
> In the dale,

Lark in the sky—
Merrily,
Merrily, merrily to welcome in the year.

As described by William Blake, spring calls day and night. It calls through the nightingale and the lark. It calls from the meadow where daisies thrust faces towards the sun, from the woodlands where violets carpet the earth, and from streams which gurgle and babble. It calls in bright sunshine and in soft falling rain.

Perhaps that call once took Jesus across open fields and meadows as new life burst forth from an old earth. He must have spent much time examining the world around him, for he often spoke of seed, flowers, and birds. He noted how plants grew—first the blade, then the ear, then the full grown corn. He thought about small mustard seeds which grew into such large plants sparrows perched on their spread out limbs. He noticed how beautiful the lilies were, and he felt close to the Father who made grain and mustard and sparrows.

Because Jesus went everywhere by foot or in a boat, he was in touch with nature. In contrast, we do most of our traveling in a car. Today do at least one errand on foot. Hear, smell, touch, and like Jesus, see more than fields of yellow mustard or flocks of sparrows.

May 14

Special Linens

SCRIPTURE: *Luke 4: 38 – 39*
KEY VERSE: *He bent over her, ordered the fever to leave, and it went away. She got up immediately and prepared a meal for them.*

When Peter invited Jesus to dine at his house, he may have forgotten his mother-in-law was in the grip of a high fever. If he suddenly remembered, it must have occurred to him that Jesus could heal her. Something in the eyes of the man beside her bed gave Peter's mother-in-law the same hope.

When the fever left her, she insisted on serving Jesus herself. Perhaps she took down the heirloom dishes reserved for feast days. She probably fingered their woven linens, choosing the best for the meal which was to become the most memorable of her life.

Like Simon's mother-in-law, most of us have experienced the healing hand of the Master on either our emotions or body. Today gratefully remember that touch as you serve a meal where he is an unseen guest, and make the table as beautiful as if he were going to sit at it.

Finger your linens, and examine them through the eyes of Peter's mother-in-law. Which would you choose for this man who gave you back your health? Tonight make it your best—perhaps the Belgian linen place mats, or the hand-embroidered tablecloth from the Canary Islands, or bring out the crocheted tablecloth handed down from your grandmother.

Serving more meals in a lifetime than we ever stop to count, we have a unique opportunity to stimulate and influence others by what we serve and the way we serve it. Tonight lovingly serve those around your table on linens you have chosen for Jesus. Although he has no plate set on the beautiful linen, he said that he would be there with those you serve.

May 15

Plan a Trip

SCRIPTURE: *Psalm 121*
KEY VERSE: *The Lord guards you as you come and go, now and forever.*

If I lift up my eyes to the hills,
where shall I find help?
Help comes only from the Lord...
The Lord will guard your going and your coming
now and for evermore.

In the movie *The Sound of Music*, the Reverend Mother advised Maria to climb every mountain, ford every stream, and follow every rainbow to find her dreams. The time came to climb those mountains. Giving Maria a last embrace, the Reverend Mother reminded her of words written long ago by the psalmist.

Unlike Maria or the psalmist who spent much of his life roaming the hills, many of us spend our lives climbing molehills, fording puddles, and following schedules. Today dream of mountains, streams, and rainbows; then make plans to climb, ford, and follow. Whether it's a realistic possibility or an unrealistic fantasy, plan a trip you would love to take.

If you have always dreamed of hiking the Swiss Alps, riding a gondola in Venice, or walking on the Great Wall of China, call airlines and ask the cost. If you long to explore old mansions in the Deep South, go camping in Yosemite National Park, or follow revolutionary landmarks in Boston, pick up a brochure at a travel agency and begin reading.

Set a date. List museums, landmarks, and natural wonders worth seeing. Calculate costs. Talk to the family. Such small steps could convert a fantasy into a possibility.

The Lord is our guardian, but we do not need a guardian to climb molehills, ford puddles, or follow schedules.

 Today as you dream of real mountains, streams, and rainbows, ask yourself what other dreams you need for your life. Since the Lord guards our going and coming, make the travel worthwhile.

Observe Children

SCRIPTURE: *Matthew 14: 22 - 36*
KEY VERSE: *Peter answered, "Lord, if it is you, order me to come to you on the water."*

> But fidgety Phil
> He won't sit still;
> He wriggles
> And giggles,
> And then, I declare,
> Swings backwards and forwards
> And tilts up his chair.

O nce upon a time these words of Heinrich Hoffman may have described a little boy named Simon. As an adult, sitting still was not Simon's style. When he saw Jesus walking on water, he gave it a try. High up on a mountain, he proposed building tents for Jesus, Moses, and Elijah. In the garden of Gethsemane, he drew his sword on an intruder.

Wiggly, bouncy, loud, fidgety Phils bother many of us. Talkative, curious, mischievous, they get on our nerves. Apparently God views them in a different light; he gave at least one fidgety disciple a special place in his kingdom.

Today try to see in the fidgety Phils what God sees in them. Observe them as they run through the park, climb monkey bars, or play in the school yard at recess time. See them touch, poke, pull, squeeze, and taste. Watch them laugh, cry, embrace, hit, make faces, or buddy up. Notice how built-in exuberance seems to propel many of them.

Exuberance and model behavior seldom go hand in hand, but this did not hinder Jesus from calling disciples who tried to walk across water, quarreled with each other, and drew swords on outsiders. Perhaps Jesus called Simon because of his exuberance rather than in spite of it.

Today see the fidgety Phils around you in a new light.

Stretch your spirit. Perhaps you can catch a bit of their exuberance.

May 17

Special Spot

SCRIPTURE: *Luke 22: 39 – 46*
KEY VERSE: *Jesus went out of the city to the Mount of Olives as he usually did. His disciples followed him.*

As wistfully as we watch the nursery tidy itself up in the movie, we know that no Mary Poppins is going to coax our houses clean. Nor will any fairy godmother wave a magic wand enabling us to live happily ever afterwards. But in place of a fairy godmother, God has shared his creative nature with us, enabling us to make our own happiness by overcoming circumstances.

The night Jesus faced betrayal, torture, and death, he could have called forth legions of angels to rescue him. Instead, he retreated to a private place to think, pray, and prepare himself for what lay ahead. When the soldiers approached, he was ready, and he calmly went to meet them.

No life is problem-free. We too know betrayal, heartache, and misunderstanding. Today take an overcoming step, and for half-an-hour or so, retreat to a private place where you regain poise and peace. Sit beneath a large pine in the meadow, on the bench under the rose trellis, or in a rocking chair on the porch. Wherever your calming place, spend enough time there to re-collect yourself.

If thoughts unwind easier when knitting needles click, take them along. Perhaps you regain serenity by reading a good book or answering a letter which has been sitting on your desk for days. Or peace may come as you quietly sit and do nothing. Do whatever renews and relaxes.

Creative renewal of our spirits is the first step in overcoming any circumstance. Whatever the stresses of this day, like Jesus, retreat to your own Mount of Olives and then calmly walk back to meet what awaits you.

Pray for Africa

SCRIPTURE: *Isaiah 42: 1 - 4*
KEY VERSE: *Here is my servant, whom I support. Here is my chosen one, with whom I am pleased. I have put my Spirit on him. He will bring justice to the nations.*

> For what are men better than sheep or goats
> That nourish a blind life within the brain,
> If, knowing God, they lift not hands of prayer
> Both for themselves and those who call them friend?
> For so the whole round earth is every way
> Bound by gold chains about the feet of God.

In some places of the whole round earth described by Tennyson, once-upon-a-time overlaps with here-and-now. Rather than running hot water for dishes or putting them in a dishwasher, millions of African women fetch water from the stream and carry it home in a bucket on their heads. These women shove no roast into an oven, but blow left-over coals to restart cooking fires.

Neither do they wonder whether an IBM-style personal computer or a Macintosh best fits their needs, for many of them have never been to school. Nor do they choose between a one-door and two-door freezer; multitudes of them have never laid eyes on either freezer or refrigerator.

Famine seems to plague the continent with appalling regularity. We have grown used to seeing pictures of starving children. However, today look at them, think about them, and feel for them. Isaiah prophesied the chosen one would bring justice on the nations. But some nations are still waiting.

Although their means are often small, each Sunday thousands of Christians in Kikongo-speaking countries sing an offering song urging believers to give according to their means. We who have been given much have much to give. Today at least give your prayers.

May 19

New Leaven

SCRIPTURE: *1 Corinthians 5: 6 – 8*
KEY VERSE: *Your self-satisfaction ill becomes you. (NEB)*

> Jack Sprat could eat no fat.
> His wife could eat no lean;
> And so betwixt them both
> They licked the platter clean.

T heir arrangement seemed so ideal they saw no reason to change it. They didn't know the cholesterol building up in Mrs. Sprat's arteries was slowly closing off the blood supply to her heart.

Paul saw the Corinthian Christians clogging up spiritual arteries with self-satisfaction. Their diet was robbing them of fellowship with God, and Paul pleaded with them to exchange the old leaven for a bread of a new baking.

However delicious fresh bread tasted last week, this week it tastes stale. Like the Corinthian Christians, many of us grow so used to the taste of stale bread we give it no thought. We need reminders that self-satisfaction ill becomes us.

Today change something which satisfies you. Even though you think you have an ideal arrangement, change around the living room furniture. Instead of reminding your child to obey, apologize for not listening to her side of the story. Rather than put a rude driver in his place with a loud honk, give him a smile and a wave.

Make any change which will shake up a bit of self-satisfaction. Remove some spiritual cholesterol from your own arteries.

May 20

Meet a Neighbor

SCRIPTURE: *John 2: 1 - 12*
KEY VERSE: *Three days later a wedding took place in the city of Cana in Galilee. Jesus' mother was there. Jesus and his disciples had been invited too.*

> The social, friendly, honest man,
> Whate'er he be,
> 'Tis he fulfills great Nature's plan,
> And none but he!

I t is said that Robert Burns, a tenant farmer and the son of a tenant farmer, exemplified Scottish ideals and morals at their best and their worst. In this bit of verse from "Second Epistle to J. Lapraik," he touches on the best.

Whatever other adjectives we might add, we could describe Jesus as social, friendly, and honest. He mingled with all kinds of people, took an interest in them, and made friends easily. When he invited some of them to follow him, they eagerly responded. When he was invited to a wedding, he went.

Jesus liked people, and they liked him. But then it would be hard to imagine the Son of God being antisocial.

Nor should we be antisocial. Today brush up on your own social skills by taking an interest in someone in the neighborhood. Meet someone you don't know. This is the month to do it, for spring coaxes us all outdoors.

We may feel awkward knocking at the door of an unknown person, but we feel comfortable speaking to her when she is out walking her dog. When she is out working in her irises, going over to chat seems more friendly than intrusive.

Today take advantage of these opportunities. Introduce yourself to a teenage boy trimming his father's hedge, a sweatsuit clad neighbor washing his car, or a new mother out walking her baby. Greet the young man playing Frisbee® with his children or chat with girls drawing hopscotch lines on the sidewalk.

The social, friendly, honest woman can also fulfill nature's plan.

May 21

Meal Surprise

SCRIPTURE: *Esther 5: 1 – 5*
KEY VERSE: *So Esther answered, "If it pleases you, Your Majesty, come today with Haman to a dinner I have prepared for you."*

In Shakespeare's *Two Gentlemen of Verona*, the hungry servant Speed said to his lovesick master:

> Ay, but hearken, sir;
> Though the chameleon Love
> can feed on the air,
> I am one that am nourished
> by my victuals,
> And would fain have meat...

Once upon a time, someone may have told a little girl named Esther that the way to a man's heart was through his stomach, for the little-girl-become-queen used food to soften the heart of the king she wanted to petition.

Today use food to reach the hearts of those who gather around your dinner table. The family may expect something familiar tonight, but surprise them. Like Esther, plan such a delightful dinner that spirits will be mellowed, tempers soothed, and congeniality restored.

Turn the kitchen counter into a salad bar and add a few surprises. Make a favorite meat loaf you have not made in months, stuffed baked potatoes which take a little extra time, and honey whole wheat rolls. Indulge sweet tastes with peanut butter pie or splurge on a rich pecan pie.

Create a different kind of surprise by covering the picnic table with a linen tablecloth, setting it with china, and eating dinner outside. Take supper to the park, watch ducks swim on the pond as you eat, and then treat them to some of the leftovers. Barbecue in the back yard, set up the badminton set, and invite friends to join you.

When Queen Esther prepared her meal, the life of her people hung in the balance. Our stakes are not so high, but we too have the power to reach hearts through stomachs.

May 22

ℐ Classic

SCRIPTURE: *James 4: 1 - 10*
KEY VERSE: *What causes fights and quarrels among you? Aren't they caused by the selfish desires that fight to control you?*

> O for a book and a shady nook,
> Either in door or out;
> With the green leaves whispering overhead,
> Or the street cries all about,
> Where I may read all at my ease,
> Both of new and old;
> For a jolly good book whereon to look
> Is better to me than gold.

Today like John Wilson, seek a book for the shady nook; but make it an old one—a classic.

Fairy tales end happily ever after. In real life we struggle ever after. Addressing the conflicts and quarrels of the early church, James told them to look inward for the causes. But while the evil within us demeans our existence, the overcoming of it dignifies our humanity.

In contrast to books which come today and go tomorrow, classics survive because they confront life as it is. In their two way mirrors, we see how we look in back as well as in front. Use one of these mirrors.

Whether Victor Hugo's *Les Miserables*, Mark Twain's *Tom Sawyer*, or George Eliot's *Silas Marner*, gain new insight into both your vulnerability and your strength. The stories told in the classics took place in different worlds and other ages, but the human heart has not changed. Take a better look at yours.

May 23

Recital

SCRIPTURE: *Psalm 149*
KEY VERSE: *Hallelujah! Sing a new song to the Lord, Sing his praise in the assembly of godly people.*

When we think of "Hallelujah Chorus," we think of Handel. But there are thousands, or even millions, of "hallelujah choruses." This song from Robert Browning's "Pippa Passes" is one of them:

> The year's at the spring,
> The day's at the morn ...
> The lark's on the wing;
> The snail's on the thorn:
> God's in his heaven—
> All's right with the world!

Like the psalmist, when Robert Browning looked beyond the muddy waters at his feet, he saw a magnificent world put into place by a loving Creator, and he shouted for joy.

In this month earth sings from treetop to brook, meadow to barnyard, and sunrise to sunset. We too feel the urge to sing and celebrate. Children lift voices in school chorales, piano students nervously sit on stage to recreate the music of the masters, violins tune up in anticipation of the maestro's lifted arm. In voice and instrument, the human spirit echoes the music of the season.

Attend a recital today, and fill your spirit with a musical expression of celebration. Check the newspaper for listings, inquire at music conservatories, or call schools in the area. You may discover a church offering an organ recital or a mall where school children will perform.

As you listen to the joyful strains of music, from the depths of your soul, echo "Hallelujah!" Through praise enhance the joy of life.

May 24

Letter to Editor

Scripture: *Psalm 9: 15 – 20*
Key verse: *The nations have sunk into the pit they have made. Their feet are caught in the net they have hidden to trap others.*

> 'I weep for you,' the Walrus said:
> 'I deeply sympathize.'
> With sobs and tears he sorted out
> Those of the largest size,
> Holding his pocket-handkerchief
> Before his streaming eyes.

We prefer Kleenex® facial tissue to our pocket handkercheifs, but like Lewis Carroll's Walrus, we cry when the occasion calls for it. We may even cry when the occasion doesn't call for it. (At least, we seem to go through a lot of Kleenex.) But sometimes we need to do more than cry.

As you read this morning's edition of the newspaper and become distressed, disturbed, or grieved, save your facial tissue. Write a letter to the editor instead.

The events of his world disturbed the psalmist. His psalms did not bring wicked nations to their knees, relieve the burden of the poor, or prevent the wicked man from doing evil, but they gave truth a chance to be heard.

Nor can we expect our letters to change what happens in the halls of congress or even on the streets where we live. But one expression encourages other expressions, and enough voices finally make a difference.

In the world of the psalmist, kings were all-powerful. In contrast, democracy places the responsibility for a healthy society upon each citizen. Many of us need to replace Kleenex tissue with action.

May 25

Identify Birds

SCRIPTURE: *Psalm 50: 10 - 11*
KEY VERSE: *I know every bird in the mountains, everything that moves in the fields is mine.*

And after April, when May follows,
And the whitethroat builds, and all the swallows ...
That's the wise thrush; he sings each song twice over,...

When Robert Browning remembered England in "Home Thoughts from Abroad," he did not remember birds; he remembered whitethroats, swallows, and thrushes. The Bible tells us when God looks on his hills, he knows every bird on them. He too sees whitethroats, swallows, and thrushes.

A toddler often spends his first waking moments naming his world. The objects in the crib, the images on the crib sheet, the pictures on the wall, the toys on the floor,

158

the clothes in the closet. One by one he must point them out to Mother who stands beside the crib. The child must name in order to know, and the more he names, the more he knows. Naming is seeing.

Like the toddler, we must name if we want to see. If we can not call it by name, the trilling bird in the treetop is only a sound. But once we name it, we enter into relationship with it. No longer is it a bird like all birds, but an individual bird which we know.

With the help of a bird book, today name the birds which pull worms from your lawn and the ones which trill from your treetops. Along with God, follow the flight of a swallow across the meadow, and watch a mockingbird perch on the back fence. Praise the Lord who knows not only every bird by name, but also each one of us by name.

May 26

Fun Calendar

SCRIPTURE: *Proverbs 16: 2 - 3*
KEY VERSE: *Entrust your efforts to the Lord, and your plans will succeed.*

> See-saw, Margery Daw,
> Jackie shall have a new master;
> He shall have but a penny a day,
> Because he can't work any faster.

If Jackie, whose stamina seemed to be limited, had tried to increase his efficiency, perhaps he would have held two pennies in his hand instead of one. Proverbs says if we commit all we do to the Lord, our plans will be fulfilled. However, without plans, we give him nothing to fulfill.

Today make plans for the Lord to help you fulfill. Summer tiptoes upon us, its arms loaded with long daylight hours. A whole season stretches before us, and we eagerly anticipate projects, fun, and travel. But thirteen weeks quickly pass, and without specific plans, we may reach the end of August feeling as shortchanged as little Jackie in the nursery rhyme.

What would you like to do this summer? Whatever it is, give it a chance to happen by putting tentative dates on the calendar. If a weekly picnic in the park would make the summer, write picnic across every Thursday or Saturday, or whatever fits between dentist appointments and committee meetings. If you promised the children an outing to the zoo, choose a date and write in big letters "zoo." If you want to entertain, make it happen by planning dates.

While tentative plans adjust to accommodate the unexpected, no plans surrenders to the unexpected. Entrust your efforts to the Lord, and expect your plans to be fulfilled.

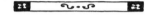

May 27

Beauty List

Scripture: *Psalm 145: 1 - 9*
Key verse: *They will announce what they remember of your great goodness, and they will joyfully sing about your righteousness.*

> Daffy-down-dilly is now come to town
> With a yellow petticoat and a green gown.

D o you remember how beautiful she was when she first appeared on your lawn? Some of her sisters came in pink gowns, and some came in white ones. But they were not the only ones to appear on your lawn this month. May sent a parade of buds, blossoms, and leaves.

Today remember God's great goodness by making a list of every beautiful gift he sent this month. Perhaps you can still see the first red tulip in the flower bed or the first lemon lilies beside the old stone wall. You may have caught the scent of the fragrant lilac each morning. A blossom filled cherry tree in the park may have lightened your own heart the rest of the day.

On your list include the birds nesting in the elm tree, the doe standing beside the road, and the porcupine waddling away into the woods. Add to it sunrises which colored mornings and sunsets which crowned evenings.

Remember the roar of the crashing surf upon the shore or the bubbling of the brook below the stone arch bridge? In your mind stand beside these marvels of nature once again. See them, hear them, sense them. List the things which thrilled you, calmed you, or inspired you.

Perhaps a hundred sights and sounds stirred your soul to new life this month. List all of them, for each was a gift from the Creator. Announce what you remember of his goodness.

May 28

Thai Restaurant

SCRIPTURE: *Psalm 139: 9 - 12*
KEY VERSE: *If I climb upward on the rays of the morning sun or land on the most distant shore of the sea where the sun sets, even there your hand would guide me your right hand would hold on to me.*

Like languages, gods changed with political boundaries in the world of the psalmist. Although his people worshipped Yahweh, to the south, north, east, and west, other gods dominated temples and shrines. But the psalmist knew political boundaries created no boundaries for the true God. Wherever he went, his God would be there to meet him.

Today take a brief flight to the frontiers of the morning by entering a Thai restaurant. Dwell a few minutes on one of the distant shores, and like the psalmist, expect God to meet you there.

In *The King and I*, Rogers and Hammerstein introduced many of us to the story-book kingdom of Siam. Although the movie mingled truth and fantasy, the kingdom was real. The kingdom is still real, but now carries the name Thailand, meaning "land of the free." A constitutional monarchy, the citizens of the country so revere King Bhumibol Adulyadej that his picture appears in almost every Thai home and restaurant, even the ones on foreign soil.

Since the Thai language has five tones, any attempt to speak phrases carries the risk of communicating something we had not wanted to say at all. However, have fun greeting the waitress with *Sah-wah-dee-KAH*, recognizing that you might be saying something other than "Hello, how are you?"

For very hot food, order a curry. If hot food is not your style, try a blander dish such as chicken and cashew nuts. For a real treat ask for the Northern Thai speciality, sticky rice and mangoes.

Enter a piece of the world twelve time zones away, and remind yourself that no time zone distances any part of his creation from the hand of the Lord. Like the psalmist, praise the Lord who knows his creation so intimately that nothing is hidden from his view.

May 29

Thrift Store

SCRIPTURE: *Matthew 13: 16 – 23*
KEY VERSE: *The seed planted among thornbushes is another person who hears the word. But the worries of life and the deceitful pleasure of riches choke the word so that it can't produce anything.*

Our purses shall be proud, our garments poor;
For 'tis the mind that makes the body rich;
And as the sun breaks through the darkest cloud,

So honour peereth in the meanest habit.
What, is the jay more precious than the lark,
Because his feathers are more beautiful?

While acknowledging the truth of these words Petruchio speaks in Shakespeare's *The Taming of the Shrew*, many of us nevertheless long for beautiful feathers to cover imperfect bodies. Eyeing poised, stylish mannequins, we fantasize that the same clothes would give us the same look.

However, none of the poised mannequins drove across town with three children and a dog in the back seat, made four sandwiches, and did three loads of laundry before 10 A.M. No one honked loudly at them when they made a turn from the wrong lane, criticized the way they ironed a shirt, or gave them a parking ticket.

It takes more than the right clothes to make real people poised, pleasant, and stylish. Even in long ago Nazareth, women must have shared our fantasies, for Jesus talked about the deceitful pleasures of wealth.

Today pull a few thorns out of your spiritual garden by declaring freedom from price tags and beguiling mannequins. Rather than drooling over expensive name-brand clothing, check out the clothing in a thrift shop or second-hand clothing shop. Along with garments too tacky to ever wear anywhere, quality clothing in excellent condition often appears on the racks.

If you like it, buy it, and proudly wear it. Perhaps it looks better on you than it did on the first person who wore it.

Vespers

SCRIPTURE: *Psalm 65: 1 - 8*

KEY VERSE: *The lands of the morning sunrise and evening sunset sing joyfully.*

> All creatures of our God and King,
> Lift up your voice and with us sing:
> Alleluia, Alleluia!
> Thou burning sun with golden beam,
> Thou silver moon with softer gleam:
> O praise Him, O praise Him,
> Alleluia, Alleluia, Alleluia!

L ike St. Francis of Assisi, this evening lift your voice in Alleluias. Long sun rays now hold a still-new green earth in softness, cradling it longer each day. Twilight lingers, warm shadows creep slowly forward, and the after-dinner hours are now daylight. This evening, pause to absorb the beauty of the moment. Then respond with joyful praise.

Praise God for a universe we can not begin to comprehend. Think about the solar system which holds the earth in place, the rotating earth, the seasons—all wonderful beyond our comprehension—and worship the One who brought it into existence. Looking upon meadows, mountains, or rising hills, wonder at the power behind such landscape. Marvel that all life on earth, including our own bodies, comes out of the dirt beneath our feet.

Then shift your thoughts to tangible sights and sounds. Hear the breeze softly blowing, the gray squirrels scurrying up the maple, the phoebe singing on the telephone wire. Remember that everything was created. Everything was given to us, not because we asked, pleaded, or insisted, but because it pleased God to please us.

In a few moments of evening vespers, praise, worship, and adore the Creator Father. Sing Alleluia!

Note Cards

SCRIPTURE: *Isaiah 37: 14 - 20*
KEY VERSE: *Hezekiah took the letter from the messengers, read it, and went to the Lord's temple.*

S ennacherib, King of Assyria, attacked and captured all the fortified cities of Judah, and with an eye on the rest of Hezekiah's kingdom, made an appeal for cooperation. The letter brought by messengers was designed to weaken Hezekiah's resistance. Holding it in his hands, a depressed, heavy-hearted Hezekiah went before the Lord in prayer.

Many of us have held an unopened letter in trembling hands, fearing the contents. Letters can add or subtract weight from our hearts. While empty mailboxes speak words of rejection, the simplest note reminds us we are still remembered and loved.

Even in the electronic age of phone and fax, the greeting card industry continues to flourish. However, rather than buying a card, today creatively lift the spirits of another with a note card you make yourself.

A gingham cat pasted onto a card may bring a smile to anyone who knows of your love of cats. A recipe copied onto the front of a folded paper may carry someone to the kitchen where you spend most of your time. Glue pressed pansies on a note card, and take someone into the garden with you.

At times we are all Hezekiahs weighed down with a threatening environment. Through a card carrying your personality through the mail, lighten someone's burden with a friendly visit.

June 1

Yard Sale Items

SCRIPTURE: *Ecclesiastes 3: 1 - 8*
KEY VERSE: *A time to keep and a time to throw away.*

> There was an Old Man with a beard,
> Who said, 'It is just as I feared!—
> Two owls and a hen,
> Four larks and a wren,
> Have all built their nests in my beard!'

Definitely, it was time for Edward Lear's Old Man to throw something away. If not two owls, a hen, four larks and a wren, then surely a beard. On the other hand, he may have made a tidy sum by putting them in a yard sale.

In his childhood, the writer of Ecclesiastes must have watched his mother collect and discard. She made a clay water jug, used it until it cracked, then threw it away. She bought sandals to protect her feet; when the leather wore out, she discarded them. Each year she made him a new tunic, but the following year she passed it on to his cousin.

Unlike Edward Lear's Old Man, we run no risk of collecting a menagerie in our beard. We do, however, collect many other things in our drawers, shelves, and closets. The time has come to lose some of them.

Our time to throw away may be another's time to collect. Today, rather than throw away, throw into a box labeled "YARD SALE." Give someone else an opportunity to

wear the lovely size eight dress which once fit. Who knows, someone may appreciate the still good cloth diapers your child once used, or the old freezer in the garage.

Or even two owls and a hen.

New Street or Road

SCRIPTURE: *Acts 8: 26 - 31*

KEY VERSE: *An angel from the Lord said to Philip, "Get up, and take the desert road that goes south from Jerusalem to Gaza."*

> As I was going to St. Ives,
> I met a man with seven wives;
> Each wife had seven sacks,
> Each sack had seven cats...

You have never seen such a sight? Then you have never traveled the road to St. Ives.

New streets and roads open new worlds. One or two streets over, the character of a neighborhood may completely change. The name of a once popular song, "On the Street Where You Live," conveys some of the nostalgia associated with the street we call our own, the one we grew up in, and the one which to a great extent shaped us.

Whether children set off for school carrying a gun, violin, or basketball largely depends on the street and the neighborhood where they live. One street produces *My Fair Lady*'s Eliza Doolittle, and another street produces a George Bernard Shaw who wrote her story.

In the 1800s, the neighborhood of Louisa May Alcott included writers like Nathaniel Hawthorn, Ralph Waldo Emerson, and Henry David Thoreau. Had she been raised in another place, the world may never have known *Little Women*. In the 1920s the streets of Harlem produced the outstanding works of black Americans such as Langston Hughes. Had he not gone to live in Harlem, we may never have heard his voice.

Today walk or drive down a new street or road and enter another world. Whether you pass grazing horses or a row of factories, feel the unseen presence of an angel opening your eyes to new perspectives. A present-day equivalent of Philip's Ethiopian may live just around the corner and three streets down. God may open a door, for angels still guide willing steps.

June 3

Small Helpings

SCRIPTURE: *Romans 14: 17 - 18*
KEY VERSE: *God's kingdom does not consist of what a person eats or drinks.*

> Little Jack Horner
> Sat in a corner
> Eating his Christmas pie;
> He put in his thumb,
> And pulled out a plum,
> And said, "What a good boy am I!"

Little Jack's mother probably told him if he were good he would have some Christmas pie. So did not a generous piece prove his goodness?

"No!" Paul cries. "The belly makes a poor god."

Measure your goodness by Paul's standards rather than those of Little Jack Horner. In our high chair days, most of us learned that, if we were good, we would get dessert. However, we left our high chairs long ago. Today look at food and the appetite in a more mature light.

While encouraging a sedentary lifestyle, modern technology increases the availability of food. Supermarket shelves, drug stores, and even gas stations tempt us to nibble on sugar-loaded snacks, and fast food places beckon with fries and shakes. Our bodies are saturated, but often our spirits are starved.

Today feed the spirit rather than the body. Tell yourself, I am made in God's image—what a good girl am I!

Then make it a point to eat small helpings which reflect caloric needs rather than the availability of food. Assume your worth rather than try to prove it.

June 4

Park Facility

SCRIPTURE: *Psalm 96: 11 - 13*
KEY VERSE: *Let the fields and everything in them rejoice. Then all the trees in the forest will sing joyfully.*

If thou art rich, thou art poor;
For, like an ass whose back with ingots bows,
Thou bear'st thy heavy riches but a journey,
And death unloads thee...

Uttering these words in Shakespeare's *Measure for Measure*, the Duke of Vienna may have spoken for many rich comrades who groaned under the burden of wealth. For long ago, when they tired of their palaces, the rich retreated to their parks. Persian kings hunted in theirs, British nobility rode their horses in parks, and French kings used theirs to escape the squalor of the cities.

In contrast to past centuries when parks were private, today most towns and all counties and states provide public parks. Regardless of socioeconomic class, we can enjoy hiking trails, swimming pools, tennis courts, swings and slides, basketball courts, picnic tables, barbecue grills, and even concerts all in the beautiful outdoors.

Perhaps the psalmist sang God's praises so enthusiastically because he spent most of his time outdoors. Today shake off the burden of possessions, go to a park, and take advantage of a once royal privilege. Throw a Frisbee® across a grassy expanse or follow a hiking trail along a row of trees. Mingle the smell of grilled hamburgers with the scent of eucalyptus or pine. Watch sunlight sparkle on water.

Count your real wealth, and along with rejoicing heavens and an exulting earth, express your appreciation in enthusiastic praise.

June 5

Outline

SCRIPTURE: *2 Timothy 1: 13 - 14*
KEY VERSE: *Keep before you an outline of the sound teaching which you have heard from me, living by the faith and love which are ours in Christ Jesus. (NEB)*

> Peter Piper picked a peck of pickled peppers,
> A peck of pickled peppers Peter Piper picked.
> If Peter Piper picked a peck of pickled peppers,
> How many pickled peppers did Peter Piper pick?

P ossibly too many. If Peter Piper had outlined his needs, he would probably have picked a peck of garden vegetables and only a handful of peppers.

But then, who outlines anything? After walking off stage with a high school diploma, most of us happily left outlines, geometry books, and chemistry test tubes in the classroom.

Paul suggested Timothy outline his teaching and ministry. Like Peter Piper and many of us, Timothy may have tended to lose the big picture among the details. Outlines organize and simplify the details, putting them into a manageable and easily remembered form. The winds of unorthodoxy continually blew through the early church, and in order to stand against them, Timothy needed to keep before him an outline of sound teaching.

Unhealthy winds still blow our way, and we often find ourselves blown off course. Today grow in your ability to concentrate on main points by outlining something you read or hear. Whether a news report, magazine article, or conversation with a friend, move beyond details to the message.

Many of us miss the point much of the time. Today do something to help yourself find it more often.

June 6

Biography

SCRIPTURE: *Acts 7: 1 - 8*

KEY VERSE: *The God who reveals his glory appeared to our ancestor Abraham in Mesopotamia. This happened before Abraham lived in Haran.*

T he childless man came out of Mesopotamia, and he remained childless in the new land. But he held on to a promise he would be the father of nations. God so wove his purposes into the events of Abraham's life that his biography continues to inspire Jews, Christians, and Muslims four thousand years later.

Five billion biographies, each one fascinating, are being created each day the world over. Only a handful will be written in ink, and fewer published. These few can open windows into the wonderful world of human existence with all its suffering and joy.

The God who worked through the wandering, childless Abraham still works among us. Through the pages of a biography or autobiography, today peek into the soul of another person, and glimpse the light of God continuing to shine on our human path.

Whether it is *This Incredible Century* by Norman Vincent Peale bringing firsthand glimpses into the past, *The Broken Cord* by Michael Dorris sharing his struggle to raise fetal alcohol syndrome children, or *Joni* by Joni Erickson Tada giving a picture of the life of a quadriplegic, any honest account of the life of another person inspires us to make more of our own life.

When Abraham was young in Mesopotamia, God had

purposes for his world and those who dwelled in it. He still has purposes, and he still calls each of us to live according to those purposes. Today learn something from another's life to help you gain a new vision of what you can be and do.

June 7

Ask a Favor

SCRIPTURE: *Luke 19: 1 - 10*
KEY VERSE: *When Jesus came to the tree, he looked up and said, "Zacchaeus, come down! I must stay at your house today."*

> Zacchaeus was a wee little man,
> A wee little man was he,
> He climbed up in a sycamore tree,
> The Lord he wanted to see.
> And as the Savior passed that way
> He looked up in the tree,
> And he said, "Zacchaeus, you come down,
> For I'm going to your house today!"

Two thousand years removed from the scene, we picture a wee little man, a sycamore tree, and a caring Savior. But those who witnessed the scene saw a wealthy man, a sycamore tree, and a stranger who invited himself to dinner at someone else's house.

Unlike Jesus, not many of us feel comfortable inviting ourselves into someone else's home. Nor do we feel very comfortable asking any kind of favor. Being on the magnanimous end of a relationship builds self-esteem, but being on the receiving end can make us feel inferior.

Jesus had no problems with self-esteem. He knew the wee little man in the sycamore tree needed to feel magnanimous. He did something for Zacchaeus by letting Zacchaeus do something for him.

172

Taking pride in our abilities, most of us are pleased when other people recognize them. Today ask a favor of someone, and grant her the dignity of sharing her gifts. We are all wee little people when we feel inferior. By asking for help today, make some wee Zacchaeus, or perhaps Zaccheia, feel bigger.

Personal Dateline

SCRIPTURE: *Galatians 1: 13 – 2: 1*
KEY VERSE: *You heard about the way I once lived when I followed the Jewish religion. You heard how I violently persecuted God's church and tried to destroy it.*

Paul had a dramatic testimony to tell. His striking conversion made a gripping story. Peter would have told a different story of his faith journey. Had Mary Magdalene told her story, it would have been still different. We each have a unique story which no one else shares, not even our siblings, for we pen the lines in our responses rather than in our circumstances.

What is your story? Perhaps you married the freckle-faced boy you met the first day of kindergarten and then set up housekeeping in your home town. Your parents may live three houses down, and life may be as predictable as the seasons, revolving around PTA, Boy Scouts, and the annual hospital fair.

Or, like Paul and Mary Magdalene, can you tell a drama of wrong directions followed by redirections? Perhaps you came from a broken home, got in with the wrong crowd, dropped out of school, married young, divorced, remarried and only slowly discovered the real you. A bout with cancer may have given you a new perspective on life.

Whatever your story, today make a simple dateline giving a picture of your life. This is your story, for only you experience your circumstances with your choices and responses.

We are not called to be Pauls, Peters, or Mary Magdalenes, but like them, we are called to turn our uniqueness into specialized ministry. Today give thanks for your uniqueness and offer it to God.

Hike a Trail

SCRIPTURE: *Habakkuk 1:2 - 3; 3:15 - 19*
KEY VERSE: *How long, O Lord, am I to cry for help, but you will not listen? I cry out to you, "There's violence!" yet you will not come to the rescue....The Lord Almighty is my strength. He makes my feet like those of a deer. He makes me walk on the mountains.*

As he described in the first three verses of his book, Habakkuk's world was falling apart, and evidence seemed to deny God's power to help. Apparently, Habakkuk was a hiker, and that seemed to make a difference. With feet nimble as a deer's, he had ranged the heights, and there he felt the power of the Creator over creation.

From the Appalachian Trail in the East to the Pacific Crest Trail in the West, and from the Natchez Trace in the South to the Potomac Heritage Trail further north, our country is laced with hiking trails. Today take advantage of one of these national, state, county, or city trails designed to introduce us to the natural beauty of our land. Hike along the beach or scale a bluff beside the majestic sea. Walk around the city park, and find the Creator's touch on every leaf and flower. Tramp through desert sands and stand on a butte overlooking the world below.

However crumbling your world, like Habakkuk with feet nimble as a deer's, experience God in the heights. Rediscover eternal strength by rediscovering the world so magnificently created by the Eternal.

Sugar-Free Dessert

SCRIPTURE: *Proverbs 19: 13 – 15*
KEY VERSE: *Home and wealth are inherited from fathers, but a sensible wife comes from the Lord.*

In the movie version of the book, the delightful Mary Poppins told an incorrigible little Michael Banks that a spoonful of sugar helps the medicine go down. All of us who have tried to force bitter medicine down a child's throat know how right she was.

But Mary Poppins was not the first to make the discovery. Five thousand years ago, farmers in India extracted sugar from the sweet cane. In the Solomon Islands, a legend attributes the origin of the human race to a sugar cane stalk developing two buds, one forming a man and the other a woman. In 1736 nobility included sugar among their wedding gifts to Maria Theresa, future queen of Hungary.

However, in the twentieth century, we risk turning sugar's blessings into an addiction. Although Mary Poppins made the phrase popular, the sensible wife described in Proverbs knows the difference between a spoonful of sugar and a cupful. When spoonfuls turn to cupfuls, more medicine usually follows.

Some doctors link sugar with such diverse ailments as cancer, hypoglycemia, and depression. A more documented relationship between sugar consumption and hyperactivity in children has led many parents to replace processed with unprocessed sweeteners such as fruits and juices.

Today satisfy your sweet tooth sensibly and creatively. Sweeten desserts with raisins, dates, or figs. Substitute concentrated apple juice or a combination of honey and fruit juice in a recipe calling for sugar. Give cookies a sweet taste with mashed bananas or applesauce and a generous addition of nuts.

Put your intelligence to work for the good of your body.

Cheerful Service

SCRIPTURE: *2 Timothy 2:3 - 7*
KEY VERSE: *Join me in suffering like a good soldier of Christ Jesus.*

> Hickory, dickory, dock,
> The mouse ran up the clock.
> The clock struck one,
> The mouse ran down;
> ...The clock struck three,
> The mouse said "Whee!"
> ...The clock struck four,
> The mouse said, "No more!"

No more! Enough is enough! Many of us can sympathize with the small mouse who gave up climbing the clock because terrifying bongs sounded every time he reached the top.

But the bongs do not single out mice. Just as we think we're about to reach the top of some ladder, frightening bongs often scare us back down. "No more! Enough is enough," we cry, throwing up our hands.

Perhaps Timothy did not expect so many bongs to sound in the Lord's service. But older and more experienced, Paul knew that hardship comes with life and urged Timothy to willingly accept his share.

Today graciously accept your share. However unpleasant, difficult, or distasteful your tasks, perform them cheerfully. Catch yourself in "I wish..." statements. They often mean we are focusing on the bongs rather than on the power of the Holy Spirit within us.

Saint-and-sinner, we all run into hardship. But while the saint overcomes, the sinner runs. Or at least we moan and complain. Today repent. Enjoy being saint-for-a-day.

Sketch

SCRIPTURE: *2 Chronicles 3: 10 – 14*
KEY VERSE: *In the most holy place he made two sculptured angels and covered them with gold.*

H ad the artist hired by Solomon actually seen an angel, or did he simply imagine the way one would look? If he had seen an angel in a vision, had he actually measured the wing span, and did it correspond to the ones he carved in the Most Holy Place?

Do you hesitate to try your hand at sketching because you suspect your sketch will not look like the original? If so, you have the makings of an artist. Consider the difference between an artist and a photographer. The photographer reproduces what his eye sees; the artist distorts. When we love the work of a particular artist, we really love his or her particular distortion.

Degas' drawings suggest delicate movement, the ones of Michelangelo picture power and vitality, and the sketches of Rembrandt capture character in even the most ordinary looking people. The carver of cherubim created a sense of holiness in the most holy place of all.

While cameras record lines and shapes, artists lift out lines here and leave out ones there, creating a feeling rather than a reproduction. By definition, each artist perceives and expresses the world in a different way.

Today set yourself free from any feeling of obligation to faithfully reproduce anything, and sketch something in the world around you. The earth, dressed in her loveliest garments, models for our benefit and even pleasantly poses. Admire and sketch.

Game Night

Scripture: *Luke 10: 38 – 42*
Key verse: *As they were traveling along, Jesus went into a village. A woman named Martha welcomed him into her home.*

> Pat-a-cake, pat-a-cake, Baker's man,
> Bake me a cake as fast as you can.
> Pat it and prick it, and mark it with a B
> And put it in the oven for baby and me.

Apparently, Martha took work more seriously than her sister Mary. Oblivious to dinner preparations needing attention, Mary sat talking with Jesus while Martha worked.

We can imagine Mary laying aside a bowl of half-shelled beans to play a Hebrew form of pat-a-cake with the baby. She may have skipped on the way to the well and tossed a stray ball back to a group of little boys. After Jesus left that night, she probably leaned on her broom handle, staring off into space as she went back over the events of the day.

If all work and no play makes Jack a dull boy, it also makes Betty, Jane, or Martha a dull girl. Many of us have learned to be good-hearted Marthas, but such devotion to duty risks trapping us in the monotonous. Secretly yearning to escape, we sometimes grow resentful of the Marys who do.

Rather than resenting a Mary in your life, today be one. Lay out a welcome mat for fun by inviting friends over for an evening of games. Dust off the Monopoly® game you have not played for years and the Pictionary® you have played a total of three times. Play pat-a-cake with the baby who tries to grab tokens off the board.

Spend an evening brushing off some of the dullness which has settled on your busy, hardworking Martha qualities. Season the evening with a touch of Mary.

June 14

Photo Frame

Scripture: *Psalm 133*
Key verse: *See how good and how pleasant it is when brothers and sisters live together in harmony!*

D ashing off thrilling adventures with her pen, Jo in Louisa May Alcott's *Little Women* dreamed of fame. Editors took little notice of her beautiful women, handsome men, and fearful villains. However, when she began recreating family scenes from childhood days, not only editors took note, but an adoring public fell in love with Meg, Jo, Beth, and Amy.

Several generations removed from the March family, we still respond warmly to the good and pleasant story of sisters living together. We may follow the story with a certain nostalgia, for sisters live together less frequently today than in past generations.

In compensation, we gather when we can. Holidays call us home, births, marriages, and graduations collect us, and family reunions periodically assemble us. Wherever we go, our cameras go, eagerly capturing the graduate receiving her diploma, the bride walking down the aisle, and the family gathering around the Christmas tree.

Today note how good it is for brothers and sisters to be together even if they can not live together. Using anything from driftwood to calico, make a frame to set off one of those moments captured on film. Use your imagination to create a special frame for a special moment.

Meg, Jo, Beth, and Amy represent the power and beauty of the hearth, even in an age where part of the hearth is here, another part there, and some of it everywhere. Although geographically divided, the heart knows how to keep it together.

Ethnic Neighborhood

SCRIPTURE: *Romans 2: 11 – 16*
KEY VERSE: *God does not play favorites.*

> Up into the cherry tree
> Who should climb but little me?
> I held the trunk with both my hands
> And looked abroad on foreign lands.

As did the lad in Robert Louis Stevenson's poem, the boy, Saul, may once have climbed a cherry tree, or perhaps a sycamore tree, to look abroad on foreign lands. The man, Paul, often saw far off lands in his mind's eyes, and longed to visit them with the Gospel. With clearer vision than many of his contemporaries, he realized that God had no favorites and sent his Son for the whole world.

Faraway places intrigue many of us as they did the lad in the cherry tree and the apostle on the move. Our generation travels, and thumbing through Sunday's travel section, we note specials to Athens, Moscow, and Bangkok. We dream of Paris, Stockholm, and Cairo. Faraway places call, and we listen.

Today travel in reverse. Visit the far-away-place in your back yard. Little Tokyo, Little Poland, Little Italy, Little India, or Little Almost Anywhere may be three stores long or three miles long, but it bears the unmistakable marks of another world and another culture. Enter one of these worlds.

Listen to the tinkle of bells, the cadence of words falling in different patterns, the pluck of unfamiliar instruments. Smell dried fish, the whiff of incense outside a store, cardamom bread coming out of an oven. Notice clothing, hairstyles, and unfamiliar scripts above shop doors.

The whole world still needs the gospel. Today briefly travel to part of it.

June 16

ℱlower Sets

SCRIPTURE: *Genesis 2: 5 - 9*
KEY VERSE: *The Lord God planted a garden in Eden, in the east. That's where he put the man whom he had formed.*

When Adam first opened his eyes, did they fall on an exquisite pink rose or a brilliant clump of red and orange impatiens? Or did they gaze on a cherry tree filled with soft pink blossoms? Whatever filled the garden of Eden, its beauty left a permanent mark on mankind.

Love of gardens characterizes people of all times. From the Hanging Gardens of Babylon to the formal gardens of Versailles, and from cottage gardens of medieval Europe to colonial gardens of the New World, flowers have lifted the spirits of nobility and peasant alike.

This month flowers turn even the most humble front yards into Renoir prints. With the addition of ready-to-bloom flower sets, today put another touch of Eden in your yard. Compliment a bed of purple perennials with pink impatiens, or plant yellow zinnias among yellow marigolds. Give your window box arrangement a new companion, or put a piece of garden in the kitchen with a hanging plant.

The garden of Eden must have held both shady nooks and sun-splashed meadows, for God created flowers for each. While fuchsias, impatiens, begonia, lobelia, and coleus appreciate shade, snapdragons, pansies, dahlias, nasturtiums, bachelor buttons, and petunias adore the sun. Select flowers which feel at home in your beds.

God must love gardens, for before he made man, he made a garden to receive him. Today greet those who come your way with a touch of beauty.

Children's Writings

SCRIPTURE: *Mark 9: 35 - 42*

KEY VERSE: *These little ones believe in me. It would be best for the person who causes one of them to lose faith to be thrown into the sea with a large stone hung around his neck.*

We can fly, we can fly, we can fly!" With these words, Wendy and John rise above the rooftops of London and sail away to Never-Never Land with Peter Pan. With them go generations of children.

Young children believe anything is possible. Peter Pan can fly and a cow can jump over the moon. Jack Frost can paint pictures on the window, and Santa can come down the chimney. Angels watch over us, and God can take care of any problem.

As we grew up, we lose faith in Never-Never Land, cows jumping over moons, and Santas coming down chimneys. However, perhaps we also lose some of our faith in angels and a God who can take care of any problem.

When we lose our childlike faith, we often lose more than our belief in fairy-tales. We lose access to God. Pointing to a child's faith, Jesus spoke words of judgment for anyone causing a little one to stumble.

Today relive a little of the sweet innocence of childhood by reading something written by a child. Perhaps still stored away in a trunk lies a smudged story you or your daughter once wrote about the tooth fairy who left a nickel. Among letters tied together with a pink ribbon may be one listing every Christmas present you received when you were ten years old. Retrieve the first poem your child ever wrote, and bring back the child by reading it.

Go back to a time when faith was strong and sure, and linger long enough to awaken childlike faith.

Historical Marker

SCRIPTURE: *Genesis 31: 43 - 54*
KEY VERSE: *Jacob took a stone and set it up as a marker.*

> O, how this spring of love resembleth
> The uncertain glory of an April day;
> Which now shows all the beauty of the sun,
> And by and by a cloud takes all away!

As Proteus indicates in Shakespeare's *Two Gentlemen of Verona*, how soon everything changes, and how quickly we forget!

Until the last minute Laban probably hoped Jacob would not take his daughters far away. But for twenty years Jacob had counted on returning to his own land, and no longer would he be detained. When Laban agreed, Jacob wisely erected a marker as tangible evidence of their agreement. In future moments of regret, Laban could not accuse Jacob of stealing his daughters or possessions. Each time he passed the marker, he had to remember that he had given his consent.

We also need markers, for we too easily confuse the past. Today stop before a historical marker and relive the story it tells. Whether a battlefield where men sacrificed their lives for their convictions, a stagecoach stop of pony express days, or the spot where gold was discovered, it represents the part others played in creating our world of today. Go back to the event, picture the people involved, and connect it to yourself.

Focusing on our own achievements as Laban did, we easily forget that our prosperity came through the labor of others. Without the many Jacobs of the past, our world would be different. Stand before some marker, and give thanks for all those who had a share in creating the world we know today.

New Recipes

SCRIPTURE: *Exodus 16: 13 - 18*
KEY VERSE: *When the Israelites saw it, they asked each other,*
"What is this?" because they didn't know what it was.

> Pease porridge hot, pease porridge cold,
> Pease porridge in the pot, nine days old.
> Some like it hot, some like it cold,
> Some like it in the pot, nine days old.

They probably preferred hot porridge, but the hurried Israelites may have expected a few meals of cold porridge. They may have even been prepared to accept it in the pot nine days old. But they never suspected that God would completely change the porridge.

Our God is a God of change, constantly introducing the new into the old. Today follow his example in the wilderness and change your porridge. From morning toast to dinner salad, use a new recipe for every dish you serve.

Change plain toast to cinnamon toast or French toast. Add applesauce, bran, or raisins to your bowl of oatmeal. Replace porridge with chocolate waffles, honey nut muffins, or a cheese sandwich. Add a cinnamon stick or touch of chocolate to morning coffee.

Dress up a noontime sandwich with alfalfa sprouts or spinach leaves. Serve sesame chicken salad instead of sandwich. Try a new meat loaf recipe tonight, add herbs to the green beans, and make pilaf. Give salad a tang with chilled grapefruit sections in mint sauce. Make apricot bars or bake apples stuffed with dates and walnuts.

For four hundred years, the Israelites ate the food of the Egyptians, but when God turned their face toward new horizons, he changed their food. Today change your eating patterns as a reminder that God is still leading us into a promised land.

June 20

Conflict Resolution

SCRIPTURE: *Ephesians 4: 1 - 6*
KEY VERSE: *Be humble and gentle in every way. Be patient with each other and lovingly accept each other.*

> I had a little pony,
> His name was Dapple Gray,
> I lent him to a lady,
> To ride a mile away.
> She whipped him, she lashed him,
> She rode him through the mire;
> I would not lend my pony now,
> For all the lady's hire.

T he little boy in the nursery rhyme appears to have settled his conflict with the lady in a sensible manner. She could not be trusted with the pony, so the boy would no longer lend the animal to her.

However, rather than solving problems, his solution would only aggravate many of ours. The lady is a family member, she accuses us of being selfish, and she tells the neighbors she has to walk because of our selfishness.

Neither did such simple solutions always work for Paul. He was often chased out of town because of his failure to resolve conflicts. However, working with all kinds of people with all kinds of agendas, he must have learned that some things work better than others. Perhaps in some humbling moment on his knees, the Spirit revealed to him that gentleness and patience sometimes work when logic fails.

Today humbly apply Paul's words to some conflict in your own life. Gently teach the lady how to treat a pony, or let her take it out when road conditions are good. Volunteer to do her errand.

Lest you never hear the end of it, spare no effort to resolve the problem.

List God's Actions

SCRIPTURE: *Psalm 136*

KEY VERSE: *Give thanks to the Lord of lords, because his mercy endures forever.*

Ladybug, Ladybug, fly away home,
Your house is on fire, your children all gone,
All but one, and her name is Ann
And she crept under a pudding-pan.

L iving through such disasters, some call them acts of God. Others see God's absence rather than his presence in tragedy.

In some of life's turns, God appears so remote that no amount of praying removes the distance we feel. At other times, an event occurs which leaves no doubt about his presence. One visible touch in a lifetime may forever assure us God is working in our lives.

In two thousand years, a handful of events gave the children of Israel confidence God was working in their midst in spite of tragic circumstances. By reciting these events from one generation to another, they held on to their faith through defeat, exile, and oppression.

Today bring back those times when God mysteriously or wonderfully worked in your life. Perhaps you saw his hand in an impulsive telephone call alerting you to a crisis, or in a check sent by one who knew nothing of your need. In a moment when all hope was gone, a job came in an unexpected way.

Whatever those touches, some so light you almost missed them and others which seemed to shout God's presence, list them. Whether five or twenty-five incidents, turn them into a psalm celebrating God's presence in your life.

Like the Israelites, survive tragedy and dry periods of faith by remembering how God has acted in your life.

June 22

Park Supper

SCRIPTURE: *Psalm 104: 13 - 18*
KEY VERSE: *You water the mountains from your home above.*
You fill the earth with the fruits of your labors.

> My mind lets go of a thousand things
> Like dates of wars and death of kings,
> And yet recalls the very hour...
> The wind came briskly up this way
> Crisping the brook beside the road...

Like Thomas Bailey Aldrich, the psalmist's mind let go of a thousand things, but the moments he spent outdoors were not among them. He long remembered the lacy pattern of leaves against the sky, a stork building her nest, and a brook trickling through the valley.

The summer solstice hands us an ideal day for such memories. Now at its zenith, the sun pours more hours of light into this day than any other. The long rays of a leisurely descending sun extend the evening and cast a golden spell over it. Profit from the long, lovely day by having supper in the park.

Spread a blue checked cloth over a park table, and enjoy your meal beside a placid lake filled with graceful swans, or eat alongside a gurgling brook in the hollow of the hills. Notice sunlight play with dandelion and milkweed, watch water ripple as insects meet waiting fish, and gaze up at a blue sky filled with cotton clouds. Like the psalmist, observe how leafy and green are the Lord's trees and how full of birds' nests they are.

Replace the strain of the day with gentle peace. Like Thomas Bailey Aldrich, in your mind let go of a thousand things, and cling to these moments when the beauty of the Lord reaches your soul.

June 23

Send a Poem

SCRIPTURE: *Acts 17:27 - 31*

KEY VERSE: *As some of your poets have said, 'We are God's children.'*

> One, two, buckle my shoe;
> Three, four, knock at the door;
> five six, pick up sticks;
> Seven, eight, lay them straight;
> Nine, ten, a big fat hen.

N ursery rhymes introduced many of us to the world of poetry. We loved to hear "One, Two, Buckle My Shoe" even when we had no idea what a buckle was. We still don't know what many of the nursery rhymes mean. Some of them never had any meaning. They are only meant to please.

The sounds of poetry have pleased man from the beginning of time, and every society honors its poets. Some poems such as the Psalms and the epic poems of Virgil retain their power to move and please generation after generation. Many of the writers of the Bible expressed themselves in poetry, and we find their words easier to remember than others.

Like us, the infant Saul may have chanted nonsense rhymes while toddling about his mother's feet. He probably began memorizing Psalms and Jewish poetry before he could correctly pronounce the consonants. When the adult Paul wanted to communicate the Gospel to the Athenians, he quoted their Greek poets.

As Paul did in Athens, respond to an almost universal love of poetry by communicating through a poem. Choose the poem for the person, for one prefers the haunting lyrics of Robert Burns while another appreciates the inspirational verse of Helen Steiner Rice. The romance of Elizabeth Barrett Browning appeals to one, and the earthiness of Carl Sandburg to another. Even people who think they don't like poetry often recite the poetry of the psalms.

With lilting, funny, or thoughtful lines of verse, add pleasure, humor, or inspiration to someone's day.

June 24

Sew

SCRIPTURE: *Proverbs 31: 21 - 22*
KEY VERSE: *She makes quilts for herself. Her clothes are made of linen and purple cloth.*

> Old Mother Twitchet had but one eye,
> And a long tail that she let fly;
> And every time she went through a gap
> She left a bit of her tail in a trap.

What was she? A needle and thread, of course. For four thousand years, women have used her to sew their apparel together.

From a shellfish found along the Mediterranean coast, the Phoenicians learned to make the purple which dyed the garments of the woman in Proverbs. She was probably an upper class lady, for only the nobility and privileged could afford the expensive purple. Whether she stitched her own garments or supervised the work of servants, the sewing was done by hand.

In the Laura Ingalls Wilder series, before Mary went off to a school for the blind, she stitched herself dresses. Until this century, almost every woman sewed a fine seam by hand and took pride in her small stitches. Now, machines—hand-operated in places without electricity— do what the hand once did. Increasingly, however, the machines whir in factories instead of homes, and many of us find ourselves slowly losing one more skill.

Today get back in touch with this ancient art with a bit of creative sewing. Make a skirt, blouse, or other garment to add to your summer wardrobe. Choose any fabric, but if you long for a look of nobility, make it purple.

June 25

Name Your Home

SCRIPTURE: *Genesis 16: 7 – 16*

KEY VERSE: *This is why the well is named Beer Lahai Roi (Well of the Living One Who Watches Over Me). It is still there between Kadesh and Bered.*

Apparently, it was Sarah's idea to bring children into the home through her slave girl. From that moment, things began going wrong in her house, and Sarah grew increasingly unhappy. When she began ill-treating the girl, Hagar ran away. However, the Lord sent an angel after the girl with a word of encouragement. Overwhelmed and relieved, Hagar called the place Beer Lahai Roi, for she had seen God and lived to tell it.

In non-western societies, names often tell a story. Thus, a Zairean with the name Mbongo Mpasi (Money Problems) always carries with him the story of his parents' financial distress at the time of his birth. The name Kwetwenda (Where are we going?) informs others his family was homeless at the time of the child's birth. When Cephas became Peter and Saul became Paul, acquaintances immediately knew something significant had happened in their lives.

When we choose names for our babies, we usually pick pleasant sounding names often unaware of any significance. However, like non-Westerners, we name our property to tell a story or give a message. An estate called Pacific Heights evokes an image of a house on a bluff overlooking the ocean, and a ranch called Drifting Sands brings to mind a desert scene. Even if we have not read the book, we can picture Nathaniel Hawthorne's *House of Seven Gables*. With its name, L'Abri in Switzerland promises a message of hope.

Today name your own home, the place where you live, grow, and meet God day after day. Play with words until you find a phrase capturing either the character of the property or the hopes and dreams of those who dwell in it. Give both strangers and friends a message through the name you choose.

June 26

Overnight Trip

SCRIPTURE: *Luke 2: 41 - 42*
KEY VERSE: *Every year Jesus' parents would go to Jerusalem for the Passover festival.*

O nly after he fled Pharaoh's palace did Moses hear God speaking in the desert. In the unfamiliar quarters of a big fish Jonah listened to God. After his conversion, Paul crystallized his faith in Arabia. In exile John received revelations from God. Getting away from the familiar stimulates most of us.

Traveling in the company of friends, every year Mary and Joseph went to Jerusalem to attend the Passover festival. The year Jesus was twelve, Luke pictures him so caught up in the words of the great teachers that he lost track of time. Those conversations probably planted many seeds of future ministry.

Today make a break with your own familiar world by planning an overnight trip into a totally different one. Go camping in the mountains where the smell of pine needles and wood smoke stimulate the senses. Watch the evening sun set over a peak and the morning one rise as you shiver beside your campfire. Hear the voice of God more clearly in the beauty of the natural world.

Or pack a quick bag and take off for the coast. After securing a motel room, spend the evening gathering shells at the edge of the surf and fingering smooth pebbles sanded by time. Treat yourself to a seafood supper and share bread with begging gulls. Take a run on the beach while day is young, and bring back a touch of your own youth.

Like Mary and Joseph and the child Jesus, go to the city for stimulation, or as Moses did, find God in the isolation of the desert. Wander a back road and spend the night in a country inn. Go into the highways and the byways where new worlds hold new food for thought.

At home, twenty-four hours is twenty-four hours. But twenty-four hours away from home is timeless. Today step out of time. Get back in touch with yourself and your Lord by going away.

June 27

Public Restroom

SCRIPTURE: *1 Thessalonians 1: 2 – 5*
KEY VERSE: *In the presence of our God and Father, we never forget that your faith is active, your love is working hard, and your confidence in our Lord Jesus Christ is enduring.*

There was an old woman tossed up in a basket,
Nineteen times as high as the moon;
And where she was going, I couldn't but ask it,
For in her hand she carried a broom...
"O whither, O whither, O whither so high?"
"To sweep the cobwebs off the sky!"

Perhaps it did not occur to the old woman to apply her broom to floors trod by human feet. But many beg a swipe of some broom, especially ones in public rest rooms.

In *To Live Again* Catherine Marshall tells of making a trip while potty-training her son. Armed with a can of disinfectant spray, she attacked the germs on public restroom toilets before taking her little son inside. We know the feeling. Entering a public restroom, we often turn up our nose and wish someone would clean it. Crumpled towels on a dirty floor, stained sinks, and smelly toilet bowls turn rest rooms into stress rooms.

Paul may have known Christians who spent their time sweeping cobwebs off the sky, for he gave thanks when the Thessalonians translated heavenly hopes into earthly labor. Today imitate the Thessalonians. Apply heavenly faith to a very earthly need and leave a public restroom cleaner than you found it.

Protecting hands with a clean paper towel, throw stray paper towels or bits of toilet paper in the trash basket where they belong. Wipe the sink or mirror with the damp towel you used to dry your hands. Inform the manager that toilet paper, soap, or paper towels need replacing.

Unlike the old woman who went seeking dirt, today take care of a little of it below your feet.

June 28

Day of Thanks

SCRIPTURE: *1 Thessalonians 5: 16 - 18*
KEY VERSE: *Whatever happens, give thanks, because it is God's will in Christ Jesus that you do this.*

> All good gifts around us
> Are sent from heaven above;
> Then thank the Lord, O thank the Lord
> For all his love.

B oth Paul and Matthias Claudius responded to God's goodness with thanksgiving. In every gift of earth, sky, and sea, these men glimpsed the unlimited love of an Eternal Father.

What spring promises, summer bountifully fulfills. Full-leafed maples generously shade lawns, petunias effusively color flower beds, and radishes grow red and round in gardens. Breezes blow, bees hum, grass grows. Spring's most audacious promises hardly measure up to summer's surfeit.

Today see these gifts, and see beyond them. See the magnanimous love which inspired them. Then give thanks. From the first ray's light on the western hills to the last glow of color in the evening sky, make this a day of thanksgiving.

Give thanks for soil and seed and the faithfulness of the seasons. Appreciate oxygen in the air, minerals in the soil, and vitamins in the plants. Thank God for the breezes which blow, the sun which shines, or the rain which falls.

Find his goodness in more than nature. Acknowledge the gift of children's laughter, curiosity, and energy. Appreciate hands to dig into the soil, feet to walk across it, and eyes to see the vegetables growing in it. Be grateful for family and friends.

Give thanks for growth which comes through difficulties as well as satisfactions, and frustrations as well as rewards. See the gift of challenges and the value of struggles. See love behind shadow as well as sunlight.

Today take nothing for granted, but give thanks for everything and multiply the pleasure of each blessing. Like Matthias Claudius, thank the Lord for all his love.

June 29

Pancake Supper

SCRIPTURE: *1 Kings 17: 10 – 16*
KEY VERSE: *"Never fear," said Elijah; "go and do as you say, but first make me a small cake from what you have and bring it out to me." (NEB)*

Aunt Jemimah did not invent pancakes; neither did the International House of Pancakes. Almost three thousand years ago, Elijah gratefully accepted pancakes for his supper.

No sacred formula determines our meal patterns, and the food we eat and the hours we eat it vary from culture to culture. In Thailand many breakfasts feature soup, and in Zaire roasted peanuts and bananas often begin the day. In Laura Ingalls Wilder's *Farmer Boy*, apple pie sometimes appeared on the breakfast table. In many European countries women serve the heavy meal of the day at noon, and in the Deep South, corn bread and buttermilk may make supper.

In the Bible story, the widow's last handful of flour fed a prophet. Tonight, with more resources than she had, turn several handfuls into pancakes for the hungry ones who appear at your supper table.

We have choices neither Elijah nor the widow had. From buttermilk pancakes to buckwheat griddle cakes, gingerbread pancakes topped with applesauce to crab-filled crepes, and chocolate waffles served with ice cream to pecan waffles topped with maple syrup, limitless possibilities can turn any home into an international house of pancakes.

Since drought dried up even the brooks, Elijah did not have the luxury of plucking a handful of berries to top his pancakes. But out in the meadow or up on the fruit stand, blueberries, raspberries, or strawberries are ours for the picking. Tonight's pancakes need not be dull.

If a small cake revived Elijah, a plate of large cakes should do the same for us.

First Aid Update

SCRIPTURE: *Mark 6: 7 - 13*
KEY VERSE: *They also forced many demons out of people and poured oil on many who were sick to cure them.*

There was an old woman who swallowed a fly;
I don't know why she swallowed a fly,
I think she'll die...

D efinitely the song writer did not possess the gift of
healing. Nor do many of us claim to possess it.

The first twelve disciples anointed with oil, healed the sick, and drove out demons. But we latter-day disciples cringe at demons, cheer the sick, and trust God and the doctors to miraculously heal our loved ones.

However, doctors are not always on the spot, and sometimes the gift of healing comes through first-aid readiness. The person who knows how to dislodge a fish bone in a choking woman has the gift of healing at that moment. Five thousand feet up in a Sierra campground, the gifted one knows how to treat a child's burn.

Today accept the gift of healing by brushing up on first-aid techniques. When life hangs in the balance of a few seconds, we don't have the luxury of thumbing through a first aid manual or waiting for a professional to appear. As summer begins, prepare yourself to deal with major emergencies until medical help arrives.

The first-aid kit of the twelve disciples seemed to contain only oil, but we have a much larger range of possibilities. With over-the-counter medications to combat them, nausea and diarrhea need not spoil otherwise delightful family gatherings. Nor must insect stings ruin an outing. Today check your own first-aid kit, refurbishing and re-supplying where necessary.

Even as medical knowledge has multiplied, the twelve disciples have multiplied into the millions. When we each study a few first aid techniques, the gift of healing goes on.

Herb Recipe

SCRIPTURE: *Exodus 12: 1 - 10*

KEY VERSE: *The meat must be eaten that same night. It must be roasted over a fire and eaten with bitter herbs and unleavened bread.*

When is zucchini more than zucchini, or salad more than salad? In *All's Well That Ends Well*, Shakespeare's Clown knows the answer:

> Indeed, sir,
> she was the sweet marjoram of the salad,
> or rather, the herb of grace.

From Shakespeare's herb of grace to Simon and Garfunkel's *Parsley, Sage, Rosemary, and Thyme*, herbs season both salads and literature. Hippocrates filled his medicine cabinet with them, and the Pharisees tithed the ones in their gardens.

In bondage to Egyptian masters, the Israelites enjoyed few privileges and suffered countless hardships. But loving wives cultivated their herbs and made zucchini more than zucchini and salads more than salads. On the night of the Passover, bitter herbs turned a meal into more than a meal.

Tonight make your own meal memorable by transforming ordinary food into gourmet fare with a touch of herbs. Season a tossed salad with parsley, rosemary, or thyme, or like the housewives of Shakespeare's world, add a bit of sweet marjoram. Use one of the 150 varieties of basil and top tonight's spaghetti with a pesto sauce. Surprise the family with rosemary flavored chicken baked with mushrooms and potatoes. Add herbs and make zucchini more than zucchini.

July 2

ℛecreation Ideas

SCRIPTURE: *1 Corinthians 9: 24 – 27*

KEY VERSE: *Don't you realize that everyone who runs in a race runs to win, but only one runner gets the prize? Run like them, so that you can win.*

> Jack, be nimble,
> Jack, be quick,
> Jack, jump over the candlestick.

T he author of the little nursery rhyme does not tell us if Jack ever became a famous high jumper or cross country runner. But if three-year-old Jack practiced jumping over the candlestick, twenty-three-year-old Jack probably jumped over many other hurdles in life.

When the athletes of Paul's day were about Jack's size, they probably began jumping over an object about the size of a candlestick. From the bleachers, the child Saul must have often watched those runners, his eyes glued to their every move. In his youth, he may have been one of them. Whether as a spectator or a participant, Saul made time for leisure and recreation.

All year we look forward to hiking the peaks of the Rockies in July, renting a cabin at the shore in August, or camping in the Adirondacks. But these big splurges usually absorb only a fraction of summer's days.

You can tuck a vacation moment into each day of summer. Exploit opportunities on your doorstep. Swim in the creek, visit old factories in the area, bring out sports equipment half-buried in the garage or attic and make specific plans to use it.

Many years after Paul sat in the bleachers, he remembered how every runner ran to win, and he encouraged the Corinthians to become spiritual athletes. This summer make leisure moments equally memorable.

Community Calendar

SCRIPTURE: *Mark 2: 1 - 5*

KEY VERSE: *Several days later Jesus came back to Capernaum. The report went out that he was home.*

> Three blind mice, see how they run!
> They all ran after the farmer's wife,
> She cut off their tails with a carving knife.
> Did you ever see such a sight in your life,
> As three blind mice?

If three blind mice were all he could talk about, perhaps the writer of the nursery rhyme had not seen a great many things in his life.

Like him, sometimes we rattle on about our own little worlds because we haven't gone very far out of them. Not everyone took the time to go see new things happening at Jesus' house. But life changed for many who went to hear the teacher.

We too have the opportunity to go see something new. Community calendars offer exhibitions, puppetry in the park, lectures on improving our self-image, autographing sessions at bookstores, and Fourth of July celebrations. A world famous cellist may be giving a concert at a community college this week, and the local band may be performing in the park.

As Jesus once visited the villages of Galilee, visiting teachers also come our way. A State Department official speaks at an open meeting of the World Affairs Council. A visiting professor from the former Czechoslovakia offers an inside view of a place the media has made familiar. A Colombian art exposition brings the opportunity to learn more about another culture.

Today enrich your summer with a community calendar event. Discover new topics of conversation.

July 4

Historical Fact

SCRIPTURE: *Proverbs 13: 14 - 18*
KEY VERSE: *Any sensible person acts with knowledge, but a fool displays stupidity.*

> Taffy was a Welshman,
> Taffy was a thief;
> Taffy came to my house
> And stole a piece of beef.

This undocumented tidbit of history could be true. Or it could be a spurious attempt to slander a good man. Unless we learn more about Taffy or the rhyme's author, we will never know.

Since childhood we have known names like Thomas Paine, Samuel Adams, and Patrick Henry, but we may not remember the role they played in the Revolution. In school, we learned about the Stamp Act, Quebec Act, and Coercive Acts which triggered the revolution, but do we still remember why they angered the colonists?

We recite famous names and events, but the Revolution often hinged on the sacrifices of people like Haym Salomon, a Polish immigrant who donated his fortune to the cause. We all know Paul Revere, but few of us know Sybil Ludington, a sixteen-year-old girl who made an even longer ride to spread the alarm of advancing British troops. A black woman, Deborah Gannet, fought as a soldier in the revolution.

From ocean to ocean, tonight fireworks light up the skies of a nation. Red, white, and blue streamers fly over parks, and hot dogs, ice cream, and soft drinks fill tables. Our patriotism waves high, for on this day in 1776 the Declaration of Independence was signed.

Today do enough research to bring the story of the American independence into sharper focus. Know why we light up the skies and watch them grow even lovelier.

A Column

SCRIPTURE: *Isaiah 10: 1 - 4*
KEY VERSE: *How horrible it will be for those who make un-just laws and who make oppressive regulations.*

> The law locks up both man or woman
> Who steals the goose from off the common,
> But lets the greater felon loose,
> That steals the common from the goose.

If it was his goose that was shut out, perhaps Edward Potts Cheyney, the indignant writer of this rhyme, had a chance to speak his piece in court. Was Thomas Jefferson thinking of such incidents when he wrote about the un-alienable rights of every human?

Time has a way of eroding lofty ideals. In George Orwell's *Animal Farm*, one pig explains to fellow pigs they are all equal, but some more equal than others. Although the founding fathers dreamed of equality, two hundred years later, some of us remain more equal than others. Like the poor of Isaiah's society, many of our poor feel trapped in a less-equal status.

Isaiah courageously addressed the evils creating such imbalances in his day. Like him, make God's concerns your concerns, and express them in writing. Yesterday we cel-ebrated the privilege of living in a free and prosperous nation. We may also have passed graffiti-filled walls and wondered what gave birth to such violence in one of the most blessed nations on earth.

In the two hundred plus years since the Declaration of Independence gave birth to a nation, what has matured and born fruit, and what has reaped heartache and violence? Why are we all equal, but some more equal than others?

Columnists make their living by reflecting on the events of our world, but we all have valid perceptions.

Today express yours. Write your own column about injustice and equality.

Or write a prayer asking God to purify and use our nation.

July 6

Under a Tree

SCRIPTURE: *Psalm 92: 10 – 15*
KEY VERSE: *Vigorous in old age like trees full of sap, luxuriant, wide spreading. (NEB)*

> Under the spreading chestnut-tree
> The village smithy stands;
> The smith a mighty man is he...

Long before Henry Wadsworth Longfellow's village blacksmith stood under the spreading chestnut tree, a shepherd boy in Israel sat gazing through the branches of a luxuriant, wide spreading tree in the meadow. Since boyhood he had sat beneath this tree, and his father had sat beneath it in his boyhood. Perhaps his children would also sit beneath it. Running his fingers over the rough bark of the vigorous old tree, he realized those who loved the Lord flourish like the tree.

Trees feed fires in one season and provide shade from scorching sun in another. They put fruit on tables and canoes on seas. They also invite us to sit beneath their boughs and dream. Perhaps the psalmist first sang his psalms playing a harp in the cool shade of a tree. Today sit beneath a tree's leafy limbs and dream your own dreams.

Watch the play of sunlight on leaves and follow a trail of ants up the dark trunk. Listen to one robin call from a top branch and hear another echo the call from another tree. Feel the soft breeze on your face. Study shifting patterns of light and shade around you. Read or knit, sketch or journal, or simply sit quietly and freshen your thoughts.

For a few minutes simply be and reclaim a part of yourself you had forgotten was there. Like the psalmist, turn your thoughts to God. Know, as he sends the sap to luxuriant, widespreading trees, he continually renews you with his spirit. In his care we all flourish.

July 7

New Ice Cream

SCRIPTURE: *Numbers 14: 5 - 10*
KEY VERSE: *If the Lord is pleased with us, he will bring us into this land and give it to us. This is a land flowing with milk and honey.*

> Things are seldom what they seem,
> Skim milk masquerades as cream.

O r as ice cream, Sir W. S. Gilbert could have added. Ice cream may not have been a part of the good life in ancient Palestine, but its ingredients, milk and honey, were among the fringe benefits of the Lord's care. Three thousand years later, they still are.

From the kitchens of the Far East, Marco Polo gleaned the recipe for ice milk and carried it back to European nobles. In the late nineteenth century, the invention of the ice cream freezer took the luxury into the homes of white collar, blue collar, and no-collar workers. Children once long deliberated before making their choice of vanilla, chocolate, or strawberry cones. Today, the most ordinary among us enjoy ice cream in more flavors than Marco Polo or European nobles ever dreamed.

How many of the hundred-plus flavors have you tried? Today buy a new flavor or create a new one. Invite friends to help crank the old fashioned freezer, and enjoy a new taste adventure together. Treat yourself to honey banana, fresh peach, or carob honey flavors. For those nagged by high cholesterol or allergic to dairy products, use tofu.

Even the Lord offers fringe benefits. Today enjoy one of them.

July 8

Inn Stop

SCRIPTURE: *Luke 10: 29 – 37*
KEY VERSE: *Then he put him on his own animal, brought him to an inn, and took care of him.*

> How many miles to Babylon?
> Three-score and ten.
> Can I get there by candle-light?
> Yes, and back again.

Just in case he can't get there in one night, the aspiring traveler would be wise to ask about inns on the way.

Wanderlust has always been a part of man's nature, pulling him away from the familiar to explore the less familiar. From ancient times, inns in India, China, and the Near East accommodated wayfarers who found themselves on the road at night. The Roman world built roads to everywhere and inns to host those who journeyed.

In the middle ages monastic orders provided havens for those traveling through dangerous territory, and by the time of the Renaissance, inns had become favorite gathering places.

Today visit one for fun. Walk along petunia-lined walkways and meander through gardens bursting with color. Sit a moment beneath a rose arbor and admire carefully groomed grounds. Enter the parlor, admire an exquisite gladioli arrangement and a glassed case of old books. Rest a moment in a chintz covered chair facing an old brick fireplace. Experience the charm of an inn designed to be welcoming and inviting.

An inn sheltered a wounded man, and in Bethlehem, an inn's stable sheltered a woman giving birth to her first child. Remind yourself God provides resting places in life's journey.

July 9

New Acquaintance

SCRIPTURE: *Acts 9: 26 – 30*
KEY VERSE: *After Saul arrived in Jerusalem, he tried to join the disciples. But everyone was afraid of him. They wouldn't believe that he was a disciple.*

We came into the world like brother and brother:
And now let's go hand in hand, not one before another.

Thus ends Shakespeare's *Comedy of Errors*. Long before a Shakespeare existed, the disciples in Jerusalem almost produced their own comedy of errors. The converted Saul tried to join their fellowship, but they were not about to be taken in by this fanatic they had heard so much about. Thanks to Barnabas, the comedy ended before it became a tragedy.

Like the disciples, we sometimes fail to recognize the stranger in our midst as a gift from God. Some live among us, but this month others come in cars with out-of-state license plates, or they descend from tour buses. We rub shoulders with them walking down the streets, browsing in gift shops, and going to church.

Whether gift-wrapped or brown-paper packaged, each comes as a gift from God, and each has a fascinating story. One adopted a blind baby, another canoed the rivers of South America, and still another spent her life teaching underprivileged children. Perhaps God sends them our way because we need to hear what they have to say.

Today speak to a tourist standing beside you in the bakery. Introduce yourself to a new neighbor. Engage a postal worker in conversation as she weighs your parcel. Receive the gifts God sends wrapped in the form of strangers.

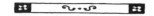

July 10

Street Find

SCRIPTURE: *Matthew 21: 1 – 9*
KEY VERSE: *He said to them, "Go into the village ahead of you. You will find a donkey tied there and a colt with it. Untie them, and bring them to me.*

One person's cast off is another's treasure. While we get rid of our mice and rats, some people of the world consider them a delicacy. We cook winter squash and throw away the seed, but in parts of Africa housewives cook the seed and throw away the squash.

The prophet Zechariah said Zion's king would come humble and mounted on an ass. For five hundred years Jewish people waited for that signal. Jesus owned no donkey, but in the street he found exactly what he needed at exactly the right time. At that moment the donkey stood idle. Perhaps its owner was glad the kindhearted teacher could use it.

Like Jesus, today meet some need with a street find. While we would hesitate to take away a tethered donkey, the discarded swivel chair or wicker love seat beside the curb leaves no such qualms. From sofas to refrigerators, and wastebaskets to dishpans, many streets hold treasures on trash day. Scrap wood gleaned from construction sites may fill wood boxes, build shelves, or make a doll bed for a child's room. Cast off bricks could line flower beds, support bookshelves, or make a walkway.

A woman clipping roses in her front yard may gladly pass along clippings of prize varieties. A farmer may share a pail of manure, and chicory growing beside the road may provide a start for flower beds.

With cleanser, paint, or bleach, transform another's trash into your treasure. Remind yourself when God provides for our needs, he does not limit himself to the contents of our pocketbooks.

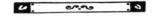

Patio Entertaining

SCRIPTURE: *Genesis 18: 1 - 8*
KEY VERSE: *He took curds and milk and the calf he had prepared, set it before them, and waited on them himself under the tree while they ate. (NEB)*

> Little Miss Muffet sat on a tuffet,
> Eating some curds and whey.
> Along came a spider, and sat down beside her,
> And frightened Miss Muffet away.

P erhaps, if Miss Muffet had sat with a friend to eat her curds and whey, it would have been the spider who fled. Once, thousands of years ago beneath a tree, Abraham shared his curds and milk, and a psychological spider fled.

Abraham could have entertained in his tent, but he chose to do so outdoors. Perhaps a pleasant breeze blew, or perhaps the views from the tree were superb. Perhaps chirping sparrows nested in overhead limbs. Perhaps he simply listened when the pleasant evening softly called.

Like Abraham, entertain outdoors tonight. Summer coaxes us to leave the house, set our curds and whey beneath a tree, and invite friends to help us eat them. A soft breeze mitigates the heat, thrushes trill from locust trees, and hummingbirds dip among snapdragons. Even the spiders of our lives seem more tame in the presence of friends.

On the patio or in the park, on a card table or on a blanket spread on the grass, serve hot dogs, crab salad, or fried chicken as graciously as Abraham served curds and milk. God rewarded Abraham for his hospitality by giving him a child.

July brings many gifts, but one of the most pleasant is a lingering twilight. Like Abraham, share it with visitors. Then watch to see how God rewards your hospitality.

July 12

Afternoon Off

Scripture: *Matthew 14: 13 - 21*

Key verse: *After sending the people away, he went up to a mountain to pray by himself. When evening came, he was there all alone.*

> I will arise and go now, and go to Innisfree...
> I will arise and go now, for always night and day
> I hear lake water lapping
>   with low sounds by the shore;
> While I stand on the roadway,
>   or on the pavements gray,
> I hear it in the deep heart's core.

Like William Butler Yeats, we may yearn to arise now and go. Perhaps not to the Lake Isle of Innisfree, but to some other spot where we can step back from the daily hassle and catch our breath. At times, Jesus had to step back. After a messenger brought news of John's death, he needed time alone with his Father.

Whether your crowd takes the shape of work or people, today step back from it. Take the afternoon off. Give yourself personal space to absorb bad news, rejoice over good news, or simply renew your spirit.

We may dream of blackberry picking, having our hair done, or rearranging the living room furniture. Perhaps we simply want to hide away with a favorite book, occasionally looking up from its pages to watch a pair of monarch butterflies playing among the dahlias.

Whatever calls, today listen and follow. Hide away for an afternoon, then return to meet the waiting crowd.

July 13

ℬefriend a Child

SCRIPTURE: *Hosea 11: 3 - 4*
KEY VERSE: *But they did not know that I harnessed them in leading-strings and led them with bonds of love—that I had lifted them like a little child to my cheek, that I had bent down to feed them. (NEB)*

> If I can stop one Heart from breaking
> I shall not live in vain
> If I can ease one Life the Aching...
> I shall not live in Vain.

Emily Dickinson obviously knew the pain of a broken heart. At times we all suffer heartache. But often we do not suspect how sharp the pain is in those around us. Nor do we make the connection between pain and violence. Every day guns take the lives of several children in the United States, usually by the hands of people known to the victims.

Hosea paints a far different picture of childhood. Here a loving father takes a child in his arms, lifts him to his cheek, bends down to feed him. Such a loving image must have come from Hosea's own father, or perhaps from his love for his own children. But when violence, rather than love, is the role model, a cycle of violence begins.

If violence begets violence, love also begets love. Love may be the only effective weapon against violence. Love invested in society's children invests in a safer future. Children hurt today may take revenge tomorrow.

Today open the door to friendship with a child. Give

extra attention to a "naughty" child at church. Take neighbor children to the zoo or park. Include your friends' children in your entertainment plans. Speak to a lonely child, be gentle with a foulmouthed one, and patient with an incorrigible one.

Hold a child in your arms, lift him to your cheek, bend down to feed him. Ease the aching of one life. Then you can say, "I shall not have lived in vain."

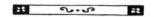

July 14

After Dinner Walk

SCRIPTURE: *Psalm 104: 22 - 25*
KEY VERSE: *Then people go to do their work, to do their tasks until evening.*

> It is a beauteous evening, calm and free,
> The holy time is quiet as a nun
> Breathless with adoration; the broad sun
> Is sinking down in its tranquillity;
> The gentleness of heaven broods over the Sea.

As described by William Wordsworth, the lingering twilight hours cast a spell on earth. Purple shadows mellow the hills and stretch across the golden meadows. Each evening the aggressive July sun turns companionable, almost playful. Then comes the holy time, quiet like a nun breathless in adoration.

The psalmist says this is the time to stop working. The rising sun sees us going about our labor, but the setting one sees us laying it aside. This evening enjoy the lingering twilight with an after-dinner walk.

The earth is full of creatures, beasts great and small, the psalmist observed. Watch for them as they, too, delight in the long summer evening. Squirrels scamper up trees, pigeons seek a last handout, and dragonflies hover over ponds. In the countryside, a doe may graze with her fawn, a porcupine waddle across the road, or a flock of wild turkeys scout the garden.

As the low sun mellows the earth, let it cast a spell over your spirit. See, hear, and be gentle and friendly. Like the breathless nun described by Wordsworth, lift your soul in adoration. Echo the thoughts of the psalmist: "What a large number of things you have made, O Lord! You made them all by wisdom."

July 15

Room Change

SCRIPTURE: *2 Kings 4: 8 - 17*
KEY VERSE: *"Let's make a small room on the roof and put a bed, table, chair, and lamp stand there for him. He can stay there whenever he comes to visit us."*

> O Woman! in our hours of ease,
> Uncertain, coy, and hard to please,
> And variable as the shade
> By the light quivering aspen made;...

As suggested by Sir Walter Scott, do we change and change about? When the lady of Shunem made a change in her house, her life changed. In appreciation of her hospitality, Elisha granted her deepest wish. He promised the following year she would hold a son in her arms.

The fulfillment of our deepest wishes begins with change. Like the rich woman of Shunem, today make a change in your house. Even if no prophet appreciates your efforts, you have family and guests who enjoy comfortable, attractive rooms.

This may be the time to change the bedroom carpet, paint the woodwork, or wallpaper the kitchen. Or new pink tiered curtains may give the kitchen a light, airy

feel. Rearranging old furniture may give the living room a new look. A Georgia O'Keeffe print may dress up the bathroom, and a teapot of petunias on the porch speak a word of welcome to guests.

Like the rich woman of Shunem, change a room and make your house more hospitable. Open a window of change so fresh breezes may enter.

July 16

New Salad

SCRIPTURE: *Numbers 11:4 - 9*
KEY VERSE: *Remember the free fish we ate in Egypt and the cucumbers, watermelons, leeks, onions, and garlic we had?*

Euphoria faded into complaints as the Israelites camped in the wilderness. Forgetting their suffering in Egypt, they idealized its "good life." Tired of manna, they wistfully remembered the salads of Egypt. Longing to bite into them, their thoughts turned to cucumbers, garlic, and onions. And watermelon! Juicy melons might make even a wilderness tolerable.

Whatever your personal wilderness experience, this month gardens overflow with the produce of Israelite dreams. Lettuce, spinach, cucumbers, radishes, green onions, and leeks abound. As if we were pharaohs and kings, daily feasts are at our command, and like Caesar demanded, we can fill our tables with radishes so thin we can see the light through them.

Today experiment with new feasting possibilities. Substitute endive and watercress for lettuce. Add mushrooms and chive blossoms to spinach, and top with an olive oil dressing. Make salad a main dish by combining chunks of chicken, fruit, greens, and a curried dressing. Discover new recipes for feasting on the gifts of gardens this month. Wildly imagine combinations never seen in a cookbook.

Deprived of salad, we might be as discontented as the Israelites. Enjoy fresh fruits and vegetables while you can.

July 17

Open Air Concert

SCRIPTURE: *Psalm 33: 1 - 4*
KEY VERSE: *Sing a new song to him. Play beautifully and joyfully on stringed instruments.*

> Music has charms to soothe a savage breast,
> To soften rocks, or bend a knotted oak.

William Congreve made the same discovery David once made while wandering over hillsides tending his father's sheep. The lad, David, found his harp could speak. When he played for the king, he soothed and healed. His instrument often inspired others to worship and praise.

We still have Davids among us. Some play harps and lutes. Others play the trombone or saxophone. Still others lift voices in song or bodies in dance. Today attend an open air concert, and listen to one of these Davids play or sing.

Spread a blanket on the grass. Load a picnic basket with fried chicken. While your children throw Frisbees® and toddlers turn somersaults, strains of a lilting harp, flute, or guitar mingle with bird song and human chatter.

Today's Davids may be touring professionals, part of a high-school or college band, or students at a local music school. Some may be using their art to praise the Lord, and some may simply be developing the gift God has given them. Whether you watch comtemporary dancers or listen to the Boston Pops Orchestra, thank God for the gift of music—and for the big and little Davids who make it.

July 18

Arrange Flowers

Scripture: *Song of Songs 2: 10 – 13*
Key verse: *Blossoms appear in the land. The time of the songbird has arrived. The cooing of the mourning dove is heard in our land.*

> "May I give to you a bunch of roses?"
> "But I've never seen you, Sir,
>   in all my life."

U nlike the unsuccessful suitor of the nursery song, the suitor of Song of Songs spoke of flowers and convinced his beloved to go away with him.

As the unfortunate man with his bunch of roses discovered, flowers alone can not inspire love. As the suitor of Song of Songs knew, they can beautifully express a love which already exists.

Flowers now appear in the countryside. Today arrange some of them for a beloved husband, child, or even for your Lord. Speak of love with an armful of wild daisies from the meadow or cultivated ones from the flower stand. Arrange them in a blue and white pitcher, raise one here, lower one there, and lovingly create an opulent touch in the house.

Express yourself in the arrangement. With a luxuriant mix of flowers and colors arranged in pyramid, round, or oval shape, create a bouquet resembling those painted by the old masters. Bring in sunflowers and give a touch of Van Gogh to the house. Put a few flowers in three levels and create the grace and simplicity of an oriental arrangement. Or pick your posies, and arrange them in a style totally your own.

Winter is past, flowers appear in the countryside, and the time has come for the birds to sing. Give to your beloved a bunch of roses.

July 19

$\mathcal{P}ortrait$ $\mathcal{P}hoto$

Scripture: *1 Samuel 1: 1 - 10*
Key verse: *Her husband Elkanah would ask her, "Hannah, why are you crying? Why haven't you eaten? Why are you so downhearted? Don't I mean more to you than ten sons?"*

The writer of Samuel created a portrait of a heartbroken Hannah. Although separated by three thousand years, we know this woman. We feel her humiliation, see tears sliding down her cheek, and hear her ask why. We see neither the color of her hair nor the color of her eyes, her height or her weight, but we see her spirit.

For centuries artists captured the spirit of a person with their brush. We never knew the little girl in Joshua Reynolds' painting *The Age of Innocence*, and yet standing in front it, we feel as though we know her. Like the writer of Samuel who painted Hannah's portrait, Joshua Reynolds takes us inside a person.

Hannahs still walk among us. By night, tears wet their pillows as they toss and turn asking God the why of barren dreams. By day, they wipe their tears, go about marketing and housekeeping, and pretend everything is okay. Only a close look at their eyes reveals the pain.

Hannah did not cry forever. Tears gave way to joy the day she held a precious newborn to her breast. Smiles broke out when she watched the child first toddle across the floor, put his shirt on backwards, and utter a complete sentence.

Today you can capture the spirit of a Hannah or Elkanah, an Eli or a Samuel, with a camera. See the pain hiding beneath a smile or joy lighting up eyes with life. Take a photograph revealing the spirit of a man, woman, or child rather than merely showing physical features. Today see what God sees in us rather than what we usually see in each other.

Quilting Pattern

SCRIPTURE: *1 Corinthians 12:14 - 19*
KEY VERSE: *As you know, the human body is not made up of only one part, but of many parts.*

> Go from me. Yet I feel that I shall stand
> Henceforward in thy shadow. Nevermore
> Alone upon the threshold of my door
> Of individual life...

Elizabeth Barrett Browning learned what Paul learned centuries earlier. Like the parts of the body or the pieces of a patchwork quilt, each believer fits into the pattern of a whole kingdom. Once we step across the doorway into that kingdom, we never again stand alone upon the threshold of individual life.

Today look at some of those patchwork quilts which transform seemingly insignificant pieces into exquisite patterns. Double Wedding Ring quilts leave hoops to enter gift shops, and Martha Washingtons hang over back country porch rails. From sea to sea, Nine Patches and Log Cabins adorn fairs. Go admire them.

Quilts were first pieced to salvage good parts of old clothing or to make use of small scraps. They revealed something about the women who stitched them. We can surmise that a frontier woman whose fingers alternated between the churn and the scrap bag conceived Churn Dash pattern. Staring at a crow on the window sill, a farmer's wife must have first have arranged her pieces in a design she called Crow Foot. Broken Dish pattern has its own story to tell, as does Corn and Beans, Our Village Green, and every other pattern.

Like these quilts which reflect the daily lives of those

who conceived them, God creates a great quilt out of our lives and individual experiences. Each square, triangle, and circle becomes significant in his great pattern.

Admire quilting patterns stitched by human hands, and think about the one stitched by divine hands.

July 21

Recent Vision

SCRIPTURE: *Habakkuk 2: 1 - 3*
KEY VERSE: *Then the Lord answered me, "Write the vision. Make it clear on tablets so that anyone can read it quickly ..."*

> Thus ever at every season
> in every hour and place
> Visions await the soul
> on wide ocean or shore,
> Mountain forest or garden
> in wind and floating cloud,
> In busy murmur of bees
> or blithe carol of birds.

Like Habakkuk, many men and women throughout the centuries have watched to learn what the Lord would say to them and through them. As described by Robert Bridges, visions still await receiving souls.

Whether their visions flash in heart-wrenching circumstances or gently slip into quiet moments of ordinary days, many still hear and feel the power of God's voice in their lives. Some inscribe their visions for contemporary heralds to publish. Today read to hear what one of these has to say.

Some like Anne Morrow Lindbergh have passed through fire; for her small son was kidnapped and murdered. While her book *Gift from the Sea* does not speak of the tragedy, her insights carry unmistakable authenticity. Writing on an island, she draws reflections from shells she finds in the surf and comes up with answers to many of the conflicts in our lives.

In *Walking on Water*, Madeleine L'Engle talks about visions which inspired her to write *A Swiftly Tilting Planet*, a story of good struggling against evil. In other books she shares the inspiration of birthday celebrations, pets, and growing children.

Read *Gift from the Sea*, *Walking on Water*, or the inspirational insights of some other Habakkuk who listened to hear what the Lord would say through him or her.

There are still visions for the appointed time, and the Lord is still speaking through us and to us. Today listen to what he is saying.

July 22

Tree Identification

SCRIPTURE: *Nehemiah 8: 13 – 18*
KEY VERSE: *"Go to the mountains and get branches—olive and wild olive, myrtle, palm, and other thick-leaved branches—to make booths as it is written."*

> Have you heard of the Sugar-Plum Tree?
> 'Tis a marvel of great renown!
> It blooms on the shore of the Lollipop Sea
> In the garden of Shut-Eye town.

If the Sugar-Plum dropped marshmallows, gumdrops, and peppermint canes, perhaps Eugene Field rightly called it a marvel of great renown. But could it be more marvelous than the trees visible to wide-awake eyes?

Wide-awake Israelites knew their trees by name. To build arbors for the feast of the seventh month, returned exiles fetched branches of olive and wild olive, myrtle, and palm, and other leafy branches. For seven days they worshipped the God who had a name as they ate, slept, and

218

celebrated beneath branches which had names.

Flipping through the pages of a tree-identification book, today see and name your trees. Walk down a lane, into the woods, or through a park, and distinguish one tree from another. Watch squirrels run up birches, hemlocks, or oaks. Listen to birds sing in lilacs, redwoods, or maples. Enjoy the fragrance of pine, spruce, or cedar.

Admire trees heavy with ripened or ripening fruit. Can even gumdrops and chocolate cats of the Sugar-Plum tree compare to the exquisite taste of sun-ripened apricots or fresh juicy peaches?

While the Israelites built their arbors on their roofs, ours grow in meadows and hills, front and back yards, parks and playgrounds. Worship beneath one today. Marvel at the wonder of trees, but also marvel at our God who fashioned miracles of limb, bark, and leaf.

July 23

Cross-Cultural Entertaining

SCRIPTURE: *Acts 17:24 - 29*

KEY VERSE: *From one man he has made every nation of humanity to live all over the earth.*

> Mary, Mary, quite contrary,
> How does your garden grow?
> With silver bells, and cockleshells
> And pretty maids all in a row.

This month we can hear Mary reply that her garden grows very well indeed. Bee balm and black-eyed Susans flourish in one corner, flax and bachelor's buttons in another, and cosmos, asters, and petunias in the center.

Whether originating in England, India, or Mexico, each flower adds color, scent, and character to the garden. Evoking Paul's description of the body of Christ, each plays its part. While one entices bees, another brings butterflies, and still another gardeners' shears.

Today enrich the garden of your life by inviting someone from another culture to join you for dinner. A pastor from Romania may be working in one of the churches in your area this month, or your community may be host to children from Ireland. An accountant from Honduras may be enrolled in a summer program of the local college. Take advantage of these opportunities to learn more about the people of the world.

Regardless of their ability to communicate in English, host the Hispanic family next door or the Laotian family new to the neighborhood. Share the evening with one who immigrated from Russia fifty years ago, but still follows the holiday traditions of her childhood.

When Mary was a child, her garden consisted of silver bells, cockleshells, and pretty maids all in a row. As she matured, she must have added more varieties to a larger plot. Today expand your cultural garden. Find a new flower to add to your silver bells and cockleshells.

July 24

Art Show

SCRIPTURE: *1 Samuel 16: 11 - 13*
KEY VERSE: *He was handsome, with ruddy cheeks and bright eyes. (NEB)*

Perhaps, like Samuel, Jesse's neighbors were impressed by tall, handsome Eliab. Recognizing a candidate for success, they probably vied with each other to obtain a marriage contract for one of their daughters.

Although also handsome, young David was seventh in line for the family inheritance, and it did not occur to Jesse to present him to Samuel. But the instant Samuel's eyes fell on the young man, he recognized a light he had not seen before. The boy was more than handsome; he had bright eyes.

For years Norman Rockwell's *Saturday Evening Post* covers called America's attention to qualities they had overlooked in each other. Filled with neighbors and friends in Arlington, Vermont, each illustration revealed bright eyes in ordinary slices of life.

Intimately knowing their village or city, local artists capture the bright eyes and bright spots of their communities. In return, communities honor them by displaying their work in greens, commons, and parks each summer. Today stroll through one of these outdoor exhibitions.

Smile as you recognize a neighbor or her cat in one of the watercolors. In the canvas of a local artist, rediscover the familiar beauty of weathered barns, Southwest buttes, or swelling waves.

Samuel must have worn thin Jesse's patience as he rejected son after son. But God had seen bright eyes in the pastures, and he knew they had the making of a king. Bright eyes still exist, and often where we least expect them. Today let local artists help you see some of them.

July 25

Morning Watch

SCRIPTURE: *Psalm 59: 16 - 17*
KEY VERSE: *But I will sing about your strength. In the morning I will joyfully sing about your mercy.*

> When night is almost done
> And sunrise grows so near
> That we can touch the spaces,
> It's time to smooth the hair
> And get the dimples ready,
> And wonder we could care
> For that old faded midnight
> That frightened but an hour.

Like Emily Dickinson, many of us survive the night because we believe in the dawn. While day is still only a thin glimmer, sit quietly and meditate on the One who forges the day and fashions the night.

Carry your thoughts beyond this small spinning mass in space and even beyond the ball of fire lighting the darkness. Think beyond the stars and galaxies, lose yourself in the cosmic picture, and worship the Lord of all the universe.

As the first glimmers of light tint the horizon pink and orange, consider the miracle of a ball of fire with an inner temperature of thirty-five million degrees Fahrenheit sending its rays 93 million miles away in eight seconds. Bow in reverence before God who fashioned not one such sun, but a universe full of them.

Intuitively, we kneel when we worship and bow our heads when we approach the One who created all that exists. Although the early Israelites had only a fraction of our scientific knowledge, what they knew so awed them they did not pronounce the name of God. Instead, they used superlatives such as The Most High, The Almighty, The Lord, The Alpha and The Omega.

Dawn turns to day; shake off the fears of night. Lift your heart in worship and praise, addressing the Lord of the universe by the title Jesus gave him: Father.

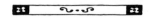

July 26

Table Touch

SCRIPTURE: *Luke 22: 7 – 13*
KEY VERSE: *"He will take you upstairs and show you a large furnished room. Get things ready there."*

> Old King Cole
> Was a merry old soul,
> And a merry old soul was he;
> He called for his pipe,

He called for his bowl,
And he called for his fiddlers three.

The king may have been merry, but one wonders if his fiddlers ever tired of the routine or if his servants grew bored of the pipe and the bowl.

If boredom existed for the disciples, it was before they met Jesus. On the road with him, they never knew what to expect. Even the prescribed Passover meal no longer had the predictability of past years. They must have often thought nothing was ever the same when Jesus was present.

Tonight drastically change the familiar setting of your own dinner table and underline your own experience that with Jesus everything is different. Bring out the sea shells you found at low tide last summer and devise a beach theme for the table, even replacing the table cloth with netting. Recreate a family trip by arranging souvenirs among the place settings. Announce a coming event through an appropriate centerpiece.

Cater to your family's interests. For kitty-loving children, decorate the table with ceramic cats and cat-shaped place mats. Enchant a small child with a Winnie-the-Pooh table or a teenage son with a sports setting.

Tonight leave the pipe, the bowl, and the fiddlers three to Old King Cole, and find a way to make newness in Christ apparent even on the dinner table.

July 27

Explore Village

Scripture: *Acts 28: 11 – 15*
Key verse: *We stopped at the city of Syracuse and stayed there for three days.*

Intery, mintery, cutery corn,
Apple seed and apple thorn,

223

Wire, brier, limber-lock,
Three geese in a flock;
One flew east, and one flew west,
And one flew over the cuckoo's nest.

D id the goose who flew east discover the taste of corn, the one who flew west the taste of apples in the orchard, and the one who flew over the cuckoo's nest only the pain of wire, brier, and limber-lock? As these three geese discovered, the directions we choose determine our experience.

Paul chose all directions. Traveling through the Roman world, he experienced the taste of east, west, and at times the cuckoo's nest. Writing to Christian congregations, he wrote with the power of firsthand experience.

Today experience a different direction by exploring an unfamiliar village. Walk along its main street, poke into its shops, and become acquainted with its atmosphere. Admire the window boxes on its store fronts, its gas-lit street lights, or whatever distinctive feature it boasts. Eat in one of the cafes which contributes to the distinctive personality of the village.

Locate its landmarks. Tiptoe into the old Congregational church where high-walled private pews whisper stories of the past. Walk through a covered bridge, stop in a museum, sit for a few minutes on a bench along Main Street.

Like Paul, communicate better because you know the world through first hand experiences.

July 28

Vegetables and Fruits

SCRIPTURE: *Genesis 1: 29 – 31*
KEY VERSE: *God said, "I have given you every plant with seeds on the face of the earth and every tree that has fruit with seeds. This will be your food.*

Every night my prayers I say,
And get my dinner every day,
And every day that I've been good,
I get an orange after food.

Perhaps Adam found as much delight in an orange as Robert Louis Stevenson did. The first meal in the Garden of Eden must have been fruits and vegetables without a dip. A handful of tender green beans and new peas from a pod may have first gone into man's mouth. Perhaps Adam curiously wiped a radish off and then popped it into his mouth or gingerly tasted an onion. Maybe the pleasant taste of an orange, mango, or strawberry finished off his first meal, bringing forth a big smile as he discovered sugar in its natural form.

From apples to bananas, escarole to cucumbers, and grapefruit to guavas, God must have enjoyed planning the tastes, colors, and textures of the Garden of Eden. But he also knew Adam's nutritional needs, and that first vegetarian diet must have met them.

Fruits and vegetables continue to supply life-giving vitamins and minerals. In their raw state, as Adam must have eaten them, they retain all the vitamins they capture from the earth and sun.

Today recreate a Garden of Eden scene by making a meal of fresh fruits and vegetables. Creatively fill trays with the best of garden and orchard, add a dip, and eat the cold supper on the lawn, beside a lake, or in the park. Enjoy your vitamins and minerals in the outdoor setting where they were first eaten.

Then, if you have been good, finish off the meal with an orange.

Play Ball

SCRIPTURE: *Isaiah 22: 15 – 19*
KEY VERSE: *Then he will bundle you tightly and throw you like a ball into a great wide land. (NEB)*

I nvested with the power of high office, Shebna and his wicked ways seemed to flourish. But the Lord noticed, and he revealed his judgment through Isaiah. He would bundle Shebna tightly, and throw him like a ball into a wide land.

Both Isaiah and Shebna perfectly understood the Lord's judgment. As a lad, had not Shebna taken pride in how far he could throw a ball? Perhaps he had often flaunted his skill before Isaiah. And in moments of anger, had he not thrown some so far they were never found?

Not only Shebna, but every Jewish lad understood this universal image. Moreover, lads of all cultures would understand, for all societies played ball. Homer made references to the popular Greek sport, upper-class Romans built ball-playing rooms in their villas, and even before Europeans introduced their ways, the Indians of the New World played a version of lacrosse.

Today become more familiar with Isaiah's image by playing ball. Shoot a basketball into the driveway hoop, or gather the family around the volleyball net. Take out the tether ball. Challenge a friend to a game of ping pong or tennis. Join a community softball game in the park, play a game of kickball with the children, or swing a golf club in the back yard. As people have done for 800 years, play croquet on the lawn.

The Lord still judges the wicked, and his judgment still resembles a ball thrown into a great wide land. Today as you watch a ball fly over a field or become lost in the bushes, give thanks that the Lord, who sees the actions of all mankind, still judges the wicked and vindicates the righteous.

New Magazine

SCRIPTURE: *Titus 2:2 - 5*

KEY VERSE: *They must set a high standard, and school the younger women to be loving wives and mothers. (NEB)*

> Curlylocks, Curlylocks,
> Wilt thou be mine?
> Thou shalt not wash dishes
> Nor yet feed the swine;
> But sit on a cushion,
> And sew a fine seam,
> And feed upon strawberries,
> Sugar and cream.

The infatuated little boy promising such bliss to Curlylocks had already learned that not all women share the same fate. He had seen some wash dishes, feed swine, and stand over the cookstove, but he had also watched the ways of fine ladies. Like them, his wife would sit on a fine cushion, sew a fine seam, and feed upon strawberries.

In many parts of the world, little boys can still observe different classes of women. One class washes its own dishes and another hires it done. Some girls still grow up sewing a fine seam, and others don't know how to hold a needle. Whether we wash our own dishes or make our own clothes often depends on our role models.

Although parents are our primary role models, they need not be our only ones. Paul urged older Christian women to school younger women to be loving wives and mothers. In our generation we have thousands of role models who can school us through the pages of magazines. Today choose a healthy one to help you grow more loving, manage your life better, or learn something new.

In the pages of *Guideposts*, discover how other people

have faced and coped with problems similar to yours. Let *Living with Preschoolers* ease the hurdle of toilet training a toddler, or with the help of *Organic Gardening*, coax more beauty out of your flower beds.

From the 6,500 magazines available to home and library, help exists for almost any problem. Let one of them reveal the secret of having curly locks, stitching crewel embroidery, or growing your own strawberries.

July 31

Balloons

Scripture: *Philippians 4: 4 - 7*
Key verse: *Always be joyful in the Lord! I'll say it again: Be joyful!*

> Oranges and lemons,
> Say the bells of St. Clement's.
> You owe me five farthings,
> Say the bells of St. Martin's.
> When will you pay me?
> Say the bells of Old Bailey.
> When I grow rich,
> Say the bells of Shoreditch.

I s that what bells say? The little nursery rhyme confuses us, and perhaps even disappoints us. When we heard the bells ringing, we had imagined they were ringing for joy. Aren't bells supposed to be joyful?

Perhaps the nursery rhyme had it wrong. Or perhaps those particular bells had not heard the good news. Or maybe they forgot. But we have heard the good news! Our lives ring with joy. Or do they?

Perhaps, like the bells of St. Clement's and St. Martin's, we become so engrossed with our oranges, lemons, and farthings we forget to announce the good news.

Today be joyful! Buy a package of balloons, blow them up, tie strings to them, and celebrate joy. Hang them on your front porch. Attach them to a stake on the lawn. Fill the house with them.

Give them away. Go to the park, and pass them out. Hand them out in the mall. Give them to the neighborhood children.

Announce your joy to the world. It may be catching.

August 1

Pearls

SCRIPTURE: *Matthew 13: 45 - 46*
KEY VERSE: *Also, the kingdom of heaven is like a merchant who was searching for fine pearls.*

> The world is so full
> of a number of things,
> I'm sure we should all
> be as happy as kings.

In his poems for children, Robert Louis Stevenson reveals some of the things which once made him as happy as a king. What makes you as happy as a queen? Each day this month, look around on a number of things, then make a calendar notation of one pearl which made you happy.

Jesus did not say how the merchant found his pearl. Perhaps he was watching fishermen prying oysters open when a bit of calcification leapt out at him. Immediately he

recognized this as what he had been waiting for, and rushed off to liquidate his assets. Whatever it cost, he had to have that pearl.

Many of us recognize polished pearls, but miss unpolished ones. Keep an eye out for them this month.

Find pleasure in plump, juicy blackberries in the meadow, hummingbirds dipping into petunias, and a sudden rainbow after a cloudburst.

Give August a necklace to wear, and string it with pearls found in the shells of each day. On the calendar, note a field of daisies caught in the morning sun, a squirrel sitting on the stone wall, a child's sudden smile. Write down the afternoon you spend on a hill, the morning at the library, and the day at the beach.

Like the merchant, be on the lookout out for valuable pearls. But, rather than buy them, claim them with memory.

August 2

Family Events

SCRIPTURE: *Psalm 90: 10 – 17*
KEY VERSE: *May all delightful things be ours, O Lord our God; establish firmly all we do. (NEB)*

> Here we go round the mulberry bush,
> The mulberry bush, the mulberry bush,
> Here we go round the mulberry bush,
> So early in the morning.

Why not go round the mulberry bush, ride a merry-go-round steed, laugh at a clown's funny face? The psalmist says the hurrying years quickly pass, leaving labor and sorrow in their wake. But he also reminds us of the other side of life. If we order our days rightly, all delightful things may be ours as well.

August's long relaxed days wait to be filled, and before they pass, order them rightly and plan delight into them.

Arrange a visit to a dairy farm at milking time. Escape sweltering heat with a picnic at the river, and invite another family to go along. Take advantage of long evenings to hike to the top of a waterfall, or follow a trail in a state park. Gather family or friends to read a Shakespeare play, or watch an open-air performance of *All's Well That Ends Well.*

Like Mary Poppins who turned "Let's tidy up the nursery!" into a game, cement family relationships with play. Mark the calendar with both a berry picking expedition and fresh pies to follow. Plan a brownies-and-ice cream break into Paint-the-Back-Yard-Fence Day. Follow clean-up day with pizza.

The hurrying years carry their share of toil and trouble. But the large hand of time makes room for all delightful things when we know how to order them rightly. Make this golden month delightful.

August 3

Language Tape

SCRIPTURE: *Acts 21:37 - 40*
KEY VERSE: *The officer replied to Paul, "Can you speak Greek?"*

Three of us afloat in the meadow by the swing,
Three of us in the basket on the lea...
Where shall we adventure, to-day that we're afloat,
Wary of the weather and steering by a star?
Shall it be to Africa, a-steering of the boat,
To Providence, or Babylon, or off to Malibar?

Where shall it be indeed? For soon little boys like Robert Louis Stevenson yearn for bigger vessels than baskets on the lea, and ticket in hand, they set off for lands beyond the meadow.

In this travel month of the world, not only will Americans be traipsing off to Malibar, Luxembourg, and Tibet, but those from Malibar, Luxembourg, and Tibet will be making their own excursions to this part of the world. We meet here, we meet there, and we meet everywhere.

Paul, the great traveler, found language a passport to friendship and opportunity. Like him, today apply for that passport. Spend part of an hour listening to a language cassette. A few key phrases in French, Japanese, or Thai could turn the next encounter with a foreign tourist into a delightful experience. Fixing the intonation in your mind with a cassette, bring forth smiles from a bus load of Japanese tourists at a rest area by greeting them with, "*Kon nichi wa!*"

As we aim cameras at Jefferson Monument, Old Faithful, or The General Sherman tree, the photographers next to us may be speaking Spanish, German, or Chinese. Gathering around Snow White at Disneyland or lining up for a ride at Six Flags, we hear exclamations in Korean, Arabic, or Lingala. The sounds of children calling out in other languages punctuate strolls in many city parks.

Whatever language you choose, you will probably hear someone speaking it this summer. At that moment, your five new phrases will open doors, and like Paul, you may find an opportunity to share your faith.

August 4

Bird Watching

SCRIPTURE: *Luke 12: 6 - 7*
KEY VERSE: *Aren't five sparrows sold for two cents? God doesn't forget any of them.*

Once I saw a little bird
Come hop, hop, hop;
So I cried, "Little bird,
Will you stop, stop, stop?"
I was going to the window
To say "How do you do?"
But he shook his tail,
And far away he flew.

Sitting at his father's carpenter's bench, perhaps the boy Jesus uttered how-do-you-do in Hebrew to little birds perched on the window sill. Perhaps he often looked up into the fig tree where sparrows chirped among the branches. Each time he marveled at his Father's love which included even these little creatures.

If a little bird perches on your sill today, say how-do-you-do. Pause to hear the blue throated one singing in the apple tree or the yellow breasted one chirping in the lilacs. Listen for small peeps in the woods, raucous cawing in the fields, and twitters in the eaves. Watch for the flash of a red wing or the sudden stir of quail beside the road, or a yellow throat barely visible in the canopy of maple leaves.

Jesus said not one of these, or the hundred billion other birds in the world, is overlooked by God. Then he added we are more important than the birds. Even the hairs of our heads are numbered.

Like Jesus, watch the birds and come closer to comprehending the greatness of your Father's love.

August 5

Daring Action

SCRIPTURE: *Ephesians 3: 20 – 21*
KEY VERSE: *Glory belongs to God, whose power is at work in us. By this power he can do infinitely more than we can ask or imagine.*

> We never know how high we are
> Till we are called to rise
> And then, if we are true to plan
> Our statures touch the skies.

Like Emily Dickinson, most of us realize we are called to rise higher than we usually do. Saul probably dreamed of rising high as a Pharisee, never imagining he would rise even higher as a Christian.

Seeing an unconverted Saul dream bold dreams, God knew a converted Paul would also dream bold dreams. God had a bigger mission field than Jerusalem in mind, and Paul was the man who would dream of taking the gospel to Asia Minor, Rome, and even far away Spain.

In contrast, many of us dream modest dreams when God yearns for us to dream daring ones. Modest dreams budge few closed windows and doors. Today push a door open with a daring dream. Give God an opportunity to do infinitely more than anything you can ask or imagine.

Add a daring action to the daring dream. Volunteer to lead a scout trip, or sign up for piano lessons. Talk to a college registrar about completing your degree. Try out for a part in the community play, sign up for a mission tour, or agree to lead a Bible study. Take charge of your finances by objecting to excessive charges for some service, and negotiate the amount you will pay.

How many of us does God look over to find a Paul bold enough to accomplish his extensive purposes? Today put timidity behind dreams rather than in front of them, and discover how much God can do in you.

Be true to plan, and watch your stature reach to the skies.

August 6

Cook Out

SCRIPTURE: *John 21: 9 - 13*
KEY VERSE: *When they went ashore, they saw a fire with a fish lying on the coals, and they saw a loaf of bread.*

After fishing all night, the disciples had nothing to show for it. As dawn tinted the lake, their rumbling stomachs matched their disgruntled moods. But on shore, Jesus knew they were hungry, and he made breakfast over a fire.

Jesus and the disciples must have often eaten outside, for much of their ministry took place outdoors. In contrast, we eat most of our meals surrounded by four walls—even when sunlight plays on meadows, twilight lingers on sandy shores, and birds hold concerts in every tree.

Women who cook outdoors may be more in touch with nature than most of us. Stirring manioc flour over an open fire, they look out on puffy clouds piling up above palm trees. Serving dinner, they hear monkeys screeching in the forest behind them, and while washing the dishes, they watch weaver birds darting into their nests.

Like these women, today meet appetites sharpened in outdoor air by cooking over a charcoal fire. Catch fish in a stream and grill them over glowing coals. Or, if you suspect the same luck the disciples had that night, buy fish from one whose pole or net brings better results.

Although they lived in a coastal country, Jesus' disciples did not go fishing every day, and Jesus did not always meet hunger with fish. Your family may prefer grilling chicken at the beach to cooking fish beside a stream. If the day is a busy one, make it hot dogs in the back yard or hamburgers in the park.

Whatever and wherever you grill, tonight stimulate and then meet appetites outdoors. Or, like Jesus, surprise the family with an outdoor breakfast.

August 7

Outdoor Order

SCRIPTURE: *Proverbs 24:27*
KEY VERSE: *First put all in order out of doors and make everything ready on the land; then establish your house and home. (NEB)*

While the plowman, near at hand,
Whistles o'er the furrowed land,
And the milkmaid singeth blithe,
And the mower whets his scythe
And every shepherd tells his tale
Under the hawthorn in the dale.

In his poem "L'Allegro," John Milton describes a pastoral scene which would have been familiar to the writer of Proverbs. In that world, the land supported the occupants of the houses, and because survival depended upon it, field work was more important than house work.

Land still supports the people who dwell on it, but not usually the small plots we call our own. Leaving the growing of food to others, we cultivate beautiful plants to feed psychological rather than physical hunger.

Today pay attention to the ways others put their out of doors in order. Jot down details which draw your eye—clumps of bee balm and snap dragons surrounded by petunias and nasturtiums or blue splashes of monkshood and delphiniums. Note arrangements worth imitating on your own plot.

Catch other details which add charm—driveways and walkways, stone walls and picket fences, trees and shrubs. Observe bird baths, benches, and swings, and note the effect of window boxes and hanging plants.

Some people put their outdoors in better order than others. Today study the ways of these gifted ones.

August 8

Edible Flowers

SCRIPTURE: *Psalm 103: 15 - 18*
KEY VERSE: *Human life is as short-lived as grass. It blossoms like a flower in the field.*

Time is very bankrupt, and owes
more than he's worth to season.
Nay, he's a thief too: have you not heard men say
That Time comes stealing on by night and day?

Long before Shakespeare's *Comedy of Errors*, in which Domio of Syracuse thought about fleeting time, the psalmist noted that like flowers in the fields, life blossoms so briefly.

As a reminder of the brevity and the beauty of life, today serve blossoms on the dinner table. Many herbal teas contain flowers like hibiscus, orange blossoms, and chamomile. But if your roses are insecticide free, do as one agriculture professor in Venezuela does. Make tea by steeping roses from your own garden, then add a squeeze of lemon juice to turn it pink.

Imitate fine restaurants, and enliven a green salad with calendula, pansy, nasturtium, wild mustard, violet, or rose petals. Pluck blossoms from your herb garden—oregano, chives, marjoram, thyme, or dill—and add both blossom and herb to a bowl of mixed greens.

In most cultures around the world, edible flowers appear on the dinner table. In Burma women fry frangipani blossoms, in Italy they stuff zucchini blossoms, and in the United States some batter-fry dandelion blossoms. In China cooks used chrysanthemums as far back as 500 B.C.

They are here today and gone tomorrow, so pluck the blossoms around you before they fade. Like the bee, butterfly, and hummingbird, nurture body and soul with their nectar. Then offer the sweet nectar of your own life to God who so wonderfully brings it to blossom.

Day Trip

SCRIPTURE: *Psalm 148*
KEY VERSE: *Praise the Lord from the earth. Praise him, large sea creatures and all the ocean depths.*

T oday praise the Lord creatively. Pack a picnic lunch and take off for the ocean or the lake, the mountains or the woods, the country or the city. Escape the heat, green beans waiting to be canned, and lawn needing to be mowed, and experience God in his magnificent creation.

While August's sun stands overhead, pouring heat upon the land, cool off in the salty surf or the rippling lake. Splash in the tide, walk along the wet sand, and build castles in the face of encroaching waves. Comb the beach for shells. Throw crumbs to the gulls. Read a book in the shadow of a large rock. Finally, watch the setting sun tint the sky and color the swelling waters.

Or cool off in the mountains, up high where the sun becomes gentle. Picnic beneath the pines, and share your sandwiches with the chipmunks. Gather pinecones and seed pods. Hike one of the trails. Breathe the scent of cedar, pine, and oak. Examine wild flowers along the trail. Watch deer disappear into the woods. Follow the flight of red birds darting among the trees. Involve yourself so much with the mountain that part of it goes back home with you.

Go sight-seeing in the city, if that is what you love. Think on kings and earthly rulers, princes and judges, young men and maidens. Consider how wonderfully we are made, then with the psalmist, recite: "Let them praise the name of the Lord, because his name is high above all others."

The psalmist saw them all: ocean depths, mountains and hills, kings and earthly rulers, and seeing, he glorified the Creator of all. Today see, experience, and praise the One who so wondrously breathed life into his creation.

Gentle Response

SCRIPTURE: *Proverbs 15: 1 – 4*
KEY VERSE: *A gentle answer turns away rage, but a harsh word stirs up anger.*

> Who is Silvia? what is she
> That all our swains commend her?...
> Is she kind as she is fair?
> For beauty lives with kindness.
> Love doth to her eyes repair
> To help him of his blindness,
> And, being helped, inhabits there.

In this song from *Two Gentlemen of Verona*, Shakespeare illustrates the power of gentle speech. Kind Silvia is the girl each swain wants to claim as his own.

One day one of them will be lucky enough to claim her, and hopefully, her gentle ways will continue when conflict creeps into the marriage relationship. For surely, the swain will have his bad days and utter harsh words he may not mean.

Pain, one of the most earthly situations, frequently wraps itself in hard, harsh words. We often react to the sting of these hurled words by throwing them back. Experience tells us they do not stay there. Gaining strength and hardness with each throwing, they return again and again.

The book of Proverbs encourages us to soften words before returning them. Harsh responses reinforce the negative self-images of those who hurl hurting words. In contrast, gentle responses set free goodness imprisoned behind pain. While vengeful words intensify the despair of already wounded spirits, soothing words relieve it.

Today repair some infirmity of soul with a gentle word.

August 11

Play with a Child

Scripture: *Matthew 19: 13 – 14*
Key verse: *Jesus said, "Don't stop the children from coming to me! Children like these are part of the kingdom of God."*

> Ring-around-a-rosy,
> A pocket full of posies;
> Ashes, ashes,
> All fall down.

Perhaps Mary and Joseph laughingly played ring-around-a-rosy with their small son, unconsciously affirming his importance. Jesus may have played similar games with small children in villages where he traveled. Children knew they were important to Jesus, for he interrupted his work to spend time with them.

Today interrupt your work to let some child know how important he is. Hold hands with a three-year-old, sing ring-around-a-rosy, and all fall down on the grass. Play hopscotch or hold the end of a jump rope for a seven-year-old. Teach these simple games to a child who has never played them.

Some children have more contact with adults in a television set than with those in their environment. No adult on television tosses a ball to a child whose eyes are glued to the screen or holds one end of a jump rope for her. They may, however, show children how to hold guns and knives. Perhaps more children who hold guns would jump ropes if more adults showed them how.

Let the children come to you today. Bless a ten-month-old with a game of peek-a-boo, or an eight-year-old with Chutes and Ladders®. Receive the Monopoly™ game the eleven-year-old holds out or the ball the four-year-old tries to hand you. Invite a child to bring her jacks or paper dolls.

Ashes, ashes, all fall down. Children who laughingly fall down on the grass stand taller on the street.

August 12

Stationery

SCRIPTURE: *Acts 15:30 - 35*
KEY VERSE: *When the people read the letter, they were pleased with the encouragement it brought them.*

> I marvelled, my Beloved, when I read
> Thy thought so in the letter. I am thine—
> But... so much to thee? Can I pour thy wine
> While my hands tremble?

E lizabeth Barrett Browning confessed that her hands trembled as she read Robert Browning's declaration of love. Perhaps the hands of the Gentile Christians likewise trembled as they read the liberating words of the church elders in Jerusalem. They must have reread them so often they had them memorized.

We all have loved ones who await word from us, and August provides raw material for letters. Someone wants to hear about lazy gulls drifting over the surf, a camping trip in the Tetons, and fish pulled out of a stream. Some loved one takes interest in the million zucchini spreading over the garden, fresh berry cobblers eaten around the dinner table, and apples growing larger on the backyard tree.

Today relate these August experiences on stationery you make yourself. Design your own letterhead. Border writing paper with gliding gulls, rolling waves, or sand castles. Paint a row of zucchini across the page. Sketch your tent among tall pines. Splash cosmos, black-eyed Susans, or peonies across the page. Share a Bible verse, poem, or song. Allow your imagination to blossom as profusely as your zucchini does.

With an expression of yourself greater than words alone can carry, today doubly bless a loved one. Even the elders in Jerusalem sent visual encouragement with their written encouragement.

August 13

Lecture

SCRIPTURE: *Proverbs 8: 10 – 21*
KEY VERSE: *I, Wisdom, live with insight, and I acquire knowledge and foresight.*

> Then the whining school-boy, with his satchel,
> And shining morning face, creeping like snail
> Unwillingly to school.

M ore than 2500 years before Jaques described the whining schoolboy in Shakespeare's *As You Like It*, the writer of Proverbs knew the type. He dreamed of a better life for his son. Urging him to run after instruction and knowledge as eagerly as some run after silver and gold, Solomon pointed out the doors they opened and the rewards they brought.

Some of us have discovered the wisdom of Solomon's words only after passing up instruction on the first round. However belatedly we discover our folly, in our generation the doors of the school house always remain open. Today look through a newspaper listing of lectures and demonstrations taking place and find an open door you would like to enter.

At the library, attend a slide show on Cuba, listen to a poetry reading, or learn about the migration habits of birds in your area. At the local art gallery, listen to a lecture on early American painters or learn to develop your own black and white pictures. At the bank, discover how to create a living trust.

Once victims of addictions, abuse, disease, and learning disabilities suffered in alienated silence. Today they have come out of the closet, banded together, and work at developing coping skills. Benefit from one of these support groups and attend a lecture on living with Alzheimer's disease, recognizing the signs of drug use in adolescents, coping with grief, or whatever touches your life.

Knowledge and wisdom still reward those who run after them. Today discover the exciting new shapes of school house doors, then eagerly step inside one.

August 14

Display

SCRIPTURE: *2 Chronicles 5: 1 - 10*
KEY VERSE: *There was nothing in the ark except the two tablets Moses placed there at Horeb, where the Lord made a promise to the Israelites after they left Egypt.*

The Lord rescued the children of Israel from bondage, opened up a sea as an escape route, and fed them while they were refugees. Freedom was not all they had anticipated it to be, and they began to doubt God. High up on a mountain, Moses experienced the power of the Lord, and when he descended he carried back two tablets of stone containing the word of the Lord.

First the tablets dwelt in an ark housed in a shrine, then later the Israelites put them on permanent display in the temple. They had settled far away from the mountain top where God spoke, but the souvenir of the experience kept it fresh.

Souvenir, a French verb meaning "recall," originated with the Latin *subvenire* meaning "to come to mind." Like Moses who carried away tablets of stone from the mountain, we carry our share of souvenirs away from the mountains we have climbed, the beaches we have run along, the cities we have explored. Also like him, we have witnessed God's majesty and power on the mountain top, in the surf, and in the kaleidoscope of humanity he designed.

Like the children of Israel who placed the Ark beneath the wings of cherubim, today creatively display your souvenirs. Arrange sea shells in a beautiful glass dish on the coffee table, and remember sensing God's majesty as you looked out across the sea. Pile cones in a basket beside the door, and recall the peace you felt high up on the mountain. Frame a map for the den wall, and bring to mind the wonders of God's creation wherever you traveled.

Let your souvenirs remind you that you too have seen the hand of God, sensed his power, and felt his peace.

August 15

Flea Market

SCRIPTURE: *Matthew 7: 7 – 8*
KEY VERSE: *Search, and you will find.*

> Cock-a-doodle-doo!
> My dame has lost her shoe.
> My master's lost his fiddle stick,
> And knows not what to do.

L ong ago Jesus told the dame and the master what to do. "Search," he said, "and you will find." However, it appears that searching did not immediately occur to the dame:

> Cock-a-doodle-doo!
> What is my dame to do?
> Till master finds his fiddle stick,
> She'll dance without her shoe.

Some of us lose a shoe and forever afterwards dance without it. Sometimes we simply give up dancing. A few of us never had a shoe, and while we envy those who do, it never occurs to us to seek one.

Jesus said that whatever we search for, we will find. Today search for a shoe in a flea market. If you don't need a new shoe, search for old silver spoons, a new bread board, or a handmade cradle. Search until you find something you need.

While our deepest needs are emotional and spiritual, rummaging through a flea market reminds us that whenever we begin searching, we begin finding. Whatever lack we perceive, we can share the happy ending of the master and dame:

> Cock-a-doodle-doo!
> My dame has found her shoe,
> And master's found his fiddle stick,
> Sing doodle, doodle-doo.

August 16

Banana Split

Scripture: *Deuteronomy 26:5 – 11*
Key verse: *He brought us to this place and gave us this land flowing with milk and honey.*

> The Pedigree of Honey
> Does not concern the Bee—
> A Clover, any time, to him,
> Is Aristocracy.

Perhaps, as for the bee in Emily Dickinson's poem, the pedigree of honey did not concern the Israelites. Honey was honey, and they marched forward to the promised land filled with it.

Their own eyes had not actually seen this promised land, but every man, woman, and child knew it flowed with milk and honey. It was the good life, and it was to be theirs.

Thousands of years later, especially when the August sun presses down, we still think of the good life in terms of milk and honey—although we prefer ours in the creamy frozen form. If children were asked to define the good life, most of them would include ice cream cones.

Moses told the children of Israel that once they entered the promised land, they were to rejoice. Today imitate them and rejoice that our forefathers also came to a land flowing with milk and honey. Celebrate in style by making banana splits—ice cream dressed in party clothes.

Everyone, including aliens, was included in these Israelite celebrations. Add zest to your celebration by inviting others to join you. With several flavors of ice cream, bananas, and a variety of toppings, including honey, invite everyone to create a banana split.

The good life is ours. Today make the most of it.

August 17

Bus

SCRIPTURE: *Psalm 16*
KEY VERSE: *Thou, Lord, my allotted portion, thou my cup, thou dost enlarge my boundaries. (NEB)*

The face of all the world is changed, I think,
Since first I heard the footsteps of thy soul
Move still, oh, still, beside me, as they stole
Betwixt me and the dreadful outer brink
Of obvious death, where I, who thought to sink,
Was caught up into love, and taught the whole
Of life a new rhythm.

As Elizabeth Barrett Browning discovered when she met Robert Browning, the face of the world changes when the footsteps of love draw near. When the footsteps of a loving Lord drew near, the psalmist also discovered the face of his world changing and his boundaries continually enlarging.

Today take a bus, and let the Lord shove back or dismantle fences around your own life. Traveling by bus relates us to others as we sit behind them, in front of them, and face them. We watch them board, ride, and leave the bus. We hear them talk to each other. We notice their clothing, hair styles, and carriage. On a bus we are with others, not passing them.

With others, life gains fuller perspective. No longer are we the center of life; we are one among millions of other centers. Those centers laugh and cry, hate and love. They use crutches and wear braces. They count their pennies and discipline their children. They resemble us and they differ from us. But they all introduce us to God, for God stamps his image in each.

Seeing new neighborhoods and new people from a seat on a bus, experience boundaries moving beneath your feet and in front of your eyes. See the face of the world change as the love of the Lord draws a bigger circle of love around you.

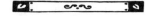

August 18

ℱurnish 𝒦itchen

SCRIPTURE: *Proverbs 24: 3 - 4*
KEY VERSE: *Knowledge furnishes the rooms with all the precious and pleasant things that wealth can buy. (NEB)*

We wonder what the writer of Proverbs had in mind when he spoke of the precious and pleasant things wealth could buy. The mistresses of those long-ago houses purchased no refrigerator, gas stove, or synthetic lace curtains, nor did they carefully choose a coffee pot, electric mixer, or flowered shelf paper in any store. Neither did they spend their coins on a toaster, blender, or mixer.

We have options those woman of three thousand years ago never had. Regardless of the state of our pocketbooks, we have no excuse for a dowdy kitchen. Today examine the coins in your purse, and use a few of them to furnish your kitchen with precious and pleasant things.

Our kitchen shops would have enraptured those women of ancient times. Even the household section of a department store would have tucked dreams into a lifetime. As they would have done, today take delight in the many charming options available to furnish your kitchen.

Exchange a few coins for sunflower-patterned pot holders to brighten a wall, or a fish-shaped mold to hang above the doorway. Replace the cracked teapot with a charming new one, buy an engaging set of hand painted ceramic canisters, or invest in a set of bright dishes to increase the pleasure of any meal.

If your purse has holes instead of coins, depend on knowledge and fertile imagination to create a more beautiful kitchen. Give curtains charm by adding ruffles, brighten the room with quickly stitched red and yellow tea towels, or fill a vase with daisies gathered beside the road. Hang a Jan Vermeer print on the wall, un-clutter the counters, and show off your cookie cutter collection.

Today furnish one room with something pleasant and precious.

August 19

Identify

Scripture: *Genesis 2: 19 – 20*
Key verse: *The Lord God had formed all the wild animals and all the birds out of the ground. Then he brought them to the man to see what he would call them.*

L ike a mother handing a dish towel to her toddler and encouraging him to dry a cup, the Lord generously grants man a toddler-size part in creation by letting him name the world. Like mother and child at the kitchen sink, we stand side by side with God when we give names to his gifts.

We also determine relationships with the names we use. While unnamed weeds irritate, named ones may nourish or heal. Once we know the name of a weed as plantain, we might turn its leaves into soup or salad, or cook its seeds like rice. Knowing nettle by name, we can remove its sting by creaming it or steaming it like spinach.

God looked on his creation and called it good. Perhaps he thought if man were allowed to name what he saw, he too would see how good it was. For the more we name, the more we, like God, call it good. Today learn to call more of creation good by learning to name more of it.

Out of the hundred plus varieties of pines, which produced the cones you brought back from the mountains? Today discover the difference between a Jefferson, ponderosa, and sugar pine cone. Find out which pines have edible seed.

Identify the shells you carried home from the beach, or the ones you bought in a gift shop. Call them cockles or arks, moon shells or whelks, scallops or clams. The Lord has filled the sea with great and tiny creatures, but many of these miracles escape us until we know them by name.

Give names to the trees on your street, the flowers in your neighbor's yard, or the mushrooms in the field. Recognize the difference between a poisonous mushroom and an edible one. In the meadow see bluebells, buttercups, and meadowsweet.

God invited us to name what he created. Today accept his invitation.

August 20

Vegetarian Meal

SCRIPTURE: *Daniel 1: 6 - 16*
KEY VERSE: *After ten days they looked healthier and stronger than the young men who had been eating the king's food.*

Hot July brings cooling showers,
Apricots and gillyflowers.
August brings the sheaves of corn,
Then the harvest home is borne.

As in Sara Coleridge's poem, in our gardens the corn reaches higher each day, its kernels growing wonderfully juicy and sweet. Tomatoes hang heavy, green beans lengthen, and cucumbers and squash run uncontrolled. Kale and chard broaden, tender young carrots and beets wait underground, and canteloupe scent the air. This month we begin to reap what we have sown.

Thousands of years ago, Daniel discovered a source of vitality in this fruit of field and garden of ancient Palestine. After being captured by the Babylonian army and selected for service in the royal court, he convinced his guard to let him continue his vegetarian diet. While his fellow prisoners languished on the rich food of the royal house, Daniel glowed with health.

In this moment when gardens magnificently reward those who sowed, try Daniel's secret to vitality. Crown the day with a vegetarian meal. Enjoy your vitamin C in a juicy red tomato picked off the vine and your vitamin A in squash, carrots, and mustard greens fresh from the garden. Take your minerals in the tall leafy greens waiting to be gathered.

Vegetables gave Daniel glowing skin, shining hair, and bright eyes. Today put more glow in your skin, sheen in your hair, and light in your eyes.

August 21

Begin

SCRIPTURE: *Matthew 17: 19 – 20*
KEY VERSE: *If your faith is the size of a mustard seed, you can say to this mountain, 'Move from here to there,' and it will move.*

Rose kissed me today.
Will she kiss me tomorrow?
Let it be as it may,
Rose kissed me today.
But the pleasure gives way
To a savor of sorrow;
Rose kissed me today,
Will she kiss me tomorrow?

Like Austin Dobson in his poem "A Kiss," perhaps we have all wondered if the first kiss would be followed by a second. We know the importance of that first kiss. Once something begins, it might continue!

Speaking of small beginnings, Jesus said even mountain-sized difficulties can be removed with mustard seed-size faith. However, glancing at a massive mountain looming in front of us, sometimes even our minuscule faith shrivels. Calculating the mountain's million shovelfuls of dirt—and not up to moving even a hundred—we often give up before we begin.

Today use whatever size faith you have to take the first shovelful of dirt out of a seemingly unmovable mountain. If the cluttered garage overwhelms you, fill your shovel with ten items and dispose of those. If your small shovel can only hold five items, put in only five. Tackle a mountain of unanswered letters by answering one letter today. If bathroom scales measure your mountain, pass up one snack today.

Even minuscule faith can move one shovelful. Today use it to move that first bit of dirt. It won't move the mountain. But maybe, tomorrow another shovelful will follow!

Old Friend

SCRIPTURE: *2 Timothy 1: 15 – 18*

KEY VERSE: *You know that everyone in the province of Asia has deserted me, including Phygelus and Hermogenes.*

Like everyone, Paul had his share of fair-weather friends, but he did not dream that Phygelus and Hermogenes were among them. As a prisoner in Rome, he counted on their help. However, as month followed month with no word from them, he finally realized they had deserted him.

Perhaps they really intended to contact Paul, but preoccupied with their own affairs, they simply forgot. Or perhaps, out-of-sight was out-of-mind.

Few of us consciously desert old friends, but caught up in the daily business of life, we too fail to follow through on good intentions. Reconstituting orange juice, making beds, separating dark and light clothes in the laundry, the morning vanishes. Urgency takes us to the dentist after lunch, common sense dictates watering potted plants, and necessity sends us to the grocery store.

Most of us have Pauls out there wondering what happened to us. Today be an Onesiphorus and take pains to search one out. Realign priorities and call someone whose friendship means more than orange juice, a dark load of laundry, or even the dentist appointment.

Paul, Phygelus, and Hermogenes once shared dreams, heartaches, and joys, and as they parted they embraced warmly with heartfelt promises. The warmth of their friendship strengthened Paul, but when it grew cold, he also felt the chill of his circumstances more keenly.

Today ward off the chill of another's circumstances with the warmth of friendship.

August 23

Craft Fair

SCRIPTURE: *1 Thessalonians 4: 9 – 12*
KEY VERSE: *Let it be your ambition to keep calm and look after your own business, and to work with your own hands, as we ordered you. (NEB)*

> Chairs to mend, old chairs to mend,
> Mackerel, fresh mackerel.
> Any old rags, any old rags...

Traveling the highways and byways, peddlers once sang those lines. Our modern-day peddlers call from booths in a craft fair. Their wares may be handmade pig-shaped cutting boards, or ceramic bowls turned on their pottery wheels. Filling the air with foot stamping music, some of them play fiddle next to a guitarist. In white aprons, they sell salsa and assemble tacos for a crowd of waiting people.

Paul would approve, for he found dignity in working hands, and he valued the approval of non-Christians who bought his tents. Whether they made tents, pottery, or furniture, he urged the Thessalonian Christians to put their hands to use.

In the Middle Ages, craft fairs combined business with pleasure as they provided craftsmen with a place to offer wares to the public. Some towns like Provins, Bar-sur-Aube, and Lagny grew rich on their fairs. Even today craft fairs contribute significantly to the economy of many small towns.

Take in one of these craft exhibitions today. Buy salsa or a pig-shaped cutting board. Admire Double Wedding Ring quilts, bright Mason jars of strawberry preserves, and hand painted wooden Santas, sheep, and geese. Finger hand-knit, bulky sweaters and smocked children's clothing. Take delight in hand-woven place mats, lap rugs, and scarves.

Like Paul, find dignity in working hands and affirm it.

August 24

List Needs

SCRIPTURE: *Psalm 4*

KEY VERSE: *Yet in my heart thou hast put more happiness than they enjoyed when there was corn and wine in plenty. (NEB)*

T he psalmist discovered that it takes more than corn and wine in plenty to create happiness. Many other people in the world have made the same discovery. They have had to find their happiness without plenty of anything.

Island of the Blue Dolphins, an award-winning classic by Scott O'Dell, recounts the story of the Lost Woman of San Nicholas who lived alone on the Island of the Blue Dolphins for eighteen years. When found, she lived in a crude hut with her dog, and she wore a skirt of cormorant feathers.

Even if we have never read the book, we know of Robinson Crusoe and the life he created on an island. In Disneyland we can climb the steps of a reconstructed Swiss Family Robinson tree house illustrating the potential to create meaningful existence with a minimum of resources. Henry David Thoreau's *Walden* continues to put us in touch with simple living.

Today list your needs. Rather than living on an island, we live in society with others, and we face greater needs than a shack and cormorant feather skirt. Capitalism creates new needs in order to create new markets, but today separate advertisement-induced needs from genuine ones.

What are these genuine needs? No two of us can make the same list, for we each have personal needs in addition to basic ones. Like the shepherd boy who had his harp, a gift of music may require a piano, violin, or voice lessons. The artist needs her paints, the seamstress her machine, and a green thumb may require a small patch of earth.

Like those in the psalm who linked happiness to prosperity, we too find happiness elusive when we confuse wants and needs. By listing your genuine needs, take a big step in the direction of happiness.

August 25

Apply Bible Verse

SCRIPTURE: *Matthew 7: 24 - 27*
KEY VERSE: *"Therefore, everyone who hears what I say and obeys it will be like a wise person who built a house on rock."*

I am a feather for each wind that blows." Like Shakespeare's King Leontes in *Winter's Tale*, at times we too feel like a feather for every wind. Realizing this, Jesus spoke of the wise man who built his house on rock where no rain, flood, or wind moved it. Today check your foundations.

In the wilderness, the children of Israel either ate their manna each day or lost it. Regardless of the amount collected, only the portion immediately eaten benefitted them.

In the pages of the Bible, God continues to provide manna for personal wilderness experiences. However, like the manna thousands of years ago, only the parts of it we actually use benefit us. Many of us grew up singing the praises of the Bible. But neither singing its praises nor memorizing it miraculously transform us into new creatures in Christ.

Nor does a lifetime of Bible study. No matter how many Bible verses we quote, we become spiritually anemic unless we eat what we collect. When anemia weakens our inner resources, even the most knowledgeable among us turn into feathers for any wind.

Today digest rather than collect. Creatively read the Bible, meditate, then act. The word of the Holy Spirit is a word of change, and when we listen to his word, something in us changes. We act in ways we have not acted before, and we speak words we do not usually speak.

If we eat it, manna changes us. It might even change the world if we all ate manna instead of collected it! Today eat what you gather. Tomorrow be stronger than any wind.

August 26

Party

SCRIPTURE: *Luke 15: 25 – 32*
KEY VERSE: *His older son was in the field. As he was coming back to the house, he heard music and dancing.*

> Tick, tock, tick, tock,
> Merrily sings the clock;
> It's time for work,
> It's time for play,
> So it sings throughout the day.

The father celebrated the prodigal son's return by throwing a party. "This brother of yours was dead but has come back to life. He was lost but has been found," he explained to the older son who heard music and dancing as he returned from the fields.

Perhaps the fun-loving son ran away because his father did not sooner hear the clock ticking time-to-play. The older brother did not outwardly rebel against unrelieved work, but he too longed to have fun. However, his father had never once thrown a party for him, and he saw no reason to attend one for his irresponsible brother.

Like the father, many of us hear the clock tick time-to-work, but fail to hear it tick time-to-play. Today plan a party. Make it a big affair or little one, a quiet or boisterous one, an elaborate or simple one. Indoors or outdoors, sit down or run-around, dress-up or come-as-you-are, make it what you want it to be; but in some way celebrate life by playing.

Blow up balloons, bring in flowers, and polish silver, or stock up on paper plates and sweep the patio. Invite the whole world to join you in the back yard, or treat the aged widow down the street to an evening out. Do anything, but do something.

Celebrate before the younger brother in you, or in those around you, goes astray. Celebrate before the older brother in you and others grows bitter. Hear the clock ticking time-to-play.

August 27

Enlargement

SCRIPTURE: *Psalm 31: 19 – 20*
KEY VERSE: *How great is thy goodness, stored up for those who fear thee, made manifest before the eyes of men for all who turn to thee for shelter. (NEB)*

> God is great,
> God is good,
> Let us thank him
> For our food.

Thank him for watermelon and canteloupe, squash and tomatoes, turnips and kale. But thank him for much more. This summer he sent sun and rain, flora and fauna, family and friend, and we have snapshots to prove it. Today remind yourself of God's goodness by enlarging one of these photos recording your blessings.

Perhaps the picture of the sea gull sitting on the rock vividly brings back a marvelous day at the ocean. Looking at its immaculate black and white feathers and the red spot on its beak, you may once again hear the surf roar and feel salty spray on your face. You even see twin sailboats gliding in the distance and hear children laughing as the surf overtakes their castle.

Take another look at the print showing the proud face of your grandmother holding a great-grandson on her lap. Beyond her face, you may see jars of bread-and-butter pickles lined up on the counter and apple pies laid out on the table. Her wrinkled features may picture a lifetime of labor and love.

The small snapshot of a lovely valley may barely show the white steepled church with geraniums on the step and a small stream behind it. Enlarge it and recall not only that valley, but all the beautiful ones you saw on your trip.

How great is the goodness of the Lord! Put the good things he sends into the big picture.

Coffee Alternative

SCRIPTURE: *1 Kings 17: 1 - 6*
KEY VERSE: *You can drink from the stream, and I've commanded the ravens to feed you there.*

I f you have already had your morning cup of coffee, you fall into the same pattern as one-third of the world. Like a crank on a mechanical toy, that first cup of coffee gets us going each morning, and other cups here and there keep us going the rest of the day.

In the fantasies of the *Nutcracker Ballet*, an Arabian lady does the dance of coffee, and perhaps the fantasy contains an element of truth. Legend attributes the discovery of coffee to Kaldi, an Arab goatherd around 850, who was puzzled by the strange behavior of his flock. Tasting the berry his goats had been eating, he experienced such exhilaration that he tried it again. Legend does not tell us if he did a coffee dance, but apparently he recommended the berry to others.

The drink was not introduced into Europe until the sixteenth century, but it gained such popularity that coffee houses soon sprang up all over London. People all over the world consume more coffee than any other beverage, making it a universal drink.

As the largest coffee consumers in the world, we in the United States keep the pot going much of the day, or we dip into our jars of instant coffee. Like the goatherd in the legend, we like coffee's stimulation, and when we feel energy flagging, we reach for another cup.

Long ago, when Elijah's energy flagged, the Lord gave him water to drink from a brook. Perhaps the act of bending down to drink from the brook helped wake him up. But later when the brook dried up, Elijah asked a widow in Zarephath for a drink of water.

Today replace at least one cup of coffee with water, herbal tea, or juice. Like Elijah, renew energy without the artificial stimulation of coffee. Wake yourself up with a brisk walk, play a game of ping pong, or engage someone in stimulating conversation. Wash walls, scrub floors, or take a shower. At least once today, find more stimulation in creativity than in a berry.

August 29

State or National Park

SCRIPTURE: *Luke 6: 12 - 19*
KEY VERSE: *At that time Jesus went to a mountain to pray. He spent the whole night in prayer to God.*

> When learning's triumph o'er her barb'rous foes
> First rear'd the stage, immortal Shakespeare rose;
> Each change of many-colour'd life he drew,
> Exhausted worlds, and then imagin'd new...

Samuel Johnson described a changing world and a man who used the changes wisely.

A red leaf on the lawn reminds us that our world is also changing. Within days we will begin picking up routines dropped here and there across summer's path. Like

259

Jesus who went away to the hills before beginning a new phase of ministry, today go away before plunging into autumn's intense schedule. Spend an afternoon in a state or national park where you can hear God's voice without interference.

We safeguard the natural wonders of our nation in our national parks, and each state uses public funds to preserve scenic treasures. States, like Minnesota with over sixty state parks, put scenic beauty within the reach of any citizen.

Prepare for the changes ahead by immersing yourself in this beauty. Walk wooded trails, picnic beside a stream, climb to a waterfall. Sit quietly, watch chipmunks scurry, and listen to blue jays jabber. Examine flowers in the meadow, lichen on the trees, and ants on the path.

Since we become like what we think about, today fill yourself with the beauty of God's world. Like Jesus, retreat into nature, and let its Creator restore your own inner power, peace, and poise.

Prepare for a new season by renewing the inner woman.

August 30

Encourage

Scripture: *Colossians 1: 3 - 8*
Key verse: *You learned about this Good News from Epaphras, our dear fellow servant. He is taking your place here as a trustworthy deacon for Christ.*

> How dreary to be somebody!
> How public like a frog
> To tell your name the livelong day
> To an admiring bog!

Although, like Emily Dickinson, we do not fancy any admiring bog, most of us need a certain amount of genuine recognition and encouragement.

Paul begins his letter to the Colossians by commending their faith, love, and fruit in the Lord. Then he acknowledges the hard work of Epaphras, their teacher in the faith. Epaphras worked for the Lord, but he may have also been trying to please the great apostle, his father in the faith.

People who encourage us often shape our lives. Most of us respond to recognition, and we repeat behaviors which bring it. Our "Big girl!" motivates the two year old to use her potty chair, put her toys away, and sit quietly in church. We never outgrow the need for recognition.

By concentrating on their strengths before addressing their weaknesses, Paul drew the positive out of many less-than-perfect congregations. Like him, use heartfelt encouragement to bring out the positive. Do you spot a less-than-perfectly-clean fork in the dish drainer? Shift your focus. Someone did the dishes, and like Paul, recognize admirable efforts, even if they are less-than-perfect ones.

True, few of us dream of fame or telling our name to an admiring bog. But still we appreciate knowing that our efforts are well received—even when they did not turn out as wonderfully as we anticipated. Today give that assurance.

August 31

Servant Role

SCRIPTURE: *Matthew 20: 24 - 28*
KEY VERSE: *Whoever wants to become great among you will be your servant.*

> To see a world in a grain of sand
> And a heaven in a wild flower,
> Hold infinity in the palm of your hand
> And eternity in an hour.

These words in William Blake's poem "Auguries of Innocence" run contrary to our desires. Rather than a grain of sand, we want the whole beach. Not a single wild flower, but the meadow where it grows fulfills our longing, or perhaps, even a house in the country.

Not the minute, but the big and showy impress us. In a poem entitled "Written in London, September, 1802," William Wordsworth laments, "The wealthiest man among us is the best..." Almost two hundred years later we still confuse greatness with bigness.

The small and menial weave the fabric of few dreams, and perhaps so many of us try to get out of such jobs because we feel small when we perform them. But our feelings derive from worldly standards rather than heavenly ones. A great chasm divides the kingdom of this world and the kingdom of heaven. The first belongs to those who give orders, the second to those who serve.

Today enter the kingdom of God through a servant role. Disinfect the toilet bowl in the boys' bathroom and clean the woodwork. Pick up sidewalk litter and scrub graffiti off a wall. Instead of going to Bible study, volunteer to watch babies so young mothers can attend. Fill a basin and wash someone's dirty feet.

William Blake saw heaven in a flower. Perhaps Jesus would also have seen it in a clean toilet bowl.

September 1

Good-bye

SCRIPTURE: *Daniel 4: 10 - 23*
KEY VERSE: *The tree grew, and it became strong enough and tall enough to reach the sky. It could be seen everywhere on earth.*

> These are the days when birds come back—
> A very few—a bird or two—
> To take a backward look.

In twenty words and three lines, Emily Dickinson captures the essence of a changing season. As another season changes, we may recognize a kind of good-bye in our own backward looks.

In the interpretation of his vision, Nebuchadnezzar heard another kind of farewell. Looking back, he longed to cling to the golden season of life, and he chose not to listen to the good-bye.

Like Nebuchadnezzar, we often try to hold on to one season when we should be reaching out for another. Before departing, the seasons of our lives gently bid good-bye. Today listen to one speak in rustling leaves. Hear its voice in a flock of geese honking overhead and the piercing chirp of the cricket. Detect it in the raucous call of a solitary crow in the meadow.

Sometimes eyes detect the good-bye before the ears. We notice lingering mist in the valley, dawn coming a few minutes later each morning, or the first red leaf on the lawn. Browning meadows, yellowing pumpkins, smoke drifting from chimneys call adieu to summer and welcome to fall.

Like Emily Dickinson, today capture one kind of good-bye on paper. In three lines and twenty words or in two journal pages, record the changes making this day different than the ones before it. Not even a powerful Nebuchadnezzar could hold back the hand of change. Today welcome change in both earth and soul. Graciously allow God to usher new seasons into your life.

September 2

New Shop

SCRIPTURE: *Acts 11: 19 – 21*

KEY VERSE: *But other believers, who were from Cyprus and Cyrene, arrived in Antioch. They started to spread the Good News about the Lord Jesus to Greeks.*

F earing persecution, many disciples learned to look both ways before speaking about Christ. Others recklessly ventured outside believing circles, taking the Good News into Gentile streets and shops. The Lord empowered these bold ones, and their explosive message split open confining Jewish containers. Their boldness fashioned a bigger container, the church.

Our streets and shops still hold potential for an explosive message to split open the confining containers of our lives. Today venture into them, and see life from another side. Browse in a funky side-street shop where a different crowd shops to different music. Speak to a shopper choosing a garment you would never wear. For fun, hold one of these dresses up to you in front of a mirror. Imagine yourself wearing it.

Wander through the kitchen store on the corner of Third and Main, admire the variety of cookie cutters and kitchen towels, and speak to a customer beside you. Walk through a new book store, a Scandinavian import store, or a music shop tucked into a little corner of the mall. Exchange greetings with Jews and Gentiles, shoppers and shop keepers.

The face of the early church changed when disciples began mingling with people in the streets. Like them, today mingle with unfamiliar people in unfamiliar places. Pick up a new thought, idea, or friend. At any moment, something new may explode something old, forcing us to create larger thoughts and actions to contain the surprising results. God may still be trying to change the face of the church.

Day of Dieting

SCRIPTURE: *Romans 14: 19 – 23*
KEY VERSE: *Don't ruin God's work because of what you eat.*

L ongaville, one of the lords attending the King of Navarre, pronounced this judgment in Shakespeare's *Love's Labour's Lost*:

> Fat paunches have lean pates; and dainty bits
> Make rich the ribs, but bankrupt quite the wits.

Today take these humorous words seriously and begin reducing the paunches. Work at putting more into your wits than into your mouth. Start a new season in shape.

Long before Longaville made his observation, Paul noted that pampering the paunches detracts from higher callings. As we often do, some Roman Christians tried to justify questionable eating patterns. However, Paul said that if they harbored inner doubts about their food choices, they were guilty of sin.

His definition of sin leaves many of us guilty. Knowing we often make wrong food choices, make this a day of dieting. Focus on the kind of food you eat rather than the amount. Since sugars and fats contribute much to paunches and little to wits, eliminate them. Choose a peach over a chocolate eclair, munch on carrot sticks instead of potato chips, and replace hollandaise sauce with zesty herbs.

Make this a vitamin-and-mineral day rather than a carbohydrate-and-fat day. Rich foods hold no monopoly on good eating, so discover and enjoy flavor, texture, and color in healthy foods. Take pleasure in crunchy celery, deep yellow squash, tangy kiwi fruit, sweet pears, and thirst-quenching watermelon.

Begin a new season with an eye on higher callings than food. Today give higher priority to wit than to paunch.

Property Investment

SCRIPTURE: *Luke 13: 6 - 9*

KEY VERSE: *The gardener replied, "Sir, let it stand for one more year. I'll dig around it and fertilize it."*

> Little Bo-peep has lost her sheep
> And cannot tell where to find them;
> Leave them alone, and they'll come home,
> And bring their tails behind them.

Perhaps Little Bo-peep's sheep returned on their own, but few other things respond so well to neglect. Not even the fig tree in the parable bore fruit until human hands improved the soil which nurtured it.

Rather than waiting for lost sheep to return or fruitless fig trees to bear, increase tomorrow's yield by adding fertilizer today. Make a property improvement which will pay off in next summer's pleasure.

Mend a broken picket fence, take out scraggly bushes cluttering the back yard, or dig dandelion roots out of the grass. Fertilize the lawn, thin saplings on the hillside, or plant a tree. Paint the old bench in the back yard, or buy a new one to set under the apple tree. Give lawn chairs a fresh coat of paint, lay a stone walkway from the driveway to the back door, or build a rose arbor. Clean out annual beds, put in mums for fall blooming, or add perennials to the flower garden.

Does the plum tree bear poorly and the apple tree not at all? Perhaps they bear the fruit of neglect. Before chopping them down, add fertilizer to the ground and give them time to respond.

What other fruitless trees in your life bear signs of neglect? While working on your property, think about some of these as well. Add some spiritual fertilizer to areas which bear poor yield, coaxing future fruit out of barren branches.

September 5

Fashion Awareness

SCRIPTURE: *Acts 16: 11 – 15*
KEY VERSE: *A woman named Lydia was present. She was a convert to Judaism from the city of Thyatira and sold purple dye for a living.*

> The morns are meeker than they were,
> The nuts are getting brown;
> The berry's cheek is plumper,
> The rose is out of town.
> The maple wears a gayer scarf,
> The field a scarlet gown.
> Lest I should be old-fashioned,
> I'll put a trinket on.

L ike Emily Dickinson, Lydia loved colors, and her eyes were quick to pick out the ones in fashion. Dwelling in a fashion-conscious society, she easily made her living selling purple, the fashionable color of the empire.

Today imitate both Lydia and Emily Dickinson and note the new fashions of the season. Bathing suits, tank tops, and sundresses now yield center stage to thick sweaters, wool skirts, and winter coats. A season changes, and styles change with it. Throw off labels and inhibitions. Try on one of the new "in" fashions, and smile at what you see in the mirror.

Lydia and other women gathered for worship beside the river. Like all women, they chatted about this and that. In addition to talk of babies, husbands, and food, they must have touched on the subject of clothing. Perhaps Lydia freely offered a suggestion here and there, helping ordinary women add a fashionable touch to daily garments.

Few modern day Lydias gather beside the river on the Sabbath, but they still make their living selling fashionable styles and colors. Today let one of them help prepare you for a new season.

September 6

Library

Scripture: *Acts 26: 24 – 29*
Key verse: ***While Paul was making his defence, Festus shouted at the top of his voice, 'Paul, you are raving; too much study is driving you mad.' (NEB)***

> Summer fading, winter comes....
> How am I to sing your praise,
> Happy chimney-corner days,
> Sitting safe in nursery nooks,
> Reading picture story-books.

Perhaps, like Robert Louis Stevenson, the child Saul also sought refuge from howling winds by reading favorite scrolls in a cozy nook of his home. Well-versed in literature, the apostle Paul used it in his defense of the gospel. Watching the scholarly prisoner pour over books day after day, the astonished Governor Festus accused him of over-studying.

Like Paul, today become better versed in literature. Summer fades, so get ready for stormy weather and dark evenings. Browse through the shelves of a library, ferreting out books to turn dark days into happy chimney-corner days. Leaf through unfamiliar authors as well as favorite ones, adding new treasures to old ones. Check out recent arrivals.

Perhaps Paul drew from the libraries of his friends, or possibly, he carried his own library with him as he traveled. His guards may have supplied him with reading materials. But whatever the source of his manuscripts, he poured over them for the two years he was in chains.

Although not in chains, inclement weather imposes certain limits on us. Books turn our limitations into opportunities. Regardless of the size of any personal cell, today create a bigger world with a trip to the library.

To-do List

SCRIPTURE: *Proverbs 3: 5 - 6*
KEY VERSE: *In all your ways acknowledge him, and he will make your paths smooth.*

I n Shakespeare's *All's Well That Ends Well*, Helena speaks words which reflect what many of us have experienced:

> Oft expectation fails, and most oft there
> Where most it promises.

Perhaps the writer of Proverbs had seen many expectations fail to materialize, for he had a word of advice about how to avoid disappointments. He said that by thinking of the Lord in all our ways, our plans would be fulfilled.

Along with nippy mornings and yellowing leaves, new expectations mark the changes in the air. Labor Day, summer's last fling, draws a line between seasons. We eagerly put our hand on the gear shift, preparing to move into high gear.

But in our eagerness, we may grind gears. Although living in a pre-transmission day, the writer of Proverbs knew that by shifting properly, he reached his destination with less stress and fewer breakdowns. His shifting went more smoothly when the Lord's hand rested on his.

Today think of the Lord in all your ways by making a list of everything you have to do in the next few weeks. Write it down. Be specific: buy pipe insulation, make a hair appointment, clean flower beds, take woolens out of moth balls, go to Bible study, give a baby shower.

Rather than assuming success, recognize that reality often shatters expectations. Like the writer of Proverbs, first think through what you need to do to turn expectations into reality. Then put it all in the Lord's hands. Make your path smoother by thinking of the Lord in all your ways.

September 8

Tea with a Neighbor

SCRIPTURE: *Ephesians 5: 15 - 20*
KEY VERSE: *Make the most of your opportunities because these are evil days.*

> There was an old woman
> Lived under a hill,
> And if she's not gone,
> She lives there still.

E ven if the old woman in the nursery rhyme lives there still, she won't forever. Nor will the old woman down the block, nor the young one next door. Before one of them goes, invite her to tea.

Many of us grew up giving tea parties with dolls circling a small table. We served pretend tea before we knew the taste of real tea. Those wee cups and saucers we found under a Christmas tree introduced us to the pleasant art of social intercourse.

Today give a small, but real, tea party. Paul admonished the Ephesian Christians to make the most of their opportunities and allow the Holy Spirit to work in and through them. Since today's neighbor may be gone tomorrow, invite her to drop in for a cup of tea today. Make tea more than tea with bannocks, muffins, or snickerdoodles.

However, since relationships characterize the kingdom of God, focus on the neighbor rather than the tea. If the day is hectic, dip a Constant Comment™ tea bag in a mug of boiling water and offer it with a warm smile. But if time allows, bring out a favorite tea pot, porcelain cup and saucers, and give the tea party of your little-girl dreams.

Paul told the Ephesians to sing and make music in their hearts. Witnessing often begins when our neighbors catch a strain of music in our hearts. Use today wisely. Joyfully and caringly reach out to a neighbor.

September 9

Lunchbox Surprise

SCRIPTURE: *1 Kings 19: 1 - 9*
KEY VERSE: *When he looked, he saw near his head some bread baked on hot stones and a jar of water. So he ate, drank, and went to sleep again.*

H is life threatened by the revengeful Jezebel, Elijah fled into the wilderness, lay down under a broom plant, and prayed for death. But instead of death, the Lord gave him a surprise lunch.

Although few of us fear losing our lives at the hands of a Jezebel, life can overwhelm us to the point where we want to give up. No lunch magically wipes out problems, but it may put heart into the one facing difficult circumstances. Today give someone's morale a lift with a lunchbox surprise.

What could change boring to exciting, delicious, or wonderful? Perhaps pizza instead of a sandwich would make a lunch box exciting. Would curried chicken and fruit salad bring cries of, "Delicious"? Try fried chicken and potato salad, and see if someone calls the lunchbox wonderful. Elicit interest by including raw vegetables and a dip.

God provided cake-like bread for Elijah in the wilderness. Follow his example by providing your own cake for some wilderness experience. Put together a three-tiered cake with nut and pudding fillings, or make a chocolate cake and relieve some of the discomfort of any wilderness. Surprise someone with a large piece of cherry pie or a generous piece of cheesecake.

Jezebel's threats could not match God's power, and neither can our overwhelming circumstances. Like Elijah we need strength to face and conquer whatever Jezebels threaten our peace. Sometimes strength comes through a simple token of caring such as a lunch box surprise.

September 10

Change Pews

SCRIPTURE: *Acts 19: 17 - 22*
KEY VERSE: *After all these things had happened, Paul decided to go to Jerusalem by traveling through Macedonia and Greece.*

> There was an Old Man in a tree
> Who was horribly bothered by a bee;
> When they said, 'Does it buzz?'
> He replied, 'Yes, it does!
> It's a regular brute of a bee!'

More than a century after Edward Lear wrote his limerick, we are still left wondering if the bee ever went away. Another question also comes to mind. Why didn't the Old Man get out of the tree?

If we ever chanced to meet him, the Old Man might look us in the eye and ask why we don't get out of some of our ruts. In another century, our descendents might still be asking the same question.

This Sunday get out of one rut—the pew-shaped one. Give up your seat at the end of the third row on the left side of the church—or whatever seat you usually claim. Sit in the middle seat of the fifteenth row on the right side of the building.

As you worship the Lord from a new perspective, also see those around you in a new light. Think about them, pray for them, and after the service, speak to them. Place the kingdom of God in a bigger circle.

Even Paul changed places from time to time. Although his ministry was going well in Ephesus, he knew other people also needed him. He decided to go on to Jerusalem, Macedonia, Greece, and even Rome.

Today get out of your tree—the one which produced your pew—and see God's kingdom from another viewpoint.

Scrap Project

SCRIPTURE: *1 Corinthians 12:27 – 31*
KEY VERSE: *You are Christ's body and each of you is an individual part of it.*

O ne wise bumper sticker proclaims, "When life hands you scraps, make a quilt." However, longing for beautiful bolts to create Cinderella dresses and Cinderella lives, many of us feel frustrated when we see only scraps in our hands. Some days we even think of ourselves as scraps.

But Paul says God creates his kingdom out of scraps. Some of us may be larger, some prettier, and some more scintillating, but none of us can claim to be more than a scrap until God fits us into the patchwork pattern of his kingdom. Paul calls us a toe, a liver, a capillary, all rather useless when unconnected.

Like God who forges a kingdom with scraps of humanity, today use life's scraps constructively. Follow the advice of the bumper sticker. Since life has probably handed you scraps, make a quilt.

If you don't have enough leftover minutes to tackle a quilt, take on a less ambitious patchwork project. Use miscellaneous scraps to make a Nine Patch pot holder. Create a hostess skirt with a patchwork design, or simply combine bright colors in a crazy-quilt pattern. Turn a few scraps into a doll quilt, or fewer ones into a patchwork book cover. Stitch patchwork place mats.

Have fun with scraps, and learn to enjoy all of life's little pieces. If God can create universes and kingdoms with little pieces, we should be able to constructively use all the scraps in our own lives.

September 12

Insect Life

Scripture: *Proverbs 6: 6 – 8*
Key verse: *Consider the ant, you lazy bum. Watch its ways, and become wise.*

> Over in the meadow where
>   the grass grows so even
> Lived an old mother frog
>   and her little froggies seven.
> "Jump," said the mother;
>   "We jump," said the seven.
> So they jumped all day
>   where the grass grows so even.

This old nursery song also tells us about other creatures who live over in the meadow. But rather than trust the rhyme, today check the meadow yourself. Investigate the insect life in the grass beneath your feet.

Measure off a square yard of lawn, garden, or field. What lies there? On your hands and knees, see what you can see. Perhaps the first clue of insect life will be the minuscule ants crawling up your hands. Separate the tufts of grass and find their nests or holes. Watch them come and go, always on the run. Discover where they are going and what they are doing.

How many ants can you find in a square foot of ground? Think beyond the small patch to the entire yard. Perhaps thousands of ants spend their lives beneath our feet. Keep thinking, taking your thoughts across the continents. Imagine the trillions and trillions of ants constantly working around the globe.

What else do you find? Depending on the terrain, you may find the mother froggie and her little froggies seven, or the mother lizard and her little lizards eight. An earthworm may appear, or a beetle may escape your poking fingers.

The writer of Proverbs says to gain wisdom by watching the ways of an ant. Today watch the ant, the cricket, the grasshopper, and all the other field creatures which fulfill God's purposes for them.

Learn from them, and ask God to help you fulfill his purpose for you.

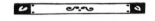

September 13

Slides or Videos

Scripture: *Psalm 98*
Key verse: *Let the rivers clap their hands and the mountains sing joyfully.*

Did you see the rivers clap their hands this summer? Or did you stand beside the roaring sea? Did you witness the hills singing aloud before the Lord?

Perhaps you heard a song in the deep colors of the Grand Canyon at sunset or in the mighty waters of Niagara Falls. Maybe the flight of a gull over a lighthouse in Georgia or a doe and her fawn grazing in the lower meadow brought strains of music to your ears. You may have heard your garden singing when cosmos created a Monet masterpiece.

Did your friends hear nature sing in far away Poland, Guatemala, or Bangkok? Reading their descriptions of a cruise down the Rhine, a ten day tour of Russia, or a tour of old plantations in Virginia, perhaps you caught a note or two of a song acclaiming the Lord.

Using images of seas roaring, rivers clapping their hands, and hills singing, the psalmist described a world full of praise for its Creator. This summer we saw a bit of what he saw so many thousand years ago, and while he captured his visions with words, we captured ours with cameras.

Tonight relive some of these memories by sharing slides, videos, or prints with friends. Invite your guests to share their own experiences recorded on film. Or bring out old slides, and once again stand beside Yosemite's Mirror Lake as it once was, walk through Washington, D.C. at cherry blossom time, or look up at Gothic cathedrals in Quebec.

Like the psalmist, acclaim the presence of the Lord our King by reliving beautiful moments.

September 14

Best Advice

SCRIPTURE: *Psalm 119: 57 - 64*
KEY VERSE: *I have thought about my life and I have directed my feet back to your written instructions.*

I n Shakespeare's *King Lear*, Edmund describes human nature in these words:

> This is the excellent foppery of the world,
> that, when we are sick in fortune,
> —often the surfeit of our own behaviour,—
> we make guilty of our disasters
>   the sun, the moon, and the stars;
> as if we were villains by necessity...

A modern day observer of behavior, Ann Landers, provides America with insight into human nature in her advice to broken-hearted wives, perplexed teenagers, betrayed men, and all who read her column.

Recognizing her wisdom, we seek light in her words for our own darkness. Yet her light is probably no greater than our own. Most of us know what is right, and if someone were to ask our advice, we could probably call forth solutions similar to the ones Ann Landers gives.

Without an Ann Landers, the psalmist did his own thinking and drew his wisdom from the Lord's instruction. Today do the same. Look through the eyes of your own experience, and be your own Ann Landers. We have all been through life's mill, and most of us are the wiser for it. Like Ann Landers, we have learned through failure, observation, and trial-and-error.

The Lord's instruction leaves none of us without wisdom, and Ann Landers' value lies in articulating what most of us already know deep inside. Today listen to the voice of the Lord speaking through your own experiences, and list ten ways of making life function more smoothly.

Write down the instruction you have received from the Lord, then begin following your own advice.

September 15

County or State Fair

SCRIPTURE: *Isaiah 55: 9 – 13*
KEY VERSE: *Rain and snow come down from the sky. They do not go back again until they water the earth. They make it sprout and grow so that it produces seed for farmers and food for people to eat.*

> Oh, dear, what can the matter be?
> Oh, dear, what can the matter be?
> Oh, dear, what can the matter be?
> Johnny's so late at the fair.

Perhaps, with so much to see, Johnny could not tear himself away until he had seen it all. Undoubtedly, he will tell his sweetheart all about it when he finally arrives with the bonny blue ribbon he promised her.

As in the nursery rhyme, fair time has come. Toggenburgs and Nubians bleat, Suffolk ewes patiently endure shearing, brown Jerseys flick their tails, and milling people pause to look, touch, and judge. Like Johnny, they linger, for there is much to see.

Isaiah notes that the rains and snows come down from

heaven and return only after they have watered the earth, making it blossom and bear fruit. Rejoicing in God's ways, each year we exhibit the finest and biggest specimens of the fruit of the land, and we make a holiday of it.

Fairs demonstrate a need beyond survival. Putting up rows of canned peaches and tomatoes does not satisfy us. We want them to look appealing, and we reward those who add that beauty to their labor. We want more than covering for our bodies; we seek well carded wool, carefully spun and beautifully woven. We do not simply want eggs; we want healthy Rhode Island Reds to lay them. We want Blue Ribbon quality in our lives.

Today go to a fair, pay tribute to blue ribbon living, and determine to put blue ribbons back into your own life.

September 16

Outreach Ideas

SCRIPTURE: *John 4: 35 - 38*
KEY VERSE: *"Don't you say, 'In four more months the harvest will be here'? I'm telling you to look and see that the fields are ready to be harvested."*

The highlight of the musical *Annie* is the orphan's stirring salute to "Tomorrow, Tomorrow." Many of us look forward to a brighter tomorrow when everything will be different. Like the magical word "someday," tomorrow holds in its hands all that today does not.

But Jesus knew if today's hand is empty, tomorrow's hand will probably also be empty. Perhaps many around Jesus shared the laid-back philosophy expressed in a popular fifties song declaring, "Mañana is good enough for me."

But Jesus told his disciples that mañana is not good

enough. Even though the calendar indicated four more months until harvest time, Jesus told the disciples to look around. The fields were already ripe for harvest.

Like the disciples of Jesus' day, we often mark time waiting for a future harvest. Today listen to Jesus speaking, look on the fields around you, and note how ripe and over-ripe they are. Be moved, and reach for a scythe in the form of outreach ideas.

Make a list of every idea which comes to mind, practical and impractical, convenient and inconvenient, sane and insane. God's ways, like a manger and a cross, sometimes appear insane to man, so write down ideas which sound wild, as well as ones which sound reasonable.

Some scythes come in the shape of hospitality, babysitting, or baking for others. Others reach further to sponsor youth groups, start young adult groups, and teach English to immigrants. Think of all the sizes and shapes needed to harvest today's crop. Mañana may be too late.

September 17

Act on the News

SCRIPTURE: *Ephesians 4: 17 - 28*
KEY VERSE: *However, you were taught to have a new attitude.*

> There was a crooked man,
> And he went a crooked mile,
> He found a crooked sixpence
> Against a crooked stile;
> He bought a crooked cat,
> Which caught a crooked mouse,
> And they all lived together
> In a little crooked house.

As in the nursery rhyme, crooked men still become entangled in crooked affairs. Headlines announcing new details of a crooked world hardly phase us, for we expect the crooked man to buy a crooked cat and to live with it in a crooked house. Some things never change.

Paul says they can and should change. With the new nature God creates, the crooked man stands upright and straightens his affairs. As you read today's paper, pray for that new nature to transform a crooked world. Stand straighter yourself by expressing God's new nature in action.

Patronize a restaurant banning smoking in its facilities. Volunteer to work with an anti-drug program such as DARE. Contribute to the local food bank. Pray more intelligently after reading *Zlata's Diary: A Child's Life in Sarajevo* (mentioned in section E-1). Support the youth of your community by attending a performance of their orchestra or a high school sports event.

With a new heart and new spirit, even reading the newspaper should take on the new dimension of action.

September 18

Nature Walk

SCRIPTURE: *Genesis 1: 9 – 13*
KEY VERSE: *The earth produced vegetation: plants bearing seeds, each according to its own type, and trees bearing fruit with seeds, each according to its own type. God saw that they were good.*

> The ripe, rich tint of cornfields,
> And the wild geese sailing high;
> And all over upland and lowland
> The charm of the golden-rod,—
> Some of us call it Autumn,
> And others call it God.

L ike William Herbert Carruth, today see God in the autumn world. Large yellow mushrooms push through a fresh carpet of leaves in the woods, red headed woodpeckers drill into dead pines, and geese stretch their wings in flight. Deep blue skies hold gleaming white clouds, and maples glow with color. Berry vines shrivel, unveiling gurgling streams behind them.

When God looked upon his handiwork, he called it good. Today draw close to the autumn world and see how good it is. Take a walk and appreciate the earthy colors replacing summer's vivid ones. Note how thick is the caterpillar's fur and the cattle's coat and how intense grows the cricket song. Watch puffy-cheeked squirrels, scurrying chipmunks, chubby gophers. Listen for the sudden rustle of quail and the quiet stir of pheasant.

Delight in bright red apples decorating the orchard, orange pumpkins still clinging to the vine, and rows of browning cornstalks. Walk through the tall grasses of the field and among milkweed pods letting go spun silver. Gather acorns strewn across the road.

Witness the satisfaction of harvest replacing the excitement of growth, and see celebration now in fruit rather than in vine. As earth crowns labor, behold, and with a heart full of praise, give thanks

September 19

Music Discovery

Scripture: *Psalm 138*
Key verse: *They will sing about the ways of the Lord: "The Lord's honor is great!"*

Suddenly, medieval music has become excitingly new, for the music world has rediscovered Gregorian chants. Stashed away for centuries, old scores once again sing of the Lord's ways.

The heart was made to praise and adore, and men and women have sung of the Lord's ways from history's beginning. In all countries, languages, and styles, music has articulated the whispers, cries, and praises of the soul. Today make your own musical discovery by listening to a new song. Hear of the Lord's ways through different voices.

Like the Gregorian chants, much of our musical heritage lies mute in archives. Our shelves also hold sound hostage. The genius of Liszt, the gifts of Bach, and the creativity of Mozart remain silent until, like the prince who kissed Snow White, we set free their sound. Today set one genius free.

Genius expresses itself in many forms and many voices. Folk songs born in Appalachia or the green valleys of Ireland, the plains of Arabia or the mountains of Bolivia, the islands of the Philippines or the African coast also voice man's struggle to know himself, his world, and his Lord. The legacy is still being written, for creativity seeks expression generation after generation.

Hear of the Lord's ways through an old Gregorian chant, a Mozart concerto, or a contemporary artist. Turn the radio dial to a new setting, check a cassette out of the library, or invest in a new CD.

The glory of the Lord is great. Today behold it through the eyes of a musician who heard notes the rest of us missed.

September 20

Switch Sides

SCRIPTURE: *1 John 2: 7 - 11*
KEY VERSE: *Only the man who loves his brother dwells in light: there is nothing to make him stumble. (NEB)*

> There I met an old man
> Who would not say his prayers;
> I took him by the left leg
> And threw him down the stairs.

The zealous writer of the nursery rhyme had precedents for his action. A zealous Saul threw into jail Christians who did not properly say their prayers. In the sixteenth century, zealous Christians did the same to Muslims who refused to properly say their prayers.

Long ago, John said we live in darkness unless we love our brother. However, throughout most of history, we have created problems by giving too narrow a definition to brother. Saying we should love our neighbor as ourselves, Jesus defined neighbor in terms of need rather than geography, culture, or theology.

Today increase your capacity to love by genuinely trying to understand someone who doesn't properly say his prayers. What kind of abuse and neglect created the gnawing anger, frustration, and hate of the criminal who set fire to an apartment building, murdered a foreign tourist, or raped thirty women? Perhaps the God he knew was so judgmental that he never dared approach him in prayer.

What drives one who interferes with your own hopes and dreams? For a moment take his or her side rather than yours, and feel need, frustration, and pain from another perspective.

Put yourself in the shoes of anyone else—the nerd, the whining child, the boring speaker on the platform. Today increase the light coming into your life with a bigger definition of brother or sister.

September 21

Color List

SCRIPTURE: *Exodus 39: 1 - 5*
KEY VERSE: *From the violet, purple, and bright red yarn they made special clothes worn for official duties in the holy place.*

Roses are red,
Violets are blue,
And God in heaven
Knows I love you.

How long did it take us to realize violets are purple or white? Perhaps this little childhood ditty has seriously hampered our ability to really see color. Having been told from a tender young age that roses are red, we may still see red even when the rose is vermilion, crimson, or cerise.

Long before the writer of the ditty described roses as red and violets as blue, and even before there was an English language forcing him to rhyme "blue" with "you," ancient Israelites saw color. We may not know the difference between violet and purple, but they knew. When they stitched vestments for those who ministered in the sanctuary, they enhanced worship with the use of color.

As autumn extravagantly crowns the year with glorious color, we respond in praise and worship. Like ancient Israelites, today increase the sense of worship by seeing color in the September world and listing every shade and hue. Call the sky azure or cerulean, sky-blue or royal blue, sapphire or lapis lazuli. Rather than impose crayon-yellow and crayon-brown on the changing hills, give colors their true names. See sulphur, amber, saffron, ochre, rust, copper, chestnut, and tawny.

Today refuse to squander nature's breathtaking diversity by fitting every hue into a primary color. See color upon color, hue upon hue. See, and expand worship and praise.

September 22

Save Paper

SCRIPTURE: *Proverbs 9: 10 – 13*
KEY VERSE: *The fear of the Lord is the beginning of wisdom. The knowledge of the Holy One is understanding.*

Jack and Jill went up the hill
To fetch a pail of water;
Jack fell down and broke his crown...
He went to bed to mend his head
With vinegar and brown paper.

Would a pizza advertisement, dry cleaning offer, or tire special also work to mend Jack's head? If so, we could mend many heads with what came in yesterday's mail, today's mail, and every day's mail.

Our generation turns the scent of pine and the home of the blue jay into millions of tons of third class mail. In the process, we pollute waterways and build up the ozone layer. And what do we do with our third class mail? We stuff it in drawers and then in the trash can. Eventually it goes to landfills, creating sometimes contaminated hills where little Jacks and Jills play.

Living in a biodegradable world, the writer of Proverbs did not concern himself with landfills and ozone layers. His knowledge of the Holy One gave him understanding, and he realized the Lord's ways are for our good. He saw the advantage of respecting God's creation.

Today pay respect to the Holy One by respecting his creation. Recycle the pizza advertisement. If you have no Jack with a broken head, save it for scratch paper, create a collage, or begin a papier-maché project. Send more than one message by using the back side as stationery. Hand it back to the mail carrier.

In a paper shuffling generation, it will be to our advantage to shuffle wisely. Today take a small step in the fight against pollution. Save a token drop of water in a vast sea of pollution.

September 23

Cultural Bridge

Scripture: *Psalm 146*
Key verse: *The Lord protects foreigners.*

> Once riding in old Baltimore,
> Heart-filled, head-filled with glee,
> I saw a Baltimorean
> Keep looking straight at me.
> Now I was eight and very small,
> And he was no whit bigger,
> And so I smiled, but he poked out
>   His tongue, and called me "Nigger."

A lthough the Lord watches over strangers in our midst, as Countee Cullen described in his poem, "Incident," we do not always do so. But today share God's concern for immigrants by visiting one, and begin to build a bridge between your culture and hers.

Before building a bridge, we have to know something about the land on both sides. Which foods appearing on our tables originated in the immigrant's culture? Your love of pita bread, tamales, or Gouda cheese may create the bridge's first cable. Since almost every English word evolved from the roots of other languages, discover which came from her native tongue.

No ethnic group has a monopoly on inventions, so respect her native land's contribution to human progress. If she is Muslim, increase her dignity by remembering that while Europe was groping its way out of the Dark Ages, Muslims were benefitting the world with medical discoveries. If she is Indian, appreciate her country's gift of our number system; if Chinese, acknowledge China's gift of silk to the world.

God looks after the stranger in our midst. Today draw closer to Him by drawing closer to a foreigner.

September 24

Notebook Cover

SCRIPTURE: *Exodus 38: 16 - 20*
KEY VERSE: *All the curtains around the courtyard were made out of fine linen yarn.*

My heart's in the Highlands, my heart is not here;
My heart's in the Highlands, a-chasing the deer;
A-chasing the wild deer, and following the roe,
My heart's in the Highlands wherever I go.

L ike Robert Burns, many of us have fallen in love with some beautiful place. Perhaps long ago, the Jungfrau in Switzerland's highland claimed our memories. Or closer to home, we felt our hearts leap when our eyes fell on a hillside of blazing maples or a field of dandelions. Beauty may be in the eye of the beholder, but—because we are made in God's image—we all long for it.

When Moses and the Israelites built the Tabernacle to hold the Tent of the Presence, they poured their resources into making it beautiful. They saw that from dawn's first rays to sunset's last ones and from the sea's swelling breakers to the heavens' twinkling stars, God crowned his creation with beauty. Instinctively they knew only a beautiful dwelling place would honor the Presence of the Creator of beauty.

Like those early worshipers of the Lord, part of our creative legacy is the power to create beauty. When we add beauty to the work of our hands, we simply reflect the image of the one who made all things beautiful. The Presence no longer dwells in a Tent within a Tabernacle, but within us.

Today add a touch of beauty to one expression of yourself. With linen, calico, or poplin, cover the journal you write in at night or the composition book where your ideas accumulate. By making more beautiful the notebook which reflects the thoughts, dreams, and plans of your soul, remind yourself the love of beauty is one of God's most precious gifts.

The present day tabernacles of God need to be as beautiful as ancient ones.

September 25

Foster-Care Inquiry

SCRIPTURE: *Esther 2: 5 – 9*
KEY VERSE: *He had a foster-child Hadassah, that is Esther, his uncle's daughter, who had neither father nor mother. (NEB)*

> Little Orphant Annie's come to our house to stay,
> An' wash the cups and saucers up,
>   an' brush the crumbs away,
> An' shoo the chickens off the porch,
>   an' dust the hearth, an' sweep,
> An' make the fire, an' bake the bread,
>   an' earn her board-an'-keep.

Like the little girl described by James Whitcomb Riley, many motherless and fatherless children must have been forced to earn their board-and-keep following Nebuchadnezzar's destruction of Jerusalem. Fortunate ones, like Esther, were taken in by foster parents who loved them as they fed them, erasing some of the traumas of the past.

In every state and town of our nation, children coming out of abusive or traumatizing situations need foster-parents who can love as well as feed them. Unfortunately, for lack of enough good foster homes, the foster care system designed to protect children sometimes increases the trauma.

We do not know how old Esther was when she went to stay with Mordecai, but we know one-third of our foster children are under the age of four. Nor do we know the extent of Esther's trauma when she lost her parents, but we know most of our foster children enter foster homes carrying more pain than clothing.

Neither does the Bible tell us Mordecai's age when he became a foster-father and then an adoptive father. Perhaps, like today, traumatized children then found healing through the love of families, single women, working women, and grandmothers or great-grandmothers in their seventies.

From a foster care agency, today learn more about the need for care providers or back-up helpers in your community. If we had more Mordecais in our midst, perhaps we would also have more Esthers.

September 26

Tell a Story

SCRIPTURE: *Matthew 13: 1 – 9*
KEY VERSE: *Then he used stories as illustrations to tell them many things. He said, "Listen! A farmer went to plant seed...."*

Tell me the stories of Jesus I love to hear;
Things I would ask him to tell me if he were here.
Scenes by the wayside, tales of the sea
Stories of Jesus, tell them to me.

Thus William Parker pictures Jesus telling stories to children. Perhaps, as Jesus traveled through the villages of Galilee, children who had already heard his stories pleaded, "The storyteller is back, Mother! May we go hear him? Please, Mother."

Those who heard Jesus remembered his stories and passed them on. Storytelling is the oldest art known to mankind, and the centuries have not diminished the role of a good storyteller. Even in a video age, live stories still grab attention and cling to the memory.

Most of us tell more stories than we realize. A five

minute traffic jam, a persistent salesman at the door, and a telephone call waking the baby turn us into storytellers as we describe the incidents. If we exaggerate in the telling, it is not because we are liars, but because we are storytellers.

Today reach a child's heart by telling a story. Describe the day you were baptized, a bike ride that ended in a broken arm, or recess time when you went to school. Share the disappointment of getting chicken pox the day before summer camp. Tell of your adventures in foreign lands, childhood vacations at the coast, your first trip to Disneyland.

Like Jesus, learn the art of storytelling, and the children will run to hear what you have to say.

September 27

Run

SCRIPTURE: *Matthew 28: 1 - 10*
KEY VERSE: *They hurried away from the tomb with fear and great joy and ran to tell his disciples.*

> Thyself and thy belongs
> Are not thine own so proper as to waste
> Thyself upon thy virtues, they on thee.
> Heaven doth with us as we with torches do,
> Not light them for themselves.

A s the Duke in Shakespeare's *Measure for Measure* observed, heaven does not light a torch for itself. Discovering the empty tomb, Mary of Magdala and the other Mary did not return home with full hearts and thanksgiving on their lips. They ran to tell the disciples.

Had we discovered an empty tomb, some of us would have tried to hail a taxi, catch a bus, or perhaps, send a messenger to alert the disciples. However wonderful the news, few of us run to tell anyone, for running leaves us out of breath.

As we enter a season of diminishing physical exercise, today increase the capacity of your heart and lungs by running. Run the length of the block, half the length of the block, or even a quarter of it if that is your comfortable distance. If you find no distance comfortable, stay in the house and run in place, saving your outside debut for another day. If running comes easy, today run further or faster or in a different direction.

Tiredness wears the edge off enthusiasm, but physical stamina gives it wings. Many of us are still enthusiastically rediscovering the empty tomb and its implications for our lives. Today get in shape to run tell someone about it.

September 28

Polish Brass

SCRIPTURE: *Ezekiel 1:4 - 13*

KEY VERSE: *I saw a storm wind coming from the north, a vast cloud with flashes of fire and brilliant light about it; and within was a radiance like brass, glowing in the heart of the flames. (NEB)*

The vast cloud had a brilliant light about it, and within the cloud was a radiance like brass. Exiled by the river Kebar, Ezekiel saw a vision of God in the radiance. Most visions of God described in the Bible speak of a similar radiance like that of precious metals.

The earth has its own precious metals, and it is beginning to display them. We catch a touch of copper in the woods, a hint of brass on the hillside, and the sheen of silver and pewter in the clouds. Blazing evening skies reveal a smelting furnace. Like a hostess preparing for a party, earth puts a shine on every vessel in its house. Today behold the glory of God in the radiance of the season.

Reflecting on the radiance of the Almighty, put a shine on your own brass. Apply cleaner to the lamp base whose rich color is hidden beneath tarnish. Bring back the high-lights of the brass candelabra which will be used more often with lengthening nights. Return the shine to the brass elephant paperweight on your desk. Polish the brass fruit bowl in the kitchen.

A new season's fickle weather already limits outside activities, but the warm glow of shining metals in hearth and home welcome us indoors. The bright colors in garden and field have passed, but they have left the richer colors of enduring metals. While the cosmos petal is fragile, here today and gone tomorrow, metal is strong and permanent, and we can depend on it. Today put a shine on one of those metals, and highlight its qualities.

As you add a touch of radiance to the house, let God touch your life with the radiance of his presence. Shine with joy.

September 29

Hand-Made Gift

SCRIPTURE: *Acts 9: 36 - 43*

KEY VERSE: *So Peter went with them. When he arrived, he was taken upstairs. All the widows came and stood around him. They were crying and showing Peter the articles of clothing that Dorcas had made while she was still with them.*

D orcas filled her days with acts of kindness and charity. Her death left a vacuum in the church—too much of a vacuum. When believers in Joppa heard that Peter was nearby, they sent an urgent request for him to come. He did, and they showed him the shirts and coats Dorcas had so generously stitched for others. Moved by her generosity, Peter called her back to life.

Do you make shirts and coats? Special wreaths or lined wicker baskets? Handmade candles or baby booties? Bread-

and-butter pickles or strawberry jam? Whatever creative expression your hands take, today generously share it with others. Give a gift you make yourself.

A gift of our hands is a gift of ourselves. Those receiving the gift receive an intimate part of who we are. All gifts express affection, but handmade ones intimately share our life as well as our possessions.

Who needs an intimate touch with you today? Some lives already contain so much that another gift is another piece of clutter. Other lives hold empty spaces where gifts fit. Still others know only a terrifying inner vacuum, and a handmade gift casts a warm glow in the emptiness. Share your gift with one who needs it.

Today fill an empty space in someone's life with a patchwork pillow, crocheted scarf, or cloth doll. Or like Dorcas, make shirts to give away. Give something from your hands to someone who has empty space to fill.

September 30

Brainstorm

SCRIPTURE: *Matthew 25: 14 - 30*
KEY VERSE: *The one who received ten thousand dollars brought the additional ten thousand. He said, 'Sir, you gave me ten thousand dollars. I've doubled the amount.'*

> Humpty Dumpty sat on the wall,
> Humpty Dumpty had a great fall;
> All the king's horses and all the king's men
> Couldn't put Humpty together again.

Rather than trying to put Humpty together again, the king's men could have scrambled him or made an omelet. The baker could have turned him into cookies or cake, the housewife could have gathered him up for pancake batter. Without some kind of fall, sooner or later he would have rotted on the wall.

Many of us spend too much time lamenting Humpty Dumpty's fall rather than using it to our advantage. Like the wise servants in Jesus' story, we will be rewarded according to how we have used our resources. Today, look at a cracked egg in your own life, and brainstorm ways to use it constructively.

Like the king's men trying to put a broken egg back together, some of us never make ends meet financially. Today, instead of trying to glue crumbling corners together again, list ten, twenty-five, or fifty ways to cut corners. Who knows? Rounded living may be more fun than square living.

Some cracked eggs come in the form of home, marriage, and relationships. Rather than wistfully dreaming of five bags of gold, brainstorm ways to use the one or two bags of gold you have.

With hard work, each industrious man in Jesus' story doubled his assets. Use the cracked eggs in your life before they spoil.

October 1

Wax Leaves

Scripture: *Acts 14: 14 – 18*
Key verse: *Yet, by doing good, he has given evidence of his existence. He gives you rain from heaven and crops in their seasons. He fills you with food and your lives with happiness.*

> I dimly guess from blessings known
> Of greater out of sight,
> And with the chastend Psalmist, own
> His judgments too are right.

Beholding the glory and goodness around us and faintly glimpsing what lies beyond, like John Greenleaf Whittier, our hearts quicken.

This month we behold glory upon glory. Sugar maples set hillsides ablaze, yellow beech capture the sun's gold, and quaking aspens light up the mountains. Even the staid oak turns its leathery leaves maroon and copper before sending them to the

ground. Sumac reddens humble roadsides, sweet gum colors city streets.

Autumn parades an unparalleled extravaganza of color, holding nothing back in the spectacle. No thoughtful prudence, no economizing of color, or modest restraint marks this seasonal affair. The earth goes all out for one moment of glory on the world stage. Finally, spent from such extravagance, it falls back to rest on its laurels for another year.

Today catch a bit of the glory before the brilliance fades. Wax red, orange, or yellow leaves in melted paraffin. Pile them in a clear glass dish or pewter platter and light up winter's dark days with a token of autumn's brilliance. Keep a single waxed leaf on the coffee table to remind yourself that the glory you have seen is but a glimpse of what is yet to come. The Lord who extravagantly colors a season also extravagantly colors our lives with his glory and grace. Today feel the touch of his brush in your life.

October 2

Muffins

Scripture: *Genesis 27: 1 - 4*
Key verse: *Prepare a good-tasting meal for me, just the way I like it. Bring it to me to eat so that I will bless you before I die.*

> Do you know the muffin man,
> The muffin man, the muffin man?
> O, do you know the muffin man
> Who lives in Drury Lane?

We may not know the muffin man on Drury Lane, but we know others. Wherever they live, they tempt us with the smell of their wares and bless us with the taste. Our appreciative hearts return the blessing.

Before meals, we often ask God's blessing on both the food and the hands which prepared it. Some foods tempted and pleased Isaac more than others. When he needed comfort and cheer in his old age, he asked for these. He gave his blessing to the son who prepared his favorite dishes.

Some foods still bless more than others, and like Isaac, we ask special blessings on the ones who prepare them. Since muffins rank high on any favorite food list, today make a batch.

Complementing crisp autumn days, hot breads prepare us to leave the hearth, and they welcome our return to it. Their substance braces us for nippy mornings; their aroma gives any day an emotional boost.

Make today's muffins special. If zucchini overflow in every basket in the kitchen, turn them into muffins. Dip into a bushel basket of apples in the garage; then stir up apple nut muffins. Try pumpkin, whole-grain, or cooked-cereal muffins. Add bananas or pineapple, dates or raisins, cooked bacon or sausage to the batter.

Coax a blessing out of the family by treating them to one of their favorite foods.

October 3

Coffee Table Book

The words God spoke through Moses lay silent. For years no one had opened the book of law, and no one remembered what it said, or even that it was in the temple. Hilkiah found the book, gave it to Shaphan, and Shaphan read it to the king. Moved to tears, the king found new direction for his life.

God still speaks through books, and some of his messages come through coffee table books which reveal the majesty of his creation. However, after the books' newness wears off, we often bury their messages and then forget them.

Move the book of Maine lighthouses from the bottom of a stack to the top of the coffee table. Relive the trip along the coast when you ate a picnic lunch below the lighthouse and fed the gulls with scraps. Smell the salty ocean air, hear the gulls, see the lobster boats bobbing offshore. Once again lift your heart in praise to the Lord who created such a marvelous world.

Retrieve the picture book of Norway a friend gave you. In pictures of graceful Viking ships and a rugged *Kon-Tiki*, hear stories of past exploits. See deep blue fjords wind their way between mountains rising sharply into a blue sky. Bow before the God of all people of all times.

Take out a book of Southwest canyons, Alsace-Lorraine houses, or Rembrandt reprints. Whatever once touched you holds the potential to do so again. Like the book of the law, what lies forgotten on the shelf brings no blessing in our lives.

Today find a book, and be thrilled, charmed, or awed by God's wonderful ways in the world. Like the king, be moved to follow His ways more closely.

October 4

Sunrise

Scripture: *Psalm 108: 1 – 5*
Key verse: *Wake up, harp and lyre! I want to wake up at dawn.*

When morning gilds the skies
My heart awakening cries:
May Jesus Christ be praised!

In the moment when darkness changes to light, quietly sit before the window and see it happen. Witness the first rays of light appear, then the first tinge of pink on the horizon. Watch the glow intensify, painting the sky in brilliant and joyous hues. Sing with joy as the sun once again brings light out of darkness.

Ancient people recognized the relationship of the sun to life on earth, and many of them responded by worshiping the sun. The Aztecs believed they had a divine mission to save the earth. Each day their priests sacrificed a human heart to ensure the rising of the sun.

Early Egyptians believed their pharaohs were sons or daughters of Re, the sun god who sailed through the sky in a boat by day and battled the powers of darkness by night. Ancient Hittites gave Arinna, the sun goddess, special honor among their deities. Many American Indians included an annual sun dance in their religious ceremonies.

The psalmist also followed the course of the sun in the heavens, beholding its rising and its setting. But rather than seeing the heavenly light as a deity, he saw it as a proclamation of the Deity. Like other ancient men, he responded to the rising sun in worship. Unlike them, he worshiped the God who created the heavens, summoning the world from one end of the sun's path to the other.

Today as the morning sky blazes day into being, respond with worship to the Lord of heaven and earth rather than anything in it. Let your heart resonate the lines of the German hymn: "When morning gilds the sky, my heart awakening cries, 'May Jesus Christ be praised!'"

October 5

Open a Gate

SCRIPTURE: *Luke 5: 1 - 11*
KEY VERSE: *Jesus told Simon, "Don't be afraid. From now on you will catch people instead of fish."*

S imon may never have dreamed of being anything other than a fisherman like his father and possibly his grand-father. He must have often gazed contentedly at his boat and felt a healthy pride at his ability to handle it well. The life of a fisherman was a good one, the sea a generous giver, and he probably never sought or imagined change. But one day he met a man who changed his career, his name, and his life.

No longer do we automatically fall into the careers of our parents, and yet our backgrounds still shape our ex-pectations and dreams. Like Simon and the other disciples, we adopt certain roles and make certain assumptions about ourselves because they fit into the pattern of life we know. If we sometimes wistfully dream of other roles, an inner voice reminds us to be realistic.

But realistic may be another word for fear. Had Simon stopped to consider a realistic response to Jesus' invita-tion, the pages of the Bible would lack a Peter. But impul-sive Simon opened the gate of the fence he had built around his life, and Peter walked through it.

Today open a gate in the yard of your own life by doing a new thing, Do an unrealistic thing, an "I-would-love-to-but..." thing, an out-of-character thing. Do you think you're not an artist? Sign up for piano lessons, a drama class, an oil painting workshop. Are you too shy to ask questions in a meeting? When the Bible study leader asks who will open in prayer, raise your hand.

Simon dreamed of fishing in the sea, but Jesus made him a fisher of men. What would he make of us if we had the courage to open unrealistic gates and walk through them? Today open one and give him a chance to take you through it.

October 6

Role Play

SCRIPTURE: *2 Corinthians 6: 3 – 10*
KEY VERSE: *People can see our purity, knowledge, patience, kindness, the Holy Spirit's presence in our lives, our sincere love, truthfulness, and the presence of God's power. We demonstrate that we are God's servants.*

> Sweet are the uses of adversity;
> Which, like the toad, ugly and venomous,
> Wears yet a precious jewel in his head.

S peaking for himself, the Duke in Shakespeare's *As You Like It* also articulated Paul's experience following his conversion. Far from a happily-ever-after fairy talc, new life in Christ brought Paul flogging, imprisonment, mobs, overwork, sleeplessness, and starvation.

In similar circumstances, many of us would give up, convinced we were not in the Lord's will. Some of us might try new prayer techniques before concluding we had misread God's call. Others might feel abandoned by God.

However, it never seemed to occur to Paul that he was not in the Lord's will. Nor do we have any indication he questioned his prayer life. But it did occur to him that each hardship provided an opportunity to demonstrate the power of the gospel through patience, kindness, and sincere love.

Problems neither make nor break us any more than they did Paul, but our perceptions of them color our responses. One person sits depressed before a mountain, while another builds a road over it. Someone else invents an airplane to fly over it, and others stubbornly tunnel through it. A few climb it and discover the joy of a mountaintop experience.

Today imagine some personal mountain through the eyes of other people. List ten people whom you admire and try to picture how each would respond if they stood before your immovable mountain. Write out imagined words or actions, and predict an outcome.

Perhaps your mountain will shrink in the process.

October 7

Foliage Drive

SCRIPTURE: *Romans 1: 18 – 23*
KEY VERSE: *From the creation of the world, God's invisible qualities, his eternal power and divine nature, have been clearly observed in what he made.*

> There is something in the autumn
> that is native to my blood—
> Touch of manner, hint of mood...
> There is something in October
> sets the gypsy blood astir;
> We must rise and follow her,
> When from every hill of flame
> She calls and calls each vagabond by name.

Like Bliss Carmen who wrote "A Vagabond Song," do you hear October calling? Today rise and follow her, and with the apostle Paul, see God's power and deity in this magnificent autumn world.

Drive into the countryside where flaming maples line dirt roads and stands of sun-splashed birch light up dark woods. Wander along a dirt lane canopied in fiery orange and flaming red. Peer through yellow leaves to a lapis lazuli sky. Listen to the crunch of leaves, and watch a red leaf twirl in a pool beneath a waterfall.

Meander through rustling cottonwoods, bright birch, and muted oak. Listen to birdsongs carried by crisp October air. Follow an old stone wall into hushed woods. Sit beside a stream.

Like candles in the night, luminous maples and golden aspen glow more intensely as darkness deepens. If the day is overcast or skies gray with falling rain, drive among these glowing lamps of autumn, for this month nature lights a fire in its own hearth.

Paul says that God reveals his everlasting power and deity to all men in the things he has made, but the wicked refuse to render him thanks. Today see what God's hand has done, catch a glimpse of the invisible attributes of the Almighty, and render thanks.

October 8

Withhold Advice

SCRIPTURE: *Matthew 7: 1 – 5*
KEY VERSE: *So why do you see the piece of sawdust in another believer's eye and not notice the wooden beam in your own eye?*

Every one can master a grief but he that has it." As Benedick discovered in Shakespeare's *Much Ado About Nothing*, advice comes easily from those who do not have the problem. Leonato, another character in the play, speaks these words:

> I pray thee, cease thy counsel,
> Which falls into mine ears as profitless
> As water in a sieve...
> For there was never yet philosopher
> That could endure the toothache patiently...

Our tendency to correct and advise others must have often dismayed Jesus. Sometimes, he may have also smiled; for with a touch of humor he noted that although we do not remove the planks in our own eyes, we generously offer to remove the specks in other people's eyes.

Few of us can resist sharing our wisdom, and giving advice seems close to second nature. Almost as soon as a problem emerges, we leap to the rescue with, "Have you tried...?", "What if ...?", or even, "You should..."

However, as Leonato observed, our wonderful advice usually falls through a sieve. Since we each made the choices which created our problems, we must each face the consequences, take responsibility, and begin making the kind of choices which bring happier results.

Today hold back any advice on the tip of your tongue. Listen sympathetically, perhaps ask questions, but do not offer solutions. Give a gift of dignity by allowing someone to work through her own problems.

October 9

Narration

SCRIPTURE: *2 Samuel 12: 1 - 14*
KEY VERSE: *So the Lord sent Nathan to David. Nathan came to him and said, "There were two men in a certain city. One was rich, and the other was poor...."*

> There was a young lady of Riga,
> Who rode with a smile on a tiger;
> They returned from the ride
> With the lady inside,
> And the smile on the face of the tiger.

Did you miss the moral of that story? Although Jesus did not use limericks, he told stories to illustrate his points. In one a man built a bigger barn, in another a woman found a lost coin, and one told about a man who had a hundred sheep. He convicted people with stories about weddings, beggars, and weeds. He talked of flour, yeast, and salt. And people listened.

Our backgrounds, hopes, and fears so color the meaning of words we often hear story messages better than direct messages. Stories place speaker and listener on the same patch of ground.

Today listen to a recorded narration, and hear a message which has eluded you in more conventional ways. View yourself through the eyes of St. Exupery's *Little Prince*, A.A. Milne's *Winnie-the-Pooh*, or Jane Austin's *Emma*.

Like David hearing Nathan's story, as we listen to the psychological and moral destruction of Shakespeare's *Othello*, we may suddenly be convicted of our own role in the downfall of another. Perhaps only then do we recognize the destructive influence another has on us.

God speaks to us in many ways, but sometimes we only hear his voice in story form. Today listen to hear what you have been trying not to hear.

October 10

Pictures to an Invalid

SCRIPTURE: *2 Corinthians 1:3 - 7*
KEY VERSE: *He comforts us whenever we suffer. That is why whenever other people suffer, we are able to comfort them by using the same comfort we have received from God.*

> 'Tis the last rose of summer
> Left blooming alone;
> All her lovely companions
> Are faded and gone...
> When true hearts lie withered,
> And fond ones are flown,
> Oh! who would inhabit
> This bleak world alone!

I n his poem, "'Tis the Last Rose of Summer," Thomas Moore identifies with the loneliness surrounding age and infirmity. As old friends die, many last roses lose their past, foresee no future, and lose interest in the present. With the consolation Paul describes, today make the bleak world less bleak for one of these roses who inhabits it alone.

Visit an elderly shut-in, and link her reduced world to a larger world by sharing some of your recent photos. A picture of a covered bridge in New Hampshire may mean nothing to her, but it will gain interest as you tell the story of your trip. Include the humorous details of things gone wrong.

Show her a picture of the forty pumpkins growing in your garden, an outrageous clown you saw at the state fair last week, or your black and white kitty curled up in a chimney corner. Take a picture of your back yard, your neighbor's children, or your wonderful geraniums. Share any picture which delights you, and impart delight to one who thinks of delight only in the past tense. Freshen the present with a breath of fresh air.

October 11

Autumn Poem

SCRIPTURE: *Psalm 96: 1 - 3*
KEY VERSE: *Sing to the Lord a new song! Sing to the Lord, all the earth.*

Season of mists and mellow fruitfulness,
Close bosom-friend of the maturing sun;
Conspiring with him how to load and bless
With fruit the vines that round the thatch-eaves run.

In his poem "To Autumn," John Keats describes the poetry of his September or October world. Today imitate him.

In flaming hills and sunburnt meadows, falling leaves and bubbling brooks, nature writes poetry for all of us. It pens its lines in circling hawks over a valley and the formation of geese rushing southward. It makes stanzas of acorns, mushrooms, and apples still clinging to the trees.

Creatively respond to nature's poetry by writing your own lines and stanzas. The psalmists says to sing a new song to the Lord, and what can be more new than the one you pen yourself?

As you look around, what do you see in the hills and fields? You may detect camel humps, curried mulligatawny, or even a Middle Eastern Bazaar. Perhaps the image of leaping flames comes to mind or a blend of cinnamon, nutmeg, and allspice. You may see a patchwork quilt or a tweed skirt.

What excites, comforts, or satisfies about the season? Do you love rows of fading cornstalk in the fields or full silos standing on the horizon? Do you look forward to picking apples when crisp air turns your cheeks red like the fruit? Do crunching leaves, apple pies, and pumpkins make the season for you?

In few or many lines, capture what you see, feel, and think. Sing a new song and offer it to the Lord.

October 12

Ethnic Event

SCRIPTURE: *Psalm 67*
KEY VERSE: *Let the nations be glad and sing joyfully because you judge everyone with justice and guide the nations on the earth.*

> In fourteen hundred and ninety-two,
> Columbus sailed the ocean blue.

When Columbus discovered the New World, Queen Isabella rejoiced at what appeared to be a magic solution to her bankrupt coffers. The New World seemed to hold promises of enriching an exhausted old one.

Other explorers followed Columbus, each intent on enriching himself as well as his country. But most of these conquistadors who destroyed civilizations and raped continents died broken men. The Old World never dreamed that the greatest wealth of the New World lay in the men and women of two new continents rather than in any silver, gold, or fountain of youth.

Five centuries later, gold and silver still gleam more brightly for many than do people and cultures. But three thousand years ago, the psalmist had a different view. His benediction included a blessing for all peoples and nations of the earth.

Living in a crossroad of continents, the psalmist must have seen many foreigners riding camels past his village. Perhaps he greeted them with, "Shalom!" or "The Lord be with you." He may have bought their wares in local markets.

Today share in the cultural wealth of the nations by attending an ethnic event in your own back yard. Drop in on a Greek festival at an Orthodox Church; taste pastries of another culture; listen to its music and admire its crafts. Join in a festive Latin gathering, clap to South of the Border music, and dine on tamales. Spend an evening watching Thai tribal girls perform on stage, or take advantage of any opportunity to know another culture better.

In the midst of some ethnic gathering, with the psalmist, pray God's grace and blessings on all the nations.

October 13

Cookbooks

Scripture: *Proverbs 31: 27 - 31*
Key verse: *Her children and her husband stand up and bless her.*

> Little Tommy Tucker
> Sings for his supper.
> What shall he eat?
> White bread and butter.

hicken and roast beef, hot breads and dumplings, raspberry ice and eclairs filled other tables, but poor little Tommy could only look forward to a supper of white bread and butter. Believing rich tables were for the "swells," he may have gratefully gulped down his white bread and butter.

Like Little Tommy Tucker's supper table, our tables may hold poor fare compared to others. Although boasting thousands of recipes in our cookbook collections, most of us use only a few in our lifetime. Perhaps we too look on some recipes and foods as the property of the "swells."

Since husbands seldom sing a wife's praises over tidy houses, clean laundry, or predictable dinners, the woman described in Proverbs must have been creative as well as capable. Unlike Little Tommy Tucker, her little Eli must have expected surprises on the dinner table.

Search through your cookbook collection with an eye for recipes which will elicit praise.

In tempting salad recipes, from jellied clam ring to cucumber-and-onion salad, find one your family will like. Expand your pancake repertoire with hominy cakes and squash pancakes. See desserts through poached, stewed, flambeed, sauteed, curried and glazed lenses.

Keep your eye on your cookbooks as well as on the other doings of your household.

October 14

Almanac

SCRIPTURE: *Matthew 2: 1 - 2*
KEY VERSE: *They asked, "Where is the one who was born to be the king of the Jews? We saw his star rising and have come to worship him."*

oming out of Middle Eastern astrology, almanacs originally charted star positions for the purpose of making weather predictions. From an early almanac, the astrologers from the East may have determined a king had been born in the land of Judah.

Today's almanacs tell us the normal January temperature in Alabama, describe social security benefits, and list the rulers of Prussia. They include a copy of the constitution of the United States, flags of all nations, and zip codes of towns with a population of 5000 or more.

The astrologers from the East who went to worship the new born king were called wise men. Perhaps we would also be wise if we used our almanacs as well as they used theirs. Today rediscover this convenient source of information on an amazing range of topics.

We may not discover the birth of a king in our almanac, but it will tell us which countries still have one. More relevant, it gives the warning signals of cancer, the number of calories in a brownie, and the amount of calcium in an egg bagel. Its information about sending packages may save a phone call to the post office, and by looking at the rates of compound interest, we may find the return on an investment without a trip to the bank.

Among all the astrologers of the East, only the ones mentioned in the Bible knew their almanacs well enough to detect the greatest cosmic event in history. Today, like these wise men, use the almanac on your shelf.

October 15

Best/Worst Experiences

SCRIPTURE: *Philippians 4: 10 – 14*
KEY VERSE: *I know what it is to be brought low, and I know what it is to have plenty. I have been very thoroughly initiated into the human lot with all its ups and downs— fullness and hunger, plenty and want. (NEB)*

I t was the best of times, it was the worst of times." Describing revolutionary France at the turn of the nineteenth century, Charles Dickens coined the phrase in his novel *A Tale of Two Cities*, but the experience is universal. The apostle Paul calls it the human lot with all its ups and downs.

His world was perhaps as tumultuous as any other. The divine light Christ brought into the world threw a shadow of persecution on those who dwelt in it. But even as Paul experienced overwork, hunger, and the disappointment of stumbling Christians, he experienced an inner power giving him strength to face any circumstance. The brilliance of Christ's light made any shadow seem small.

Like Paul, today take stock of your own ups and downs. The human lot exempts none, apostle or agnostic, from pain, betrayal, and loss, but neither does it leave any unblessed. Make a list of the ten best and the ten worst experiences of your life.

You may find the worst of times also the best of times. The year you lived in a shabby apartment on almost nothing may have brought more happiness than bigger houses and paychecks later in life. Having your car repossessed may have been the most humiliating experience of your life, but perhaps you experienced God in special intimacy during that time.

Note how light and shadow compliment each other in your life, adding depth and beauty to your soul. Accept the ups and the downs, knowing there is a place for each.

October 16

A Play

SCRIPTURE: *Jeremiah 13: 1 - 11*
KEY VERSE: *These were the words of the Lord to me: Go and buy yourself a linen girdle and put it round your waist, but do not let it come near water. (NEB)*

All the world's a stage,
And all the men and women merely players;
They all have their exits and their entrances;

L ike Jaques who spoke these words in Shakespeare's
As You Like It, Jeremiah felt himself a player in a cosmic drama directed by God. Judah had once been close to
the Lord, but had wickedly turned away, and the Lord pronounced judgment through a drama Jeremiah acted out
with a linen girdle.

In the first act, Jeremiah bought the girdle and wore
it around his waist. In the second, he hid the girdle in a
crevice among the rocks. In the last act, he retrieved it but
found it spoiled. Seeing the spoiled girdle with their own
eyes, the people of Judah saw themselves as God saw them.

Ancient people often used drama to interpret their
existence, especially in relation to their deity. Thousands
of years ago, Egyptians used drama in religious rites, and
early Christians relived the Easter story with a portrayal of
the empty tomb. In the Middle Ages, actors performed the
entire story of the Bible through a series of plays, enabling
audiences to vicariously experience its drama.

Plays continue to reveal hidden truths to us. Whether
a vehicle for entertainment, social commentary, or the ex-
ploration of the psychological make up of man, they help
us better understand ourselves and our world. Today
make plans to attend a play and examine yourself in a
new mirror.

Sometimes only a spoiled girdle can show us the condition of our soul.

Favorite Books

SCRIPTURE: *Luke 4: 16 – 21*
KEY VERSE: *The attendant gave him the book of the prophet Isaiah. He opened it up and found the place where it read: "The spirit of the Lord is with me..."*

B ack home in Nazareth on the Sabbath day, Jesus went to synagogue as he had always done. This time he read the lesson. When he was handed the scroll of Isaiah, he did not hesitate. He knew what it said and what it meant.

The boy Jesus must have loved to read, for the adult Jesus thoroughly knew the scriptures. Apparently, he had favorite ones, for he mentioned some more than others. The Isaiah passage must have been one of those favorites, and perhaps the shape of his divine mission evolved through the reading and rereading of it.

The books we love paint a portrait of who we are. Whether we grew up admiring the self confident Nancy Drew in Caroline Keene's series or the sensitive and gentle Beth in Louisa May Alcott's *Little Women* determines to a great extent who we are today. Today list the ten books which have most influenced your life.

Which long ago stories still stir nostalgic memories? Was *Winnie-the-Pooh* by A.A. Milne a bedtime must, or did you grow up on fairy tales like "Beauty and the Beast?" Which books do you continue to read and reread? Which do you recommend to others?

If you love the "Anne of Green Gables" series, there's a little of Anne in you. If Rosalind Carter's autobiography is a favorite, something in her personality meets a kindred spirit in you. If Alan Paton's *Cry, the Beloved Country* still moves you, like him, you respond compassionately to suffering.

Your list paints one more portrait of who you are. Understand yourself better by looking at the books which helped shape your life.

October 18

Invest Money

SCRIPTURE: *2 Corinthians 8: 1 - 9*
KEY VERSE: *While they were being severely tested by suffer-ing, their overflowing joy, along with their extreme pov-erty, has made them even more generous.*

> Simple Simon met a pieman,
> Going to the fair;
> Says Simple Simon to the pieman,
> "Let me taste your ware."
> Says the pieman unto Simon,
> "Show me first your penny."
> Says Simple Simon to the pieman,
> "Indeed, I have not any."

I ndeed, in today's world many Simons have not any. Per-haps all worlds have had their share of hungry Simons.

Impoverished Macedonian Christians experienced un-relieved hunger, and they constantly struggled to make ends meet. Hearing of starving Christians in other places, they insisted on reaching into near-empty pockets to help them.

Like the Macedonians, today reach into your pocket and find coins for a worthwhile project. Help a teenager earn money for college by subscribing to one of his maga-zines. Turn a dowdy church nursery into a pleasant atmo-sphere by adding curtains, toys, or a rug. Invest in friend-ship by taking an acquaintance out to lunch.

Relieve Simple Simon's hunger by buying him a pie. Or take pies to the local food bank. Make a contribution to a church camp, enabling youth to experience God more inti-mately. Redirect the lives of lost youth by sending a check to an organization working with gangs on the streets of New York City, Mexico City, or Bangkok. Improve a schoolhouse in Haiti by using your savings to participate in a work project.

Today invest part of your money in eternity.

Knitting

SCRIPTURE: *Proverbs 31: 23 – 26*

KEY VERSE: *She dresses with strength and nobility, and she smiles at the future.*

Baa, baa, black sheep, Have you any wool?
Yes sir, yes sir, three bags full.
One for my master, one for my dame,
And one for the little boy who lives down the lane.

And what did the dame do with her wool? First she spun it, and then she knit it into stockings to keep her feet warm on the icy floors of her drafty house.

Although feet at this end of the century climb into heated automobiles and re-enter heated rooms, handknit wool socks still warm the coming and the going. The same wool which insulates lambs when icy winds whip across the fields insulates human feet walking through the fields.

Before long, the icy winds come. Like the woman praised by the writer of Proverbs, prepare ahead of time.

Today begin knitting a pair of wool socks to ward off the freezing temperatures soon arriving. Buy a pattern, follow the directions until they lose you, and then ask for help to turn the heel or whatever.

Or take the chill off low temperatures by knitting a thick sweater or woolen vest. With your needles, turn yarn into a jump suit to warm a toddler or a blanket for a baby on the way. Make a pair of slippers, or work on an Afghan.

Knit the first row, purl the second. Knit and purl, a little now, a little then, adding stitches to your needle in extra moments. Like the woman in Proverbs, give a satisfied smile because you have begun to face winter.

October 20

Seeds

SCRIPTURE: *John 12: 23 - 26*
KEY VERSE: *I can guarantee this truth:A single grain of wheat doesn't produce anything unless it is planted in the ground and dies.*

> Are you sleeping, are you sleeping?
> Brother John, Brother John!
> Morning bells are ringing.
> Morning bells are ringing.
> Ding dong ding! Ding dong ding!

B rother John is not the only one sleeping. The earth also sleeps, and under the ground, tiny seeds lie waiting for morning bells to ring. When the bells sound their ding dong dings, miracles emerge.

Today hold a miracle in your open hand. Examine an apple seed, and imagine the full grown tree. Split the tiny seed open and look inside. This turns into stems and leaves, trunks and bark, leaves and fruit? Can it be?

Now put an apple seed and an orange seed side by side. Is it possible that one contains the blueprint for an apple tree and the other an orange tree? No, we want to say about the unimpressive looking seed. It is not possible.

But we live with the impossible. The blueprints are there, whether we see them or not. As you contemplate the impossibility of the reality, lift your thoughts to the Creator. Who is he, this One who designs such impossible realities? Slowly quiet your spinning mind and begin to comprehend the meaning of reality: every touch of God's hand creates a miracle.

We pray for miracles. We wait for miracles. But in every direction, morning bells are ringing. It is time to wake up and begin seeing the miracles around us—and to begin believing in the ones within us.

October 21

Food Stand

SCRIPTURE: *Ruth 2: 1 – 16*

KEY VERSE: *Ruth, who was from Moab, said to Naomi, "Please let me go to the field of anyone who will be kind to me. There I will gather the grain left behind by the reapers."*

After leaving the drought-stricken Moabite country, Naomi and Ruth found Bethlehem in a state of excitement over its barley harvest. In large swathes, reapers gleaned fields while others ran back and forth filling water jars. Following close behind the reapers, women gathered everything they missed, and Ruth excitedly joined them.

Gathering among the swathes, Ruth must have given thanks that she and her mother-in-law would again eat. Perhaps her heart would have missed a beat if she had known the field of Boaz held her future as well as her food.

Like the people of Bethlehem, we often walk down our streets thinking of food. Far from barley fields, we rush towards a corner stand where steam rises and people queue. At one stand a bratwurst sausage or foot long hot dog may pass to our waiting hands while another offers sauerkraut or perhaps chili sauce with its frankfurters. A South American vendor may pile shredded cabbage and crisp onions on his hot dogs.

The stand may not be a hot dog stand. It may be a windowed van offering burritos, tamales, or tacos. Perhaps it is a knish cart or a hot pretzel stand. It may be shooting popped kernels into a glassed box while the aroma of buttered popcorn bids pedestrians to stop. Egg rolls may be the speciality, or arepas or kibe.

Like Ruth, today find your food in new territory. Join the queue before a stand offering some food you have not yet tried. Although Boaz does not stand behind the cart, Jose, Antonio, or Ling does. Speak or smile to this entrepreneur who takes pride in his product. Warm the day with something in the stomach, and warm your heart with this touch of life on the other side of the stand or cart.

October 22

Learn from Another

Scripture: *1 Corinthians 12: 4 - 11*
Key verse: *There is only one Spirit who does all these things by giving what God wants to give to each person.*

> Ye banks and braes o' bonny Doon,
> How can ye bloom sae fresh and fair?
> How can ye chant, ye little birds,
> And I sae weary fu' o' care?

Robert Burns wondered why the flowery banks bloomed and the little birds sang when his own heart was breaking. But God created every flower to bloom and every bird to sing, and each bloom and each song he made fair.

He made the rose and the peony fair, the violet in the woods and the daisy in the meadow sweet. He beautifully sculpted the conch shell and the murex, the cockle shell and the abalone, and into the rainbow he poured splendid color after splendid color. With limitless creativity, he touches all creation with beauty.

He has most lavishly poured his gifts into the crown of his creation, the human created in his likeness. We are his great Rainbow Coalition, and the more we appreciate the unique gifts of each other, the more of the rainbow we see.

Today see more color in the rainbow by learning something from another person. During a casual conversation, draw out the thoughts or knowledge of the other until a new insight penetrates past understanding. Learn something from the homeless lady sitting on the curb, the clerk who rings up your purchase, or a colleague whom you dislike. Ask a neighbor how to prune roses or mulch leaves.

Paul says there are varieties of gifts, but the same Spirit. Today discover how generous that Spirit is in his distribution of gifts.

October 23

Birthday Book

SCRIPTURE: *1 Thessalonians 3: 6 – 10*
KEY VERSE: *We can never thank God enough for all the joy you give us as we rejoice in God's presence.*

> So study evermore is over-shot;
> While it doth study to have what it would,
> It doth forget to do the thing it should.

T hese words in Shakespeare's *Love's Labour's Lost* describe many of us. Always reading about love, we neglect simple, everyday acts which would turn it into reality.

Already beset by difficulties and hardships, Paul must have waited for Timothy's return with trepidation, fearing more discouraging news. The word Timothy brought made his spirits soar. News of the Thessalonians' faith and love came as a breath of life, and he wondered how he could express his thanks.

We also wonder how we can express thanks to those who fill our lives with joy. As Shakespeare's Biron noted, we often fail to put feet to our emotions. The extensive line of late-birthday greeting cards gives an indication of how often we slip up even on birthdays.

While every birthday marks the anniversary of one of God's gifts to the world, the birthdays of our loved ones mark the anniversary of gifts God gave us. Although love does not hinge on remembering birthdays, when we celebrate the birth of a loved one, we express thanks to God as well as to the loved one.

Today create a birthday book to help you remember

the birthdays of those you love. For each person on your birthday list, reserve a couple of pages in a notebook for jotting down ideas for gifts and celebrations.

Like Paul, wonder how you can show your appreciation for loved ones and then give wings to your desire.

October 24

Historical Novel

Scripture: *Jeremiah 6: 16 - 21*
Key verse: *This is what the Lord says: Stand at the crossroads and look. Ask which paths are the old, reliable paths. Ask which way leads to blessings.*

> I have a little shadow
>   that goes in and out with me,
> And what can be the use of him
>   is more than I can see.
> He is very, very like me
>   from the heels up to the head;
> And I see him jump before me,
>   when I jump into my bed.

We all have them, but unlike Robert Louis Stevenson, we don't all pay attention to them. If we look closely, we see more than one following us. What is the use of them? Begin reading a historical novel, and find out. Examine long ago shadows very, very like you from the heels up to the head.

In his novel *Love is Eternal*, Irving Stone pictures an Abraham Lincoln with glaring weaknesses and wonderful strengths. This celebrated president stood his wife up on their wedding day, suffered severe bouts of depression, and mourned the loss of a child. Yet we remember him for the moments when he stood tall.

In the pages of *Two from Galilee* by Marjorie Holmes, we walk roads lying two thousand years behind us.

Thinking the thoughts of Mary and feeling the fears of Joseph, the long ago event takes on the reality of the here and now.

Tiptoe into one of these shadows. Walk through village streets in the Middle Ages, travel the seas in a Viking ship, or stand in the shoes of the first president of the United States. Go to China with Hudson Taylor, to the battlefield with Florence Nightingale, or to the cotton fields with George Washington Carver.

Standing in one of these shadows of the past, see how very, very like you it is from the heels up to the head. What is the use of it? Some shadows mark a path of blessings. Today study the markers.

October 25

Pray for the Church

SCRIPTURE: *Matthew 28: 16 – 20*
KEY VERSE: *So wherever you go, make disciples of all nations: Baptize them in the name of the Father, and of the Son, and of the Holy Spirit. Teach them to do everything I have commanded you.*

> This is the way the ladies ride,
> Tri, tre, tre, tree,
> Tri, tre, tre, tree!

We all know how the ladies ride and even how the farmers ride. But how does the church ride?

Jesus did not leave a manual telling the church how it should ride. He left no blueprint, set of guiding principles for development, or even a neat theology. The only commission he gave was to make disciples, baptizing them and teaching all that he had commanded. The Great Commandment, to love God above all and one's neighbor as one's self, summed up his teaching.

Although publishers pour forth models telling the church how to ride, sometimes we spend more time off the horse than on it. Engrossed in budgets and carpets, furnaces and copy machines, meetings and power struggles, we find little time to mount the horse and ride.

Today pray your church will spend as much time on the horse as off it. Pray for the community where men and women work and struggle, marry and divorce, suffer and try to escape through addiction in the shadow of the church. Pray for teenagers who cut classes, break into cars, and express distorted frustration within sight of the church. Pray for children who copy the inappropriate behavior of the adults in their lives.

Pray your church will quickly go, make disciples, baptizing them and teaching them all the Lord commanded.

October 26

Charm List

SCRIPTURE: *Song of Songs 5: 10 - 16*
KEY VERSE: *His eyes are like doves beside brooks of water, splashed by the milky water as they sit where it is drawn. (NEB)*

In a series of charming images, the bride in Song of Songs describes her bridegroom. Her description tells little about the bridegroom's actual appearance, but from doves beside brooks of water to lapis lazuli and topaz, we learn what appeals to her. We can almost hear the words she spoke when she first laid eyes on him. How charming!

He must have had the same thought when he first saw her. Even before he knew her name, perhaps he loved the girl whose eyes so easily lit up with pleasure. Because she found the world charming, she too was charming.

Whether in a winsome personality or an old flower garden beside a plantation manor, most of us love charm.

We use the word to describe a little boy blowing a kiss to his mother, a New England lighthouse standing above a crashing sea, and a Victorian Bed and Breakfast.

Today, like the bride, become more charming by thinking about charming things. Make a list of everything which puts a sparkle in your own eyes.

Do you find it hard to resist taking pictures of daffodils, bright faces of children, or old churches? Does your family laugh when you show them still another picture of a sea gull poised at water's edge? When you think of charm, do you think of towns like Old Town San Diego, historic Santa Fe, or a small Vermont village cloaked in snow?

What streets draw you and what people do you love to be around? Do you pause before a field of lambs or before a charming little corner shop? Or like the bride, do you love lapis lazuli and topaz?

Find the world charming, and it will find you charming.

October 27

Hospitality

Scripture: *Hebrews 13: 1 - 6*
Key verse: *Remember to show hospitality. There are some who, by so doing, have entertained angels without knowing it. (NEB)*

Not many of us have seen winged angels, but apparently all angels do not wear wings. In Hebrews we read that by showing hospitality, we may entertain an angel without knowing it.

Today open your door to an angel without wings and invite her to enter. Do not expect her to look like an angel. Welcome her in any dress she happens to wear, any tongue she speaks, and in any personality she has.

She may knock at your door with the literature of a sect group in her hands. Rather than peer through a half-closed door, today invite her inside for a cup of tea. Then explore common areas of faith.

The angel may not knock at the door, but simply sit beside you in a meeting. She may live only three houses down and shop alongside you in the supermarket. She may need fellowship, but be too shy or polite to mention it. Today take that initiative and invite her into your house.

Ask her to come for dinner, drop in for a chat, or stop by for afternoon tea. If she is elderly and without transportation, offer to pick her up. If she is a young mother, invite her to bring the three-month-old baby and two-year-old toddler. If she is a bag lady, have lunch with her.

Invite more than one angel. Volunteer to host the next Bible study or committee meeting. Offer your home for the next youth group party or as a place where the Girl Scouts can meet. Suggest having the fall potluck dinner at your house.

Open your home to whatever angel God sends your way.

October 28

Accessory

Scripture: *Genesis 24: 50 – 60*
Key verse: *The servant took out gold and silver jewelry and clothes and gave them to Rebekah. He also gave expensive presents to her brother and mother.*

> Ride a cockhorse to Banbury Cross
> To see a fine lady upon a white horse;
> Rings on her fingers and bells on her toes,
> She shall have music wherever she goes.

What is the appeal of rings on our fingers and bells on our toes? In the most primitive societies necklaces adorn bare bodies, and with shiny colored beads the Old World purchased much of the New World. Ankle bracelets appear beneath veil-covered bodies in Muslim countries, and in South America mothers pierce the ears of infant daughters. In our generation young brides flash diamond rings.

Rebecca may not have flashed a diamond ring as she traveled to meet her promised husband, but she may have felt herself a fine lady as she fingered the silver and gold ornaments he sent. Perhaps she often smiled as she thought about how beautiful she would look on her wedding day.

We can not change the features nature gave us, but we can add our own sparkle with an ornament. Like Rebecca, today make yourself more beautiful with an accessory. Buy a new bracelet, a lace collar, or a silk scarf. Fit your hands into a new pair of knit gloves or your feet into warm leather boots. Wrap your neck in a bright wool scarf. Wear your grandmother's pearls.

Even the browning earth adorns itself with the bright red barberry and brilliant red sumac. Meet approaching winter with some touch of glitter or some hint of gaiety. Today be a fine lady.

October 29

Call Congressman

SCRIPTURE: *Psalm 82*
KEY VERSE: *Defend weak people and orphans. Protect the rights of the oppressed and the poor.*

> A wretched soul, bruis'd with adversity,
> We bid be quiet when we hear it cry;
> But were we burden'd with like weight of pain,
> As much, or more, we should ourselves complain.

A driana's words in Shakespeare's *The Comedy of Errors* describe us better than they do the psalmist. Whatever his own problems, he raised a cry on behalf of the bruised, destitute, and downtrodden.

Today imitate him by raising your voice on behalf of some of the bruised in our world. With a letter or phone call, let your congressman know your concerns for the destitute and the downtrodden, the weak and the orphan.

Based on how they affect the underprivileged, explain why you agree or disagree with his votes and stances. Object to a trade embargo which punishes the poor but rewards wealthy policy makers of some small nation. Question freebies which interfere with just decisions. Applaud a bill creatively dealing with crime, poverty, or education.

The bruised of the world come into our living rooms daily through newspapers and television. Rather than bid them be quiet or turn a deaf ear, today listen to what they are saying. Look them in the eye, hear the words they speak, and feel some of the pain they express.

Like the psalmist, look at our world through God's eyes and demand justice in his name. Be one who helps create a more just world rather than one who waits for a just world to dawn.

October 30

Community Portrait

SCRIPTURE: *Acts 19:35 - 41*

KEY VERSE: *The city clerk finally quieted the crowd. Then he said, "Citizens of Ephesus, everyone knows that this city of the Ephesians is the keeper of the temple of the great Artemis. Everyone knows that Ephesus is the keeper of the statue that fell down from Zeus."*

> The farmer in the dell,
> The farmer in the dell,
> Heigh ho! the derry oh,
> The farmer in the dell.

D oes the farmer in the dell describe your community? Or is yours one of bulldozers and skyscrapers, or yellow school buses and shopping malls?

A play of birth, life, and death, Thornton Wilder's *Our Town* won a Pulitzer Prize in 1938 and became one of the most popular plays of the century. But the title alone conjures up a certain nostalgia for our own home town.

Like people, towns possess character and personality. A lively commercial town, Ephesus derived its prestige from its role as temple-warden of the great goddess Artemis. When Christians introduced a different deity, tradesmen making their living off the goddess rose up in alarm.

How gospel-friendly is your town? Today capture your community's personality with a photo representing the values of its citizens. A snapshot of a child licking an ice cream cone may provide a portrait of your family-centered community with opportunities for church outreach.

If your town is in transition, how does this affect the ministry of your church? Perhaps a picture of a sign in a foreign language, an abandoned grocery cart in an empty lot, or a group of immigrant children in the park may symbolize your changing population. Perhaps a street jammed with pedestrians, a Joshua tree in the desert, or a silo on the horizon describes your community.

Today look at your familiar world from an angle of a camera lens and recognize unique opportunities for ministry.

October 31

Receive Children Warmly

SCRIPTURE: *Mark 10: 13 – 16*
KEY VERSE: *Jesus put his arms around the children and blessed them by placing his hands upon them.*

Up and down, up and down;
I will lead them up and down:
I am fear'd in field and town;
Goblin, lead them up and down.
Here comes one.

R ather than the goblins Puck mentions in Shakespeare's
A Midsummer Night's Dream, ours come in a mid-
autumn night's fantasy. Tonight mommies will lead many of
our little elves, fairies and goblins up and down the streets.

A Peter Pan in construction paper leaves and a small
fairy waving a foil-wrapped wand may appear at your door.
Raggedy Ann and a small hobo could visit holding out little
hands for a treat. Disguised by a fierce-looking mask, a tall
teen carrying a half-filled pillow case may ring your bell.

Because this is the night when they come to us, Hal-
loween offers a unique opportunity to relate to children.
The way we receive them says much about who we are
and how much we value them. Tonight show how much
you care by reaching out to all who come to you.

If Jesus were to open a door to cries of "Trick or treat!"
we can easily imagine a smile on his lips and twinkle in his
eyes. Find Jesus-like ways to welcome, love, and delight
children with healthy treats which do not leave them hyper
the rest of the week. If your community or church offers
trick-or-treat alternatives, volunteer to help with these safe
and chaperoned activities.

Whatever you do, tonight receive children warmly and
joyfully. Make your love the real treat.

November 1

Dried Arrangement

SCRIPTURE: *Luke 13: 18 – 19*
KEY VERSE: *It's like a mustard seed that someone planted in
a garden. It grew and became a tree, and the birds nested
in its branches.*

No shade, no shine, no butterflies, no bees,
No fruits, no flowers, no leaves, no birds—
November!

Thomas Hood may be right. Yet, God's hands are not idle. Furry cattails adorn the roadside, silky milk-weeds shimmer in the sun, and paper-like leaves cling to the beech.

Jesus talked about mustard growing in the fields. Only their branches now remain, but today gather these bits of November art. Fill a corner of the living room with a bas-ketful or create an airy centerpiece for the table. If you lack mustard, use dried grasses from the meadow or sheaves of wheat from the field.

Turn your thoughts to God's kingdom with any dried arrangement. Place a jar of acorns on a bed of leathery oak leaves. Pile sycamore and sweet gum balls, small pine cones, and eucalyptus pods in a glass bowl. Stand beech limbs in a tall vase, or balance a tumbleweed in a wooden salad bowl.

Eagerly accept the gifts November scatters through-out woods, meadows, and roadsides, then fill an empty corner of the house with graceful lines and warm col-ors. Just as eagerly, accept the gifts God scatters in your own life filling empty places with his grace and warmth.

The kingdom of heaven is like a mustard seed which grew to become a tree. Today put the dried stem of mustard, or another specimen of nature, where you often look. Re-mind yourself the seed of the kingdom grows within you.

Local History

SCRIPTURE: *Joshua 24: 25 - 28*
KEY VERSE: *Joshua told all the people, "This stone will stand as a witness for us. It has heard all the words which the Lord spoke to us. It will stand as a witness for you. You cannot deceive your God."*

> One little, two little, three little Indians,
> Four little, five little, six little Indians,
> Seven little, eight little, nine little Indians,
> Ten little Indian boys.

Who were these little Indian boys? What were their names, and what did they play, eat, and wear? Our knowledge of little Indian boys and little settler boys is often rather sketchy.

Perhaps any Israelite boy of Joshua's day could tell a stranger what the great stone under the terebinth in the sanctuary meant, or what happened at Shechem the day it was placed there. Perhaps, for several generations afterwards, Israelite boys still remembered. Gradually, they forgot, and one day the stone had no meaning. Then they forgot God as well as the stone.

Like the Israelites, we erect stones and pillars, but so soon forget why. Today become familiar with the work of God's hand in the history of your area. Learn something about the little Indian boys who once played where your children now play, the little settler boys who followed, and the ways their fathers cooperated or struggled with each other.

Discover the story behind your town's name. Perhaps, like Bethlehem, the name reveals the purpose of the first settlers. It may tell a story of the land, or reveal the nationality of its settlers.

A witness to past event, the stones, markers, and names

around us stop speaking when we no longer hear what they are saying. Today listen to one of them.

November 3

Political Platform

SCRIPTURE: *Micah 6: 8 - 16*

KEY VERSE: *God has told you what is good; and what is it that the LORD asks of you? Only to act justly, to love loyalty, to walk wisely before your God. (NEB)*

In an election campaign, we may feel more manipulated than informed. Using Micah's words as a guide, today create a platform you think he would endorse.

Practicing justice may mean adding policeman to the streets, but it may also mean offering job training programs in high schools and providing therapists for children at risk in elementary schools. Come up with your own creative solutions for protecting the innocent, but also ones for helping criminals and potential criminals with constructive coping skills.

Do you have practical ways of addressing the growing gap between the rich and the poor in our society? Would you advocate new tax laws, fund preschools for children of working mothers, or control health care costs? Or do you see other ways of righting an imbalance which existed even in Jeremiah's day?

What kind of foreign policy would promote global justice? Whatever the issues of this campaign, look at them from the perspective of the Lord who is Father to each of us.

Today list ten ways to build a healthier society which fits comfortably into a kingdom fashioned by the Lord of heaven and earth.

November 4

Coffee Break

Scripture: *Luke 5: 27 – 35*
Key verse: *They said to him, "John's disciples frequently fast and say prayers, and so do the disciples of the Pharisees. But your disciples eat and drink."*

With only three years to accomplish a divine mission, many of us would turn into work-aholics. To the chagrin of the Pharisees, Jesus took time out to leisurely eat and drink.

Today stop working long enough to take a coffee or tea break. From the booth of some little shop, sip caffeine-free apple tea, steaming Colombian coffee, or a generous cup of café au lait. Drink hot chocolate in a bakery where the fragrance of cardamom bread and Danish pastry mingles with the aroma of the beverage you hold in your hands.

Enjoy the blustery November world beyond the shop window. Watch a stray leaf fly across the street and a sparrow light in the leafless tree outside the shop. Admire the pageant of thick sweaters, bright caps, and knit scarves passing by the window. Notice bright cheeks, windblown hair, and the sprightly step of autumn shoppers.

Sip your coffee alone, listening, watching, and losing yourself in the awareness of a world bigger than your own experience. Or meet a friend and create your own world around a small table, experiencing your own laughter and making your own chatter.

On your way home, enjoy the simplicity and strength of a November day. Admire copper and pewter woods, and look up into dark clouds promising snow or rain. Take note of growing woodpiles preparing warmth for winter's cold. Watch a slate-colored river wind between hills.

Take time out to stay in touch with the world around you.

November 5

Candle Holders

SCRIPTURE: *Exodus 25: 31 - 40*
KEY VERSE: *Make a lamp stand out of pure gold. The lamp stand, its base, and its shaft, as well as the flower cups, buds, and petals must be hammered out of one piece of gold.*

> When icicles hang by the wall,
> And Dick the shepherd blows his nail,
> And Tom bears logs into the hall,
> And milk comes frozen home in the pail,...

As Shakespeare describes in *Love's Labour's Lost*, the winds now blow more fiercely each day bringing darkness with them. Heavy masses moving across the horizon turn blue skies pewter and then steel. More frequently rain hides the world behind gray drizzle or thick rolling fog, and icicles may hang by the wall. The dark season arrives.

The Israelites also had their long dark season. But one day the Lord lit their darkness, and to worship him, they forged elaborate lamp stands to hold the light in the Tabernacle containing the Tent of the Presence.

Today counter November's darkness with your own light, and prepare a fitting receptacle for it. Bring out the set of wooden candle holders stored on the top shelf of the hallway closet, polish the brass candelabra, or dust off the wrought iron one and light up your living room.

Perhaps candle holders already adorn the mantle or dining room table. Give light new importance with a new container. Replace the blue and white pair with the crystal set. Move the copper ones from the bedroom to the living room and pewter ones from the dining room to the family room. Call attention to the Light which conquers the darkest night.

Like the Israelites, honor the light in your life with a lovely receptacle.

November 6

New Soup

SCRIPTURE: *2 Samuel 17: 24 - 29*
KEY VERSE: *When David came to Mahanaim, Shobi, son of Nahash from Rabbah in Ammon, and Machir, son of Ammiel from Lo Debar, and Barzillai from Rogelim in Gilead brought supplies and food for David and his troops.*

When David and his men were on the point of exhaustion, three men arrived with provisions. David never forgot the difference those provisions made, and when he later recounted the story, he included the names of the three men. We know Shobi, Machir, and Barzillai because they took grains, soups, and meats to David at a critical time in his life.

When winds howl and ice coats the world, bowls of steaming soup and thick slices of warm bread still revive exhausted bodies and souls. Rather than coming from a grocery shelf, this kind of hearty soup comes from a slow cooking pot in the kitchen.

In past ages, that pot continually simmered on the back of the wood stove, winter and summer alike. Into it went meat trimmings, outside leaves of lettuce and cabbage, and bits of vegetables remaining from the dinner table. *Pot-au-feu* refers to this simmering pot of leftovers. Its aroma greeted all who entered cottage or castle.

Today greet those who enter your house with that rich aroma. Find a new recipe, and make a hearty soup which warms both bodies chilled by outside temperatures and spirits chilled by inner ones. Whether a thick bean or lentil soup like David ate or an Indian mulligatawny, enjoy creating it from start to finish. Chop onions and carrots, tomatoes and potatoes, and bring some of yesterday's sun into a November day.

In this season when earth takes away, add your own color, warmth and welcome to the day. Like David, perhaps the starved and weary ones around you will not forget what you have done.

November 7

Writing Exercise

SCRIPTURE: *Psalm 131*
KEY VERSE: *My soul is content as a weaned child is content in its mother's arms.*

> An epicure dining at Crewe
> Once found a large mouse in his stew.
> Said the waiter, "Don't shout
> And wave it about,
> Or the rest will be wanting one, too!"

We smile because the thought of wanting a mouse in our stew is so ridiculous. But we also smile because the unknown author of the limerick surprised us. We expected another ending to the tale.

We like to think that when we speak, people hear. But our words are seldom as surprising as those of the limerick, and they often slip by unheard. The psalmist often used unexpected images which we hear and remember. The image of a weaned child clinging to its mother is one that stays with us.

Today do a simple exercise to improve your communication skills. Write one sentence about anything, then write nine more, using different images to say the same thing. Begin with the obvious, then play with words to see what they can do:

Icicles hung from the branches of the rhododendron bushes.

The last rays of November sun colored long thin icicles.

Crystal icicles hung over an iced world.

Icicles took the pale hues of the weak sun's last rays.

Bumpy glass icicles threatened to shatter the frozen air of the twilight...

How many sentences did the psalmist write before he had the beautiful image of a weaned child? We do not know, but we know that those who play with words learn how to make them speak as well as talk.

November 8

Cooperate

SCRIPTURE: *Galatians 5: 13 - 22*
KEY VERSE: *But if you criticize and attack each other, be careful that you don't destroy each other.*

> The lion and the unicorn
> were fighting for the crown;
> The lion beat the unicorn all
> around about the town.
> Some gave them white bread,
> and some gave them brown;
> Some gave them plum cake
> and sent them out of town.

Of course, the lion and the unicorn were not the first to fight for a crown. As in this case, such fights usually leave a lot of losers and very few winners.

Even the Galatian Christians were attacking each other to the point where Paul warned them not to destroy each other. They forgot that love was the heart of the gospel.

Perhaps the lion would rather have died than see the unicorn wear the crown. The unicorn may have felt he could not bear the humiliation of seeing the crown on the head of the lion. So neither wore it, for both were chased out of town. Whether they parted ways or kept fighting until one or both were dead, we don't know.

It would please us to think that, along the way, some-

one talked to them about cooperating rather than compet-
ing. They could have shared the crown. If someone had
gone a step further and urged them to serve each other,
both could've been crowned with dignity.

Today look at some relationship which brings out the
worst in both you and the other person. With the help of
the Holy Spirit, shift your focus from competition to cooperation. Graciously hand over the crown of contention.
Then reach for another crown—the one shaped like love.

November 9

Earliest Memory

SCRIPTURE: *Genesis 42: 5 - 8*
KEY VERSE: *Even though Joseph recognized his brothers, they
didn't recognize him.*

> For the long nights you lay awake
> And watched for my unworthy sake:
> For your most comfortable hand
> That led me through the uneven land:
> For all the story books you read:
> For all the pains you comforted:
> For all you pitied, all you bore,
> In the sad and happy days of Yore...

T he touch of that loving hand stayed with Robert Louis
Stevenson long after his pain left him. Dedicating *A
Child's Garden of Verses* to his nurse, Alison Cunningham,
he describes detail after detail of her loving care. He remembered his nurse's touch the rest of his life.

Joseph also kept childhood memories. He retained the
expressions and features of his brothers so well that many
years later he immediately recognized them.

What is your earliest memory? Recording everything
we feel, see, hear, and even smell, the memory holds all the

secrets of the past. Today nudge yours and see how far back it will go. Pain may underline some memories, as it did for Joseph and Robert Louis Stevenson. We may still feel the childhood terror of a scratching sound in the night or the confusion of a new baby's arrival.

A Child's Garden of Verses opens a window into the world of the sick little boy who had to substitute imagination for activity. Our memories, whether painful, funny, or touching, open windows into a world we once knew. Today enter that world, look at the child, and better see the adult.

November 10

Save Electricity

SCRIPTURE: *Matthew 25: 1 - 13*
KEY VERSE: *The foolish bridesmaids took their lamps, but they didn't take any extra oil.*

> Blow, wind, blow; and go, mill, go,
> That the miller may grind his corn;
> That the baker may take it,
> And into rolls make it,
> And send us some hot in the morn.

For the first time in history, our society takes energy for granted. While once the miller waited for wind to run his mill, we wait for nothing. Energy is ours when we want it.

In the story Jesus told, all ten girls who went out to meet the bridegroom took their lamps, but five took extra oil and five did not. The wise ones may have known the bridegroom so well they anticipated a late arrival, while the foolish ones simply assumed all would go as planned.

Because our lamps have plenty of oil now, many of us assume the supply will last as long as we need it. Today, like the wise ones, prepare for the possibility of running out of oil.

At least once, find a way to save electricity. If you don't need a light, don't turn it on. If another load of laundry isn't necessary, don't do it. Line-dry clothes rather than toss them in the dryer. If the dishwasher isn't full, don't run it. Take a shorter shower. Turn the burner off as soon as the teakettle boils.

Jesus said the kingdom of Heaven would be like the late arrival of the bridegroom. Perhaps if we are wise enough to set aside extra oil on earth, we will also set aside extra oil for our spiritual life.

November 11

Pine Pillow

SCRIPTURE: *Isaiah 41: 17 – 20*
KEY VERSE: *I will plant cedars in the wastes, and acacia and myrtle and wild olive; the pine shall grow on the barren heath side by side with fir and box. (NEB)*

How do we detect God's presence in our midst? In one of the darkest periods of Israelite history, God gave his people a sign to reassure them of his presence. He said he would open rivers among sand dunes, turn wilderness into pools, and plant trees in the wastes. Pine would grow in the barren heath.

Our barren heath has also been covered with pine. Today look out on the pine, and see how God has kept his promise. Whatever our personal darkness, we can know he is still with us, for pine still grows in our midst.

Walk among the pine. Layers of dried needles carpet the woods, cushioning steps and releasing clean pine fragrance into the air. Before winter snows create their own cushiony cover, gather a basketful of pine scent for the house. When windows and doors close tight for a season, keep a fresh sign of God's loving care indoors.

Add gentle fragrance to the living room with a patchwork sofa pillow filled with dried pine needles. Make a needlepoint pillow cover or an eyelet one. Stuff a calico cat and set it on the trunk in the hallway. Stitch a burlap cow or plaid dog to fill with the scent of pine. Stop the seepage of cold air underneath the door with a long needle-stuffed snake.

Keep the bedroom fresh with small pine sachets tucked among underwear, hanging in the closet, or lined up on the dresser. Put fragrance into a huge rabbit or purple elephant doorstop. Throw a pine pillow on the bed.

However dark the season of the year, or the season of life, know our God has not forsaken us. The pines around us shout his presence.

November 12

Share

SCRIPTURE: *Luke 12: 32 – 34*
KEY VERSE: *Sell your material possessions, and give the money to the poor. Make yourselves wallets that don't wear out! Make a treasure for yourselves in heaven that never loses its value! In heaven thieves and moths can't get close enough to destroy your treasure.*

> This little pig went to market,
> This little pig stayed home.
> This little pig had roast beef,
> This little pig had none,
> And this little pig cried,
>   "Wee wee wee!" all the way home.

When people asked John the Baptist how to repent, he told them the man who had two shirts must share with the man who had none. Like the little pigs in the nursery rhyme, we would prefer another way to repent. We have not two, but five, ten, or twenty shirts.

Yet, John was not the only one to stress sharing. Jesus said we must invest in a heavenly kingdom rather than in earthly possessions, and he told some disciple candidates to first go sell their possessions and give the proceeds to the poor. Few of us would measure up to his requirements.

Ask yourself what you must do to realign your life to Jesus' teaching. Living in a materialistic society, glitter flashes from every direction, distracting us from any simple answers. Begin heeding Jesus' words by sharing some possession.

If you have two coats, give one away. If you have two one-quart saucepans, donate one to a family who lost everything in a fire. If you have an extra bed, offer it to a foster child. If you have roast beef, share with one who has none.

In some way, today show that you have heard Jesus' words and store your treasures in heaven.

November 13

Math Problem

SCRIPTURE: *Exodus 22: 1 - 5*
KEY VERSE: *Whenever someone lets his livestock graze in a field or a vineyard, and they stray and graze in another person's field, he must make up for what the damaged field was expected to produce.*

> Multiplication is vexation,
> Division is as bad;
> The rule of three doth puzzle me,
> And Practice drives me mad.

We don't know if ancient Jewish boys and girls shared the feelings of this sixteenth century student or not. However, math was a part of Jewish life. They may have learned their numbers by listening to their fathers count the years their Hebrew slaves had served, calculating the time remaining before setting them free in the seventh year.

The law of Moses required complicated math calculations. Accidently allowing his livestock to graze in his neighbor's field, a man had to make restitution. By using geometry, farmers in ancient Egypt accurately re-established boundaries destroyed by the flooding Nile.

In contrast, we can survive with little knowledge of mathematics. Banks figure our interest, computers total grocery purchases, and gas pumps instantly record the amount of our purchase. Small computers even balance our checkbooks. However, like ancient people, we may have more control of our own lives if we know how to make our own calculations.

Today work a multiplication or long division problem just to prove you can still do it. Give yourself a column of figures to add, or see what you can still do in an old algebra or geometry book. Rescue some ancient knowledge from the tombs of history.

November 14

Municipal Concern

SCRIPTURE: *Nehemiah 5: 1 - 13*
KEY VERSE: *Then some of the people, the men and their wives, complained publicly about their Jewish relatives.*

> It's the same the whole world over,
> It's the poor wot gets the blame,
> It's the rich wot gets the pleasure,
> Ain't it all a bloomin' shame?

T he anonymous song writer was not the first one to feel sorry for himself. Although it may produce a bit of charming doggerel, self-pity does not change our situation for the better.

Over two thousand years ago, the returned exiles had cause to feel sorry for themselves. Destitute, desperate, and powerless, they were mortgaging fields and pledging children to put food on the table. They wisely united and made their concerns known to the governor. Once Nehemiah was informed of the situation, he immediately took action.

Like Nehemiah, we are often unaware of what is happening on our very doorsteps. Or, like the anonymous song writer, perhaps we know very well, but fail to move beyond the complaining. Today attend a municipal meeting and become a better informed citizen.

Sit in on a session of the city council and listen to common people verbalize their complaints. Attend the monthly meeting of the cultural arts commission and learn more about the opportunities available in your community. Drop in on a meeting of the town library committee, and give your input about new books for the library.

Do as did the common people of Nehemiah's time. If it's a bloomin' shame, do something to change it!

November 15

New Game

SCRIPTURE: *Genesis 1: 24 – 28*
KEY VERSE: *God made every type of wild animal, every type of domestic animal, and every type of creature that crawls on the ground. God saw that they were good.*

> This old man, he played one,
> He played nick-nack on my thumb.
> With a nick-nack, paddy-wack,
>   give the dog a bone,
> This old man came rolling home.
> This old man, he played two…

The old man could have simply gone home. But he didn't. He played nick-nack on the way home.

Perhaps we love to play because God loves to play. He plays with color, shape, and sound. Does a ladybug have spots because he liked the way black spots look on a red body? Or does a zebra have stripes because he thought it was fun to make him that way? Why does a rhinoceros have a horn or an elephant a trunk?

Genesis tells us that when God created every type of wild animal, domestic animal, and creature that crawls, he looked them over and saw that they were good. The funny-faced monkey looked good to him. The pocketed kangaroo looked good and the humped camel looked good to him, too.

Today spend some time playing, and like God, play with new combinations. Retrieve a game you have not touched in years. Or buy a new one and initiate it after the supper dishes have been washed. Invite a friend to bring over a game, or join the children in their game on the living room rug. Create your own game—one as wild or bizarre as stripes on a zebra and spots on a ladybug.

It is hard to imagine a sober God fashioning a long neck on a giraffe or painting bright colors on a toucan. If our God is a God of play, when we play we are becoming more like him. Today become more God-like by becoming more playful.

November 16

Wife/Friend List

SCRIPTURE: *Ephesians 5: 21 – 33*
KEY VERSE: *Place yourselves under each other's authority out of respect for Christ.*

> She rose to his requirement, dropped
> The playthings of her life
> To take the honorable work
> Of woman and of wife.

The wife Emily Dickinson describes must have pleased her husband, for she dropped everything to give herself to him. In that generation of fixed roles for men and women, wives knew how to please their husbands for they knew what was expected of them.

But times have changed. As Jane Nelsen points out in her book *Positive Discipline*, no longer does Dad automatically obey his boss, Mom automatically obey Dad, nor the children automatically obey either Mom or Dad. We all find ourselves pioneering a new trail of equality and mutual respect.

How do we please our husbands, our children, or our colleagues when all the guidelines have vanished? Today think about qualities and traits which strengthen relationships because they are based on love and mutual respect rather than a specific code of conduct.

What is your picture of a loving wife who pleases her husband? What kind of mothering meets the needs of children and adolescents growing up in a changing society? What kind of emotional support do your friends need? Make a list of healthy ways to relate to and please the significant people in your life.

Before heading further down the trail, write out a few guidelines to make the going smoother.

November 17

Current Book

SCRIPTURE: *2 Peter 1:5 - 7*
KEY VERSE: *With all this in view, you should try your hardest to supplement your faith with virtue, virtue with knowledge. (NEB)*

Fie, foh, and fum,
I smell the blood of a British man.

Humorous words, such as these spoken by Edgar in Shakespeare's *King Lear*, often stay with us even when we have no clue to their meaning.

Working in the Asian churches, Peter had seen how often even Christians distorted the meaning of things they didn't understand. Thus he urged the Asian Christians to try their hardest to supplement their faith with virtue and their virtue with knowledge.

Even virtuous Christian stances become lopsided when based on too few sources. Today supplement your Christian virtue with knowledge by reading a current book addressing an important issue from a new angle.

Seek help for some nagging or embarrassing problem. If a loved one suffers Alzheimer's disease, a drinking problem, or has been without work for months, turn to a recent book for updated information and help. If a child cuts classes or refuses to study, balance his experience with a look at the nation's education system through the eyes of those who teach or administer.

Many of us are strong on political opinions, but short on information. Open a good biography of the president and see the political process from the inside out. Pick up John Kenneth Galbraith's latest book of political reflections and gain a longer and wider perspective of politics.

In the giant melting pot of our nation, some forces tear society apart and some work at healing it. Gain understanding of what drives destructive forces and what motivates constructive ones.

Today take a step to balance some Christian stance standing precariously on too few legs.

Pray for South America

SCRIPTURE: *Revelation 7:9 - 17*

KEY VERSE: *After these things I saw a large crowd from every nation, tribe, people, and language.*

> The Queen of Hearts, she made some tarts
> All on a summer's day.
> The Knave of Hearts, he stole those tarts
> And took them clean away.

E ach year in the United States, almost a million people without sufficient funds take so many tarts they later file bankruptcy petitions. After wiping the slate clean, they happily go off after fresh tarts. Nations, however, seldom enjoy the luxury.

Many struggling countries bought tarts on credit, but few creditors wipe the slate clean. More often lender nations offer new loans, enabling debtors to pay the interest on yesterday's tarts, even if they can not pay for the tarts themselves. Or, they give the debtor more years to pay, freeing up money to pay interest on the tarts.

Conditions attached to new loans often fail to take into account that yesterday's tarts do not satisfy today's hunger. Making debt payment a priority usually means cutting back on basic services to the bottom rung of society.

Many peasants in South America without electricity, sewage, or health care are losing patience. Many look to another revolution or coup to bring them their fresh tarts.

In John's vision, he saw a vast throng of tribes, peoples, and languages standing in front of the throne of the Lamb. Since our global neighbors here will also be our neighbors there, today begin improving relationships in your neighborhood.

Pray for Central and South American leaders who struggle to maintain good relationships with more powerful nations without sacrificing the well being of their own people. Pray for the millions of children growing up on the streets, hawking the legal and the illegal to earn a dollar. Pray that education will become a tool for justice rather than a tool for personal enrichment. Pray that the church will implement God's kingdom in the midst of a worldly kingdom.

November 19

Night Walk

SCRIPTURE: *Isaiah 40: 26 - 27*
KEY VERSE: *Look up at the sky and see. Who created these things? Who brings out the stars one by one? He calls them all by name.*

As Isaiah walked beneath a starry sky, he must have considered who created it all. Perhaps, on many of those nights, he carried his burdens with him wondering if the Lord had forgotten Israel. But the longer he looked at the heavens, the more he knew that the one who kept them also kept Israel.

Now that night falls quickly, stars may appear even before the dinner hour. Tonight go walk beneath the stars. Dressed so warmly that bitter winds can not bite the body or sting the ears, walk into the night and hold hands with it.

Walk quietly, hush troubling thoughts of today and anxious ones about tomorrow, and listen to God speak in the night. As your eyes adjust to the darkness, admire a world softened by darkness and semidarkness. If the moon is out, enjoy its fullness or its small sliver of light. Watch clouds sail past, growing light at one moment, dark at another. Watch for the bright eyes of deer or raccoons or neighborhood cats.

The night makes up half our life. Like ancient peoples, become acquainted with the night which speaks so eloquently of a loving God.

ℐpologize

SCRIPTURE: *Matthew 5: 21 - 26*
KEY VERSE: *Leave your gift at the altar. First go away and make peace with that person. Then come back and offer your gift.*

> A word is dead
> When it is said,
> Some say.
> I say it just
> Begins to live
> That day.

L ike Emily Dickinson, we have given birth to words which have lived to a ripe old age. We uttered some of the words carelessly, without taking into account the length of their life. The minute some words leave our mouth, we are sorry. But once spoken, they take root and grow.

Although we may not be able to call back unkind words, we can express regret for having said them. Perhaps some careless words have not walked off too far to add an amendment to them. Today run after them.

Most of us would rather confess our shortcomings to God than apologize to the person we have hurt. Jesus said confessing our trespasses to God does not cancel the debt. Before offering our gift on the altar, we must go make peace with the brother we have offended.

Like his assertion that anyone nursing anger against his brother must be brought to judgment, these words about making peace seem extreme. But God knows we have to make peace with an offended brother before offering our gift to Him. Once we make peace we have less reason to nurse anger or be brought to judgment.

Today make peace with someone. Say you are sorry for what you said or the way you said it. Lovingly apologize, and let the injured one know her feelings are more important than the issue which provoked your anger.

November 21

Apron

SCRIPTURE: *Psalm 145: 14 – 21*
KEY VERSE: *The eyes of all creatures look to you, and you give them their food at the proper time.*

> A was an apple-pie;
> B bit it;
> C cut it.
> But we all know who made it.
> Mother, of course!

When the psalmist pictured God graciously giving food to all creatures, perhaps he was picturing the dinner table in his mother's house. Like God, mothers not only give food when it is due, but give with an open and bountiful hand. Summer or winter, we provide what our family desires.

When God provides our food, he does it beautifully. He wraps vitamins in bright red tomatoes, small round peas, and long orange carrots. He decorates squash vines with large yellow blossoms and sends bean vines spiraling upward. He paints the fish we eat with every color of the rainbow.

As you provide for your family, today add an extra touch of beauty by wearing a pretty apron. If the psalmist's mother wore an apron, she probably wove it herself from flax. Make one for yourself from any fabric which pleases you and your family.

Add cheer to mealtime preparations with a bright orange, red, or yellow apron. Combine calico prints and solids, add ruffles, and feel feminine as you pop muffins into the oven. Give yourself the feel of a princess with a delightful eyelet ruffled apron.

Feel beautiful as you roll crust, fill it with apples, and bake the pie. Look beautiful as you serve it. When the clock strikes mealtime, reward those who lift hopeful eyes your way with beauty as well as food.

November 22

Generic Thanks

SCRIPTURE: *Psalm 103: 1 - 5*
KEY VERSE: *Praise the Lord, my soul, and never forget all the good he has done.*

> Father, we thank Thee for the night,
> And for the pleasant morning light,
> For rest and food and loving care,
> And all that makes the day so fair.

The prayers of the Pilgrims may have resembled this simple child's prayer. Half their number had died in the first year on a new continent. By our standards, they had every reason to petition rather than thank God.

But great people give thanks for simple things. The psalmist praised the Lord for his blessings of love, strength, and forgiveness. The apostle Paul gave thanks when he was hungry, cold, and persecuted. Facing a hungry multitude, Jesus gave thanks for two fish and five loaves of bread.

We may give thanks for a running car, working washing machine, and color television set, but we are the first century to be able to do so. We thank God for liberty and freedom to worship. Without either the early church experienced the overwhelming joy of knowing a living Savior.

This Thanksgiving count your own blessings as many others in all ages have had to count them. Give thanks only for blessings available to every other person in the world, regardless of economic, political, or geographical situation. Do not include your bed, for the homeless lady on the street has none. Leave out the food you eat, for the starving child in Somalia has none. Do not even include schools or hospitals, for remote villages of Africa have access to neither.

Make a list of generic blessings, and discover in it a source of power for thankful living in any situation. Like Job, discover what blessings remain when possessions, health, and success have vanished.

November 23

$\mathcal{B}$ath $\mathcal{T}$reat

SCRIPTURE: *Esther 2: 9 - 18*

KEY VERSE: *Each young woman had her turn to go to King Xerxes after she had completed the required 12-month treatment for women. The time of beauty treatment was spent as follows: six months using oil of myrrh and six months using perfumes and other treatments for women.*

C osmetics may have changed Jewish history. They may have changed more of all history than we ever dreamed.

Obviously Esther was a beautiful woman in spirit as well as looks, for she attracted the notice of Hegai, the guardian of the king's women, and received his special favor. However, in spite of her natural beauty, she was given a full twelve months of beauty treatments before she could go in to the king.

Perhaps we would all be as beautiful as Esther if we were treated six months with oil of myrrh, and another six months with perfumes and cosmetics.

Unlike Esther who had maids and cooks to prepare her banquet, our wonderful feasts arrive one peeled potato after another. The huge turkey often slips into the oven as the sun slips up over the hills, and we stay on our feet the rest of the day. Our feasts take something out of us.

Today put something back into yourself. Few of us have the luxury of a year's beauty treatments, but pamper tired muscles with a bubble bath. Add a sachet of borax or flower petals and peppermint. Pour perfumed bath oils into the water and be queen for an hour. Feel tension ease and then disappear. Feel yourself becoming softer, prettier, more poised.

Pat yourself dry, then pamper your body with perfume, sweet smelling lotion, or scented powder. Like Esther, enjoy having a woman's body.

November 24

Crossword Puzzle

SCRIPTURE: *Romans 12: 6 - 8*
KEY VERSE: *God in his kindness gave each of us different gifts.*

> If all the world were paper,
> And all the sea were ink,
> And all the trees were bread and cheese,
> What should we do for drink?

Or what would we wear? And how would we build our houses? And, without a pen, how would we write? We can clearly see it wouldn't work.

But then, neither does it work to fit every person into the same mold. We need each other, and we need each other's gifts. Just as words only have value in the context of language, our gifts only have value in the context of others. As language fits words together into meaningful patterns, God fits each of us, and each of our gifts, into a pattern of his choosing.

Today fit words together in a crossword puzzle, and remind yourself that our value lies in our connection to others. Work today's puzzle in the newspaper, noting how useless a word is until it intersects with another. Or make your own puzzle, choosing words because of their connecting-potential and rejecting ones that fail to interconnect.

352

Give your puzzle a context by working a family history or family tree into it. Make a puzzle with biblical names or the names of people attending your church. Review your travels by choosing key words from family trips.

Notice the incompleteness of blank spaces. Remind yourself that God has given us each gifts to fill in some blank, and when we fail to use them we leave his puzzle incomplete. No one else's gift matches our space, and we can not fill in the blank meant for another person.

Today fit words together until all the blanks are filled, then grant each person you meet a place in God's great plan.

November 25

Jump Rope

SCRIPTURE: *1 Corinthians 6: 19 – 20*
KEY VERSE: *You were bought with a price. So bring glory to God in the way you use your body.*

> Then it's hop, hip, hop,
>   with our tinkle and our winkle,
> And it's flop, flip, flop, with our ding dong ding!
> With our ringing and our dinging,
> And our muffy-cruffy flinging,
> Down the road we'll go a-swinging,
>   with our ting-a-ling ling.

Don't we wish! But few of us are in shape for such wonderful hopping, swinging and flopping—especially in this feasting season of the year.

When Thanksgiving and Christmas arrive, we pour out our best efforts in the kitchen and then saturate ourselves with rich and sumptuous foods. In addition to feast days, all winter we stave off cold with hot biscuits and muffins, mashed potatoes and gravy, hot cereals and brown sugar. Eating cheers the great dark season of our lives.

Jesus also feasted, attended parties, and celebrated Jewish festivals. Once he made food a priority for a hungry crowd. But he walked to the wedding feast, and he returned on foot. As a boy he walked from Nazareth to Jerusalem to attend the great Passover Festival. He was walking from Judaea to Galilee when he rested by the well in Sychar.

Unlike Jesus, most of us do not follow feasting with vigorous exercise. We ride rather than walk, and we often follow feasting with reading, knitting, and watching snow flakes fill the sky. Our feasts usually leave pounds on our bodies and cholesterol in our arteries.

Today attack some of the pounds and cholesterol with a jumping rope. Jump ten, twenty, or a hundred times, whatever increases stamina without overexerting heart and muscles.

Jesus knew he had a purpose to fulfill. God has given each of us a purpose too. Use your jump rope to put your body in better shape so you can fulfill the one He has for you.

November 26

Clothing Labels

SCRIPTURE: *Acts 10:34 - 48*
KEY VERSE: *All the believers who were circumcised and who had come with Peter were amazed that the gift of the Holy Spirit had been poured on people who were not Jewish.*

Thinking of the Lord as their God and the Messiah as their Savior, Jewish Christians did not expect the Lord to pour out his Holy Spirit on Gentiles. But God vividly demonstrated to Peter and the other Jewish Christians that his Spirit transcends all national boundaries.

Today emulate the Holy Spirit who thinks in global terms, and do a simple exercise to get more in touch with the world. Examine your clothing labels and make a list of every nation which has contributed to your wardrobe.

The blouse you are wearing may have been made in Sri Lanka, the sweater in Romania, the pants in Guatemala, the shoes in Korea, the socks in Hong Kong, and the underwear in Bangladesh.

Locate the countries on a map, and with the help of an almanac or encyclopedia, put each in a context. Uncover some fact which will put a face to a place on the map.

Picture these unknown men, women, and children who have cut, stitched, and packaged for you. Study their faces bent over their work, feel their hunger at midday, and ache with their tired bodies at the end of the day. Pray that God's Spirit will be poured out on each one.

Review your connections. Touching Romania on the map, remind yourself that a woman there knitted a sweater for you. Putting your finger on Italy, imagine the man who stitched the leather in your boots. Looking at Bangladesh, recall that the head of a household earned a few cents sewing together the pieces of your pants.

Then speak the words, "These are my Father's children."

November 27

Keep the Sabbath Holy

SCRIPTURE: *Nehemiah 13: 15 - 22*
KEY VERSE: *In those days I saw people in Judah stomping grapes in the winepresses on the day of worship. I saw them bringing in loads of wine, grapes, figs, and every other kind of load. They piled the loads on donkeys and brought them into Jerusalem on the day of worship. I warned them about selling food on that day.*

> Row, row, row your boat
> Gently down the stream.
> Merrily, merrily, merrily, merrily
> Life is but a dream.

L ife may seem a dream as we row gently down the stream, but it's only a Sunday illusion. Monday through Friday, we're back in the real world. Saturday we're caught up in preparations for Sunday's outing.

Then comes the question: Do we skip church? If the "stream" is a few hours away, we won't have any time left if we wait until after the service.

Even when we want to keep the Sabbath Day holy, we are no longer sure how to do it. Once the church handed out rules. Everyone knew what was an acceptable Sabbath activity and what was not. Each generation relaxed the rules a little, until even the last one, church attendance, has disappeared.

Perhaps keeping the Sabbath Day holy has never been easy. To people buying and selling on the Sabbath, Nehemiah said they were profaning it, following in the same pattern as their fathers. Ordering the gates of Jerusalem closed from the beginning of the Sabbath until its end, he put a stop to the commerce.

How do we keep the Sabbath holy when all guidelines have vanished? Today creatively think through God's purpose in instituting the Sabbath and what activities legitimately contribute to that purpose. Spend one Sunday trying to realign yourself to his purpose. Keep one Sabbath holy.

November 28

Conversation Preparation

SCRIPTURE: *Proverbs 18: 1 - 8*
KEY VERSE: *A fool does not find joy in understanding but only in expressing his own opinion.*

MOTH: They have been at a great feast of languages and stolen the scraps.
COSTARD: O! they have lived long on the almsbasket of words!

With these words in Shakespeare's *Love's Labour's Lost*, Moth and Costard poke fun at the verbose Sir Nathaniel and Holofernes. The writer of Proverbs must have also known men and women who had lived long on the alms basket of words. Interested only in expressing their own opinions, they had no time to listen to what others had to say. Solomon described them as fools who found no joy in understanding.

Some of us talk for the love of talking. Having nothing to say, we nevertheless rattle on, unaware that others have stopped listening. But not Paul. He commanded King Agrippa's attention with a matter of crucial importance which concerned the king.

Few of us will rub shoulders with King Agrippas, but in the coming holiday season, most of us will converse with others in our role as either a hostess or a guest. Today prepare for some of those conversations. Think of ways to draw out the gifts and experiences of others.

We come alive when talking about subjects we love, and every person we meet this holiday season has some love waiting to be shared. A couple who just returned from a mission trip to Haiti may be hoping someone will ask about it. A college freshman may be eager to describe dorm life, and an eighty-year-old just as ready to tell about her latest ski trip.

When asked why we moved to the area or why we chose our profession, school, or church, most of us respond positively. Today give thought to ways you can get better acquainted with others, and make a list of helpful questions. This holiday season find more joy in gaining understanding than in expressing your own opinions.

November 29

Fruit Treat

SCRIPTURE: *Song of Songs 2: 3 – 6*
KEY VERSE: *Strengthen me with raisins, and refresh me with apples because I am weak from love.*

> Christmas is coming,
> The goose is getting fat,
> Please put a penny
> In the old man's hat.

The goose is not the only one getting fat in November and December, for he is accompanied by plum pudding and pecan pie, divinity and nut-studded fudge, pie á la mode and double chocolate brownies. Even before the goose has finished waddling in his pen, we have begun waddling to the closet for a larger-size something to relieve the uncomfortable snugness in our middle.

Today creatively provide holiday treats which satisfy a sweet tooth without increasing a cushiony layer of fat. Like the bridegroom in Song of Songs, tempt tastebuds with fruit treats rather than starchy ones.

Replace artificial flowers on the coffee table with a big bowl of fresh fruit. Stock the refrigerator with bananas, apples, and oranges, and keep a dish of them on the kitchen counter for hungry people who collect there. Add a thoughtful touch to the guest room with a bowl of bright red apples.

Create nibbling delights with dried fruit and nuts. For dessert, serve baked apples stuffed with nuts and raisins. Top off a rich meal with slices of kiwi fruit, fruit compote, or ambrosia.

While the goose is getting fat, creatively find ways to keep the mistress healthy and trim.

November 30

Door Wreath

SCRIPTURE: *Isaiah 9: 2 - 7*
KEY VERSE: *The people who walk in darkness will see a bright light. The light will shine on those who live in the land of death's shadow.*

> The holly and the ivy
> When they are both full grown,
> Of all the trees that are in the wood,
> The holly bears the crown:
> The rising of the sun
> And the running of the deer,
> The playing of the merry organ,
> Sweet singing in the choir.

Ancient Egyptians bestowed honor with garlands of flowers, leaves, and foliage. The Greeks honored athletes with garlands, and the Romans used them to venerate their officials and warriors. Christians chose evergreen wreaths to symbolize everlasting life.

With its green leaves and red berries, Northern Europeans turned the holly wreath into an expression of both faith and joy. Entering the season of unparalleled joy and celebration, today announce your joy to the world by adorning your front door with a wreath.

Proclaim joy with the red and green holly, or express everlasting life with another evergreen. Or choose to express your joy creatively rather than traditionally. Make a wreath with dried herbs from your summer garden or pine cones and acorns collected from your driveway. Treat birds to a tasty wreath, or delight visitors with the fragrance of a bay leaf or cinnamon stick wreath.

Joy to the world, the Lord has come! Today post the news on your front door.

December 1

Advent Wreath

SCRIPTURE: *John 1: 1 – 5*
KEY VERSE: *The light shines in the dark, and the dark has never extinguished it.*

> Deck the halls with boughs of holly,
> Fa-la-la, la-la, la-la, la-la,
> 'Tis the season to be jolly,
> Fa-la-la, la-la, la-la, la-la.

As we enter Advent, begin decking the halls and singing the fa-la-las. For more than fifteen hundred years, Christians have used these weeks before Christmas to prepare themselves to receive the Christ Child. This year, with millions of others around the world, prepare your own heart.

Bend holly to the shape of an advent wreath, then insert four candles in the greens and a fifth one in the middle. Or make your wreath pine, fir, or hemlock. Give it an honored place on the table or mantle, or like many European Christians, hang it from the ceiling.

Beginning the fourth Sunday before Christmas, each evening light the candles for a few moments as you meditate and pray. Light one candle the first week, then light another candle each succeeding week, symbolically increasing the light as you approach the manger. Bring the light to its climax on Christmas Eve by lighting the Christ candle in the wreath's center.

Darkness frightens. But Good News has come. Christ is the Light shining in the dark, and no amount of darkness  can ever extinguish it. Celebrate! Deck the halls. Sing hallelujah and fa-la-la. Light candles. However dark the world, let the light shine!

December 2

Christmas Card

SCRIPTURE: *Isaiah 11: 2 - 5*
KEY VERSE: *The spirit of the Lord will rest on him.*

> Jingle bells, jingle bells,
> Jingle all the way;
> Oh, what fun it is to ride
> In a one-horse open sleigh!

Have you ever ridden in a one-horse open sleigh, and heard bells jingling all the way? Not many of us have. But we love the image. Along with Santas, reindeer, and snowmen in the malls, "Jingle Bells" opens the doors of the holidays, and inside we glimpse fun, presents, and good will.

Rather than jingling, heaven's bells must have rung joyfully the night the angels sang. No sleigh carried this heavenly host to earth. They came on the wings of divine love, and they announced the greatest cosmic event of all time. The Creator entered his universe in human form bringing the news we yearned to hear: He loves us! He loves all of us!

Why not sing Jingle Bells? Why not celebrate with fun and laughter? Hundreds of years before the Messiah appeared, Isaiah heard the faint sound of bells pealing across the centuries. He detected the presence of the Divine in their message, and he heard the sounds of laughter and joy.

Today put the lighthearted joy of Jingle Bells in perspective. Design a Christmas card which points to the cosmic event demanding both worship and rejoicing. Sketch, paste, or pen words, but share the Good News. The Lord of Lords, the King of Kings, the one who holds us in his hand also tenderly cradles us.

He loves us! He loves all of us!

December 3

Doll Dress

SCRIPTURE: *Isaiah 11: 6 - 9*
KEY VERSE: *And little children will lead them.*

> What child is this who, laid to rest,
> On Mary's lap is sleeping?...
> This, this is Christ the King,
> Whom shepherds guard and angels sing;
> Haste, haste to bring him laud,
> The babe, the son of Mary.

So much fuss over a child! But the birth of a child caused angels to leave heaven, wise men to leave their country, and shepherds to leave their fields. God has given children the highest place in the kingdom, and to approach a child is to approach the heart of God.

At the beginning of this advent season, bring the Christ Child closer by focusing on a child in your midst. Make something to help occupy little fingers which find Christmas a long wait.

Turn a scrap of cloth into a little doll dress, add a ruffle, a bit of lace, and a small bow, and give it to a little girl in your life. Perhaps she lives next door and loves dressing and undressing dolls. In this season of the Child, encourage her to lovingly attend the little child she so vividly sees in her dolly, and tell her about the precious child who once lay in a manger.

The little girl may be your daughter. If so, look on as she dresses her doll, and behold in her bright eyes the eyes of the Child of Nazareth. Tell her about that child and the night he was born. Cuddle her and hear angels singing.

On behalf of the Father of all children, turn a scrap of cloth into a blessing for one child. Then lead her to the edge of the manger as you encourage her tender love for her own dolly.

December 4

Pray for a Loved One

SCRIPTURE: *Luke 1: 5 - 17*
KEY VERSE: *The angel said to him, "Don't be afraid, Zecha-riah! God has heard your prayer. Your wife Elizabeth will have a son, and you will name him John.*

> Once in royal David's city
> Stood a lowly cattle shed
> Where a mother laid her baby
> In a manger for his bed...

After David built the royal city, his descendants waited a thousand years for the Messiah. After the Babylonian exile, they waited six hundred years. By the time He arrived, ten of Israel's original twelve tribes had disappeared, already assimilated into foreign cultures. By our calculations, the Messiah came too late. But God's time table is not our time table, nor are his ways our ways.

The story of the first Advent begins with a barren woman. Well advanced in years, Elizabeth and her husband Zechariah continued praying for a child even when they knew they were too old to have one. Why? Perhaps in their hearts they knew it was never too late for God.

Today think of concerns which have been breaking your heart for years. After so much praying without any apparent results, petitions easily deteriorate into empty habits rather than living hopes. The Christ-message is that it is never too late for God. No clock or calendar limits him. As he works out his purposes in human history, he holds eternity in his hands.

Once again, put a seemingly hopeless situation in God's hands. Lift up to him the child who has not yet experienced the saving power of Christ. Intercede for the alcoholic husband. Plead for the bitter friend, the depressed parent. Pray for the deepest grief of your heart.

In this season of gifts, give the best gift of all to a loved one—the prayer of faith in a God who never stops his work of redemption.

December 5

Christmas Literature

SCRIPTURE: *Luke 1: 18 - 25*
KEY VERSE: *The Lord has done this for me now. He has removed my public disgrace.*

> Infant holy, infant lowly,
> For his bed a cattle stall;
> Oxen lowing, little knowing,
> Christ the babe is Lord of all.

M any of us grew up on fairy tales. A fairy godmother turns Cinderella into a beautiful princess. A prince kisses the sleeping Snow White and she awakes to live happily ever after in his castle. Beast turns into a prince when Beauty falls in love with him.

We yearn for a magic touch to turn us into a princess and our misery into happiness ever after. The Christmas story makes our dreams come true. The mighty Lord of the universe comes not to a palace, but to a lowly manger. He sent his messenger not to the halls of the great, but to an elderly, barren woman. The heavenly host sang not to royalty, but to shepherds in the fields. The fairy tale of fairy tales became reality. The ruler of the universe came to live with the little ones of the world.

Christmas literature like *A Christmas Carol* reflects this fairy tale element. In Dickens' story, the love of the impoverished Cratchets defeats the ill will of the powerful and wealthy Scrooge. Today read this or another Christmas story identifying the fairy-tale-come-true element. Or re-read a fairy tale, and see how closely the manger fits our deepest longings.

The Lord of the universe who came to live among the little people still keeps them close to his heart. This advent season, lift your head, relax your face. Your prince has come. You are the princess of your dreams.

December 6

St. Nicholas Day

SCRIPTURE: *Luke 1: 57 – 66*
KEY VERSE: *When the time came for Elizabeth to have her child, she gave birth to a son.*

Jolly Old Saint Nicholas, lean your ear this way,
Don't you tell a single soul what I'm going to say.
Christmas time is coming soon,
   now you dear old man,
Whisper what you'll bring to me, tell me if you can.

A child had been born! Elizabeth's child! Zechariah's child! All Elizabeth's mothering instincts now swelled up in her breast, and going about his priestly duties, Zechariah's face kept erupting in a smile. He was finally a father, and father to the child who would prepare the world for the Messiah.

According to tradition, St. Nicholas, a fourth century bishop, prepared children for the gift of the Christ Child by visiting them with his own gifts and admonitions. Centuries later, children still receive their gifts in his name, for our Santa Claus comes from Sinter Klaas, the Dutch word for St. Nicholas. In some European countries, children receive their presents on St. Nicholas Day, December 6, leaving Christmas free to focus on the Christ Child.

Imitate the bishop of long ago. Instead of giving some child on your list a present on Christmas morning or Christmas Eve, give it today. Then make it a step to the manger by telling the child the story of the best gift of all.

Christmas time is coming soon ...
now you dear old man...
Whisper what you'll bring to me, tell me if you can.

You don't have to whisper. Tell it lovingly: "The gift of love, little one. The gift of the Christ Child."

December 7

Hostess Ideas

Scripture: *Isaiah 40: 3 - 11*
Key verse: *A voice cries out in the desert: "Clear a way for the Lord. Make a straight highway in the wilderness for our God.*

> O come, O come, Emmanuel,
> and ransom captive Israel
> that mourns in lonely exile here
> until the Son of God appear.

For hundreds of years, God urged his people to get ready for the Messiah. Then he came. The Son of God appeared! However, many were still not ready. Sweeping, cleaning the house, and cooking, they failed to notice the presence of the Divine in their midst.

We go all out to celebrate the birth of the Messiah, gathering family and friends around us for the day, or sometimes for the season. We run from mall to mall in search of the perfect gift, and sparing no effort, we turn the house into a holiday delight. Christmas Day finds us in the kitchen preparing for a wonderful feast, or in the bathroom, making sure guest towels are out and the sink is clean.

We prepare in every way we can, but often the more we prepare, the more tired and stressed we feel when the day of celebration arrives. Aching feet sometimes claim more attention than the Christ Child.

Today come up with hostess ideas which encourage fun and minimize stress. Plan several simple meals to balance the time load of elaborate ones. Make a list of outings and activities guests can do on their own. Look for tasteful, but simple, ways to give a holiday feel to the house. Think ahead, and list everything you can do in advance.

We wait, we anticipate, and then the event arrives. This year clear a way for the Lord. Sweep away some of the stress blocking the view.

December 8

Helping Hand

SCRIPTURE: *Luke 1: 67 - 79*
KEY VERSE: *You, child, will be called a prophet of the Most High. You will go ahead of the Lord to prepare his way.*

> O Morning Star, how fair and bright
> Thou beamest forth in truth and light,
> O Sovereign meek and lowly!
> Thou Root of Jesse, David's Son,
>   my Lord and Master,
> Thou has won my heart to serve thee solely!

The infant had the look of a little Zechariah, but to everyone's amazement, his father shook his head. This child was no ordinary child; this child had been born for a purpose. He would be called John.

As he made the announcement, the Holy Spirit came upon Zechariah, filling him with prophetic words. God, in his tender compassion, would send the Morning Star from heaven to rise upon his people, to shine on those who lived in darkness, and to guide their feet into the way of peace. And Zechariah's son would be the Lord's forerunner pointing people in the direction of the light.

The Morning Star has risen! We know, for our lives

catch the reflection. Today give others a glimpse of it.

Putting your own agenda in second place, reach out to someone else. Hold a baby for a harried mother trying to manage both baby and purchases at the cash register. Baby-sit for a young mother so she can go shopping. Help the child who begs you for help. Read three books to the cranky child under your feet. Give someone a ride. Listen to a long drawn out story.

The light has dawned. Today walk in it. Prepare to receive the Christ Child by acting more Christ-like.

December 9

Kitchen Gift

SCRIPTURE: *Isaiah 25: 6 – 9*
KEY VERSE: *On this mountain the Lord of Hosts will prepare a banquet of rich fare for all the peoples. (NEB)*

> Good tidings we bring to you and your kin
> Good tidings of Christmas and a happy new year.
> Oh, bring us some figgy pudding,
> Oh, bring us some figgy pudding,
> Oh, bring us some figgy pudding,
> And bring it right here.

With an extravagance of love, the Lord has prepared a banquet of rich fare for all the peoples. No one is left out, whoever they are and wherever they are, for this is a banquet for all the nations and all the earth.

Today help the Lord distribute the food of that banquet. As a symbol of his rich fare and unlimited generosity, give a gift from your kitchen to someone who is not on your Christmas list.

Make a figgy pudding for the school custodian and take it right to him. Give the church secretary a jar of your mango chutney. Surprise a clerk at the corner store with a batch of peanut butter cookies. Let the family next door know you are making so much pizza you'll send some over tonight. Double your Swedish tea ring recipe and give one to a shut-in. Make enough cookies, muffins, or whatever to share with anyone who comes to the door today.

If the day is definitely too rushed to bake, share the strawberry jam or bread-and-butter pickles you made last summer. Spoon some of your instant spiced tea mix in a small jar, wrap a ribbon around it, and send it home with one of the children playing in your yard. Whip up eggnog for an invalid.

Today imitate God's generosity as you stand before the manger.

December 10
Photo Agenda Book
SCRIPTURE: *Isaiah 42: 6 - 7*
KEY VERSE: *You will give sight to the blind, bring prisoners out of prisons, and bring those who live in darkness out of dungeons.*

> Love shall be our token;
> love be yours and love be mine;
> love to God and all men,
> love for plea and gift and sign.

Christina Rossetti's words in "Love Came Down at Christmas" describe the path to the manger. It will not be empty, nor will it be easy. The going will often be slow because those ahead of us are going so slowly. Sometimes they block the path. If we try to rush past them or squeeze in between them, we find ourselves falling off the path.

Isaiah describes this band of pilgrims. They can not see and must find their way by groping. They are captives from the prisons, and the chains on their feet impede progress. They speak unknown languages, so we may become frustrated in our attempt to communicate. By the time we arrive at the manger, we will find ourselves in the company of a great crowd of humanity.

Today internalize God's deep affection for the part of creation he made in his image. Using photos collected over the years and a blank sketch book, make an agenda book. Draw a month by month calendar on the first twelve double pages, and use the next fifty-two double pages for a week by week calendar. Glue or tape a photo to one side of each double page.

In the faces of family and friends, see people on the way to the manger. Each week remind yourself that the manger has meaning only when translated into love for those who share the path.

December 11

Downscale

SCRIPTURE: *Isaiah 58: 6 - 8*
KEY VERSE: *Share your food with the hungry, take the poor and homeless into your house, and cover them with clothes when you see them naked. . . . help your relatives.*

> Flocks were sleeping,
> Shepherd keeping vigil 'til the morning new
> Saw the glory, heard the story,
> Tidings of a gospel new.

N ewspaper editors paused, sextons stood near their bells, and a commonwealth waited excitedly as Queen Elizabeth went into labor. News of the birth of the crown prince set off the bells, typesets, and tongues of a nation.

In contrast, as described in "Infant Lowly," the King of the Universe, Lord Almighty only announced the birth of his son to a band of shepherds watching their flock by night.

The event of God coming to be among us was heaven's great downscaling.

Thailand displays the ornate cradle of its crown prince in a glassed room of the royal museum in Bangkok. God chose a makeshift manger filled with straw to cradle his son. The one who was in the beginning with God, and through whom all things came to be, left behind the power to create worlds. He took on the body of a helpless infant placed in the hands of a young girl and her carpenter husband.

The birth of a Messiah in a stall illustrated God's priorities. Unlike God, most of us upscale rather than downscale at Christmas. Today imitate God and find some way to downscale. Send the money saved to an orphanage in Mexico, give it to a struggling seminary student, or invest it in a long distance phone call to a forgotten one far away.

Celebrate the birth of the Messiah by celebrating his priorities.

December 12

Shut-In

SCRIPTURE: *Isaiah 58: 9 - 12*

KEY VERSE: *If you give some of your own food to feed those who are hungry and to satisfy the needs of those who are humble, then your light will rise in the dark...*

> Hail the heaven-born Prince of Peace!
> Hail the Sun of righteousness!
> Light and life to all he brings,
> Risen with healing in his wings.

Darkness reaches towards its apex, leaving so few hours of light to accomplish so much. But with a flick of the switch, light shines on our dark hours, and we continue working. We light our candles, and turn the tree lights on. For what is a holiday without the glow of soft lights? After the holidays, the lights go away and the glow disappears.

Charles Wesley dwelt in another light, one which needs no flick of the switch to bring light and life to all. He called it the Sun of Righteousness.

Long before Charles Wesley wrote his song, Isaiah told Jewish people how to find the light which would one day be concentrated in a manger. If they would satisfy the needs of the humble and feed the hungry from their own plenty, then their light would rise like dawn out of darkness.

Today follow Isaiah to the manger, and find the Light still shining twenty centuries after it appeared. The humble still dwell among us. Some walk next to us and work beside us, and some sit all day behind the windows of their apartments. Visit one of these shut-ins in the community.

If her eyes no longer make out the print on paper, read the Christmas story aloud. Or leave a Christmas cassette with her. If her arthritic hands can no longer hold a pencil, address and stamp her Christmas cards.

Carry light to one living in darkness, and watch light rise out of some dark spot in your own life.

December 13

Celebrate the Light

Scripture: *Isaiah 49: 5 – 6*
Key verse: *I have also made you a light for the nations so that you would save people all over the world.*

> O little town of Bethlehem,
>   how still we see thee lie;
> Above thy deep and dreamless sleep
>   the silent stars go by.
> Yet in thy dark streets shineth
>   the everlasting light;
> The hopes and fears of all the years
>   are met in thee tonight.

On lawns, in parks, and in the malls, stars top nativity scenes. Neither the stable nor the town of Bethlehem could contain the light which shone that night. Long before it came, Isaiah prophesied that it would shine on all nations of the world. In this advent season, the celebration of the Light takes place in almost every tongue and land.

In Scandinavian countries where darkness reigns much of the winter, light takes on added significance. Commemorating a woman who cared for the poor in Scandinavia and parts of Europe, many families celebrate the Light on December thirteenth, Santa Lucia Day. On this almost darkest morning of the year, the youngest daughter, dressed in white and wearing a halo of candles, walks to her parents' bedroom and serves them breakfast by candlelight.

As a reminder that the Everlasting Light shines on all nations, today observe this Scandinavian custom of Santa Lucia Day. Make a wreath of candles on a Styrofoam™ base, and let your daughter serve a special Christmas bread at breakfast, afternoon tea, or after evening devotions. If a church in your community celebrates Santa Lucia Day, attend the special service.

Or simply light several candles, and pause to let the Light overcome some of your own darkness.

December 14

Prison Ministry

SCRIPTURE: *Isaiah 61: 1 - 2*
KEY VERSE: *He has sent me to heal those who are broken-hearted, to announce that captives will be set free and prisoners will be released.*

> Silent night, holy night,
> Son of God, love's pure light
> Radiant beams from thy holy face
> With the dawn of redeeming grace...

R edeeming grace! Of all peoples, who longs for such news more than the prisoner?

The Messiah whom Isaiah foretold would bind up the brokenhearted, proclaim liberty to the captive, and proclaim release to those in prison. When he came five hundred years later, the Messiah used Isaiah's words to describe his mission.

Why prisoners? Are they any more important to God than the rest of us? They seem to be, for Jesus said that when he comes in his glory, he will separate the sheep from the goats according to whether or not they visited him in prison.

Perhaps we should not be surprised, for the Christmas story leaves us asking, "Why a manger? Why shepherds on a hillside? Why a young country girl?

Return to the manger with Isaiah. Reach out to one of the incarcerated swelling jails and prisons. Even if we do not personally know a prisoner, many of us have secondhand knowledge of one. If we lack even that, pastors can put us in touch with one.

Send a Christmas card or write a letter to a known or unknown prisoner. Collect a group to go caroling in a prison. Drop off a gift, instructing the prison warden to give it to a forgotten, depressed, or lonely inmate.

Today hold out a ray of the Light of redeeming grace.

December 15

Forgotten One

SCRIPTURE: *Isaiah 49: 14 – 15*

KEY VERSE: *Can a woman forget her nursing child? Will she have no compassion on the child from her womb? Although mothers may forget, I will not forget you.*

Be near me, Lord Jesus, I ask thee to stay
Close by me forever, and love me, I pray;
Bless all the dear children in thy tender care,
And fit us for heaven to live with thee there.

M any years ago a psychiatrist wrote a book entitled *A Few Buttons Missing*. That could describe many of us. And even if a few of us do have the full quota of buttons, they don't always match.

But the Christ came with good news! We don't have to have all our buttons to enter the kingdom. There are not even any minimum requirement of buttons. On the contrary, God often puts the ones with the fewest buttons first in line.

As expressed in "Away in a Manger," we long for the Lord Jesus to love us and stay close by us forever. But sometimes, we cross our fingers behind our back. Looking into the faces of some who have lost most of their buttons, we wonder if he has forgotten some of his creation. They look forgotten, and they act forgotten.

Isaiah says we can uncross our fingers. Even when we forget, and even when they forget, God does not forget!

Today visit one of the seemingly forgotten people in your community, and let your presence announce the good news that she is not forgotten. Whether she lives at home or resides in an institution, whether most of her buttons are missing or most of them are still there, affirm her worth by taking time to be with her. Perhaps take a child with you, for often children open doors closed to adults.

Go and chat. Laugh. Tease. Or just listen. Along with the Christ Child who got there before you, be present. As you leave, look down. You may discover one of your own missing buttons back in place.

December 16

Welcome the Nations

Scripture: *Isaiah 60: 1 - 3*
Key verse: *Nations will come to your light, and kings will come to the brightness of your dawn.*

> Thru long ages of the past,
>> prophets have foretold his coming;
> thru long ages of the past,
>> now the time has come at last!
> Jesus, Lord of all the world,
>> coming as a child among us,
> Jesus, Lord of all the world,
>> grant to us thy heavenly peace.

As far as we know, the Babylonians did not await the coming of a Messiah. Nor did the Romans or the Egyptians. Only the Jewish people looked and waited for him.

But when the Christ came, he came for all people. Isaiah knew it would happen that way. Centuries before the Messiah came, he saw nations marching towards the Light. The night the infant lay in a manger, a star appeared over where he lay, and the journey of nations began.

Only shepherds from the hillside and foreigners from the East bowed down before the new born King. The shepherds symbolized God's concern for the little ones, and the wise men's visit underlined the message that Israel's light was to shine on the nations.

While we cannot all carry the light to the nations, we can all receive their refugees. Like the holy family who fled in haste to Egypt, many are undocumented aliens brought our way by God.

Today hold your light high. On the street and in the malls, greet foreigners with a warm smile. Offer assistance. Invite an alien in for tea or take her a batch of cookies. Host a foreign student for the holidays. Today welcome the nations to the light.

December 17

Shopping

SCRIPTURE: *Micah 5: 1 – 4*
KEY VERSE: *You, Bethlehem Ephrathah, are too small to be included among Judah's cities. Yet, from you Israel's future ruler will come for me. His origins go back to the distant past, to days long ago.*

> In the bleak mid-winter, frosty wind made moan,
> Earth stood hard as iron, water like a stone;
> Snow had fallen, snow on snow,
> In the bleak mid-winter, long ago.

C hristina Rossetti wrote about Palestine's bleak mid-winter, but few of us know much about that middle-eastern climate. However, we know our own. Frosty winds, snow, and ice rush us from the car into the mall. In spite of ever-present images of jolly St. Nicholas and the sounds of Rudolph the Red-nosed Reindeer, malls are not always jolly. Crowds, crying children, and rude people wear on our nerves. Many times we climb back into the car with a throbbing head.

The crowded streets of Bethlehem must have held many throbbing heads that bleak mid-winter night. Along with Mary and Joseph, others trudged the streets seeking accommodations, and many must have lost patience and goodwill as innkeeper after innkeeper turned them away.

Making her own way through the crowd, every few minutes Mary must have stiffened with pain, then relaxed, and perhaps smiled at one who had noticed. The crowd had no way of knowing who the child within her was, but she knew. Between pains, the knowledge must have caused her to sit taller on her donkey and even smile to herself.

Like Mary in the crowded streets of Bethlehem, to-day do what you must do with dignity. Give a sympathetic smile to a frustrated, rude shopper. Step out of the way for a disheveled woman pushing ahead of you. Speak gently to a whining baby. Be patient with a fumbling clerk.

God still makes his appearance on crowded streets. Many in the crowds do not know who the child in the manger was, but you know. Walk taller and speak more softly.

December 18

Open House

SCRIPTURE: *Luke 1: 26 - 38*
KEY VERSE: *The angel went to a virgin promised in marriage to a descendant of David named Joseph. The virgin's name was Mary.*

> News, news! Jesus Christ was born to save!
> Calls you one and calls you all
> To gain his everlasting hall.
> Christ was born to save, Christ was born to save!

Call them now! Tell your neighbors and friends your house will be open today, and you would be delighted if they took a fifteen minute break from their full schedules.

Like fourteenth century Christians who sang the carol, "Good Christian Friends, Rejoice," it is our turn to rejoice. It's time to spread the news! Jesus Christ was born to save!

For a thousand years, prophet and priest kept alive the tradition of a Messiah before Gabriel appeared to Mary. But now the time had come, and an angel carried the news. He told a young girl she was to give birth to the Christ Child.

A thousand years of waiting! A thousand years of yearning for a Savior lay behind the incarnation. Then suddenly the power of the Holy Spirit overcame the young girl, and God himself was in our midst. He came to save the people, one and all. What news for every race, tongue, and nation!

Invite friends to rejoice with you. Light candles, play soft Christmas music, and bring out holiday treats. Serve eggnog or punch, or make it coffee or tea. Reward those who come with snickerdoodles or Russian tea cakes, brownies or peanut butter cookies. Put out the fudge. Put out anything. Put out everything.

Rejoice, for it's time to celebrate. Great news has come to all the people!

December 19

Express Wonder

SCRIPTURE: *Matthew 1: 18 - 25*
KEY VERSE: *She will give birth to a son; and you will name him Jesus (He Saves), because he will save his people from their sins.*

> Away in a manger, no crib for a bed,
> The little Lord Jesus laid down his sweet head...
> The cattle are lowing, the baby awakes,
> But little Lord Jesus, no crying he makes;
> I love thee, Lord Jesus, look down from the sky,
> And stay by my cradle till morning is nigh.

Tiptoe up to the manger, and take a look at the sweet little head. Watch the rise and fall of the infant's chest as he softly breathes. Notice how small and perfect the little mouth and nose are. Smile as he begins to suck in his sleep.

Now glance at Joseph's face. How would you describe that look? Perhaps a mixture of awe and unbelief? And love. Already his face glows with it.

And Mary? She's so young! But look at her face. You can hardly draw your eyes away from her radiant features.

Now tiptoe back out of the stable, and look up into the heavens. Do you see the star? Of course, you do. How could anyone miss it? Gazing at it, begin wondering. Who are we that this should happen to us? Why would the Lord of the universe so honor us with such intimacy? Who is this God, holding galaxies and solar systems in his hand, and loving such a minuscule speck as man? What does he see in us?

Write four to fourteen unrhymed lines expressing the awe and wonder swelling up in your breast.Then offer your lines to the Christ Child.

December 20

A Mother

Scripture: *Luke 1:39 - 45*
Key verse: *She said in a loud voice, "You are the most blessed of all women, and blessed is the child that you will have."*

> O how lovely, O how pure
> Is this perfect child of heaven;
> O how lovely, O how pure,
> Gracious gift to humankind!

But isn't every newborn? Although this French carol is talking about Mary's child, it could speak for any newborn placed into any mother's arms. Contemplating the miracle of life conceived in Mary's womb and in all wombs, today give special consideration to young mothers.

If only we could keep our little ones as lovely and pure as they come! But our mistakes almost immediately infect them. However, above all callings, motherhood has the most impact upon future generations. The degree of patience we have, the gentleness with which we respond to frustrations, and the wisdom in dealing with everyday situations eventually bless society or injure it. Most of us add a little of both.

The stress of holiday demands adds to the challenge of mothering. Today ease a bit of some mother's tension. Free up a harried mother's afternoon by inviting her children to decorate Christmas cookies with you. Distract neighbor children with a new coloring book and give their mother a free moment to finish wrapping presents. Breathe a prayer for a mother who slaps her child in the mall, and ask God to grant her strength for her demanding calling.

As Elizabeth supported Mary, today support some young mother on her way to the manger.

December 21

Christmas Concert

Scripture: *Luke 2: 1 - 7*
Key verse: *She gave birth to her firstborn son. She wrapped him in strips of cloth and laid him in a manger because there wasn't any room for them in the inn.*

> He is born, the holy Child,
> Play the oboe and bagpipes merrily!
> He is born, the holy Child,
> Sing we all of the Savior mild.

Among four thousand years of nights, this night stands out. For in Bethlehem in the land of Judea, Mary gave birth to the Christ Child, her first born son. God entered our history. Emmanuel, God With Us, lay in a manger, and his infant body was wrapped in swaddling clothes.

Earth did not know: neither Emperor Augustus who issued the decree placing the birth of the Christ Child in Bethlehem, nor the innkeeper who found a place for Mary to deliver her child. But the heavens knew, and angels burst into joyous song. The Divine trusted his glory and his grace in human hands.

He is born! Play the oboe and the bagpipes, the old French carol proclaims. Play tambourines and flutes, the drums and trumpets, the piano and organ, we may add. With every instrument give voice to a joy words cannot express.

Today attend a Christmas concert and listen to the instruments or voices. Let music penetrate your soul deeper than words can reach. Feel joy rising up until your heart all but bursts from fullness.

If you can't attend a concert, hear the notes of one on radio, television, or recording. Take out Handel's "Hallelujah Chorus," play it, and hear the echo of hallelujahs in your own soul.

He is born! Today tune the instrument of your heart to heaven's joy.

December 22

Caroling

SCRIPTURE: *Luke 2: 8 - 14*
KEY VERSE: *All at once there was with the angel a great company of the heavenly host, singing the praises of God. (NEB)*

> The first Noel the angels did say
> Was to certain poor shepherds
>   in fields as they lay;
> In fields where they lay keeping their sheep,
> On a cold winter's night that was so deep.

Shepherds? The Lord of the universe must have seen the high priest and the Sanhedrin at prayer in the great temple in Jerusalem. Why didn't the angels sing there? Wouldn't the Almighty have found it politically expedient to send his heavenly choir to the emperor in Rome? Even an appearance to Herod, the local king, may have advanced the Messiah's cause.

But no! The King of all creation sent his heavenly host to a band of shepherds out in the field keeping watch over their flocks by night. Although centuries of composers have gained from the appearance, what did it gain the Lord?

The Lord of Lords needs no gain. Whenever Emmanuel, God With Us, appears, the influential have no advantage over the lowly. To the contrary, the Christ came especially for those who have nothing but their hearts to offer him. Shepherds from the fields received the honor of being the first to kneel before the Christ Child.

Tonight go caroling, but imitate God's unique and creative perspective. Shepherds no longer tend sheep on our hillsides, but others without influence dwell among us. Like the heavenly host who exploded in song, take the manger's song to those who need it most. Announce the news above all news: on a night two thousand years ago, Emmanuel, God With Us, came and he is still here.

December 23

Family Time

SCRIPTURE: *Luke 2: 15 - 18*
KEY VERSE: *They went quickly and found Mary and Joseph with the baby, who was lying in a manger.*

> What child is this who, laid to rest,
> On Mary's lap is sleeping?
> Whom angels greet with anthems sweet,
> While shepherds watch are keeping?

Only two days left—so little time to do so much! Mary's child may have been sleeping, but ours are underfoot. The busier we are, the more they demand our attention.

Never mind. Today imitate the original nativity scene. Regardless of what still has to be done, realign your priorities and shift the family to first place. Give them the attention they demand. Give them the love they need.

On this night in Luke's account of the drama, a couple becomes a family. Mary's attention is focused on the newest member. She must diaper the newborn, nurse him, and even in her sleep she must keep an ear tuned to his cry.

Joseph has his own concerns. Without the help of relatives, he cares for Mary, prepares food, and gathers firewood. When the infant stirs, he quickly pats him back to sleep before his tired wife awakes.

As Mary and Joseph did in long ago Bethlehem, make this family time. Stop wrapping presents and play with the whining child at your feet. Even if it takes twice as long, let your toddler help you make cookies. Whether the moment is convenient or not, look up and listen to whoever has something to tell you. Sit down with your husband and drink a cup of tea.

Rather than cleaning the stable, Mary lovingly nursed the baby at her breast. Today stop cleaning the stable, or even the inn, and put the needs of your family before your own.

December 24

Simmer Spices

SCRIPTURE: *Matthew 2: 3 - 12*
KEY VERSE: *When they entered the house, they saw the child with his mother Mary. So they bowed down and worshiped him. Then they opened their treasure chests and offered him gifts of gold, frankincense, and myrrh.*

> So bring him incense, gold, and myrrh,
> Come, peasant, king, to own him;
> The King of kings salvation brings,
> Let loving hearts enthrone him.

This is it! We do it today, or we don't do it at all. Adding last minute touches, we straighten the falling angel on top of the tree, rearrange carefully wrapped presents, and add a sprig of holly to the greens on the coffee table.

Today add still another touch. Like the wise men, re-member the appropriate response to the Deity is worship, rather than decoration.

The wise men, along with other peoples of the ancient world, burned incense in the worship of their deities. Now a star proclaimed a new one, and they took their incense. Bowing before him, they offered frankincense and myrrh as an act of worship. They may have sensed that this deity was "the" Deity.

We may not have frankincense and myrrh, but we have spices. Today combine some of them—perhaps cinnamon sticks, whole cloves, and dried orange peel—or buy a prepared mix. Keep the mix simmering on the stove all day.

The small infant in the creche set competes with a festively decorated house for our attention. As the aroma of spices follows you through the house, lift your heart in adoration.

Approach the Christ Child and enthrone him King of Kings.

December 25

Stable View

SCRIPTURE: *Luke 1: 46 – 56*
KEY VERSE: *He fed hungry people with good food. He sent rich people away with nothing.*

> Joy to the world, the Lord is come!
> Let earth receive her King;
> Let every heart prepare him room,
> And heaven and nature sing...

Tree lights glow. Canticles, cantatas, and the strains of Isaac Watts' "Joy to the World" fill the house with music. Roasting turkey spreads its aroma, and the digestive juices are already flowing. The day is complete. All is perfect!

But wait! What happened to the Christ Child?

He is in the stable where he always was. If we want the best view of him, we must go there. The Word became flesh and dwelt among us. We beheld the face of God, and it was the face of Love. As we looked more closely, we saw it faced the direction of the ones who needed it the most.

Turn your face in that direction. Whom do you see? Perhaps it is an alcoholic neighbor who has been abandoned by his family. It may be one of the homeless men temporarily staying in the town shelter. It could a new family in your community who faces a Christmas away from loved ones.

Whoever you see, bring him, her, or them into your home today. Be welcoming, warm, and inclusive. If you exchange gifts, quickly wrap up another one. Give your guest the place of honor, and the Christ Child will leave the stable and join you. Celebrate the birth of the Savior in the presence of one of the needy ones who are so close to his heart.

December 26

Meaningful Moments

SCRIPTURE: *Luke 2: 19 – 20*
KEY VERSE: *Mary treasured all these things in her heart and always thought about them.*

> The noble Duke of York,
> He had ten thousand men,
> He marched them up to the top of the hill,
> And he marched them down again.
> And when they were up, they were up,
> And when they were down, they were down,
> And when they were only half way up
> They were neither up nor down,

Where are you today? Up or down? Or, like the Duke of York's men, neither up nor down? Now that we have gone up to the top of the hill, some of us are not sure where we are. Today take time to anchor yourself.

After the event, Mary had a baby to bathe, feed, and cuddle. But as she held him to her breast, or looked into his face as he slept, she must have gone over the events of the night. Perhaps they filled her with more questions than answers. Maybe she began to understand why the birth happened in a stable, why shepherds rather than priests worshipped the child, and why foreigners knew about the event when those next door did not.

Like Mary, spend some time today thinking about what has happened. You may have sought the Christ Child in new ways and new places this year. What brought the greatest joy? When did you feel closest to him? At what moment did new light break through an ancient celebration?

Since most of us have no baby to remind us of the night in the stable, fix the events of the season in your memory by making a list of meaningful moments. Ponder them and treasure them up in your heart.

December 27

Talk About It

SCRIPTURE: *Luke 2: 36 – 38*
KEY VERSE: *At that moment she came up to Mary and Joseph and began to thank God. She spoke about Jesus to all who were waiting for Jerusalem to be set free.*

> I know a man named Michael Finnegan.
> He wears whiskers on his chinnegan.
> Along came a wind and blew them in again.
> Poor old Michael Finnegan, begin again....

No, we have no whiskers on our chinnegan, but the winds of time do blow away our fragile memories. Perhaps that is why each year in December we begin again.

Unlike Anna, who spent almost three-quarters of a century worshipping night and day in the temple, we live in complex environments which distract us from holy thoughts. Anna had no remains of turkey to de-bone, no linen tablecloth and napkins to launder, and no cluttered living room to clean. She could easily rush off to tell what she had seen.

We are no Annas. We live neither in convents nor temples. Nevertheless, we can imitate her enthusiastic response to the Holy Family. Yesterday you made a list of meaningful moments of the season. Today carry it one step further, and talk about them.

Sit down with the family, or with friends, and let everyone share their memories. Some events of the season were funny, and perhaps a few ridiculous. There may have been surprises—both good ones and bad ones. As you share, focus on the inspiring times when God's love seemed so near and so real.

True, next December we will begin again. But keep the flame of this Christmas burning as long as you can. Winds will blow, but by talking with others about the Christmas season, put a few thoughts under shelter.

December 28

Return

SCRIPTURE: *Luke 2: 39 – 40*
KEY VERSE: *After doing everything the Lord's Teachings required, Joseph and Mary returned to their hometown of Nazareth in Galilee.*

> Yankee Doodle went to town
> Riding on a pony,
> Stuck a feather in his hat
> And called it Macaroni.

Eventually, Yankee Doodle had to go back home and admit that a feather was a feather. Whatever the mountain top, we all have to go back home where feathers are feathers and macaroni is macaroni.

The angels left, the shepherds returned to their fields, and the wise men went back to their own country. Mary and Joseph returned to Nazareth. Apparently, the future held no more angelic messages for them. On the contrary, they raised their child among familiar routines, friends, and neighbors.

Today go back to your Nazareth. Walk through the neighborhood and see this place where you live. Here you live and relate; here you grow and become. Here you find the kingdom of God and your place in it.

Speak to children trying out new roller blades, jump ropes, and sleds. Wave to neighbors leaving or entering their homes. Smile at the people you pass. Noting decorations still lingering in windows and doors, think about how the incarnation touched, or can touch, each home.

We belong to a community. The mountain top gives us a panoramic view, but we work down in the valley. We miss the message of the incarnation and nativity unless we take it back to Nazareth.

December 29

Highlights of the Year

SCRIPTURE: *2 Timothy 4: 6 - 8*
KEY VERSE: *I have fought the good fight. I have completed the race. I have kept the faith.*

> I slept and dreamed that life was beauty;
> I woke and found that life was duty.

The anonymous rhyme writer was right, wasn't he? But he cut off his rhyme too soon, for there's more to the picture.

Knowing his time was running out, Paul looked back. Since his conversion, hardship, persecution, and even hunger had been his lot. But he had no regrets. He had run the great race and had kept the faith.

Before the year slips into history, do as Paul did. Look back. We all have our duties, and they may take up most of the year's space. Like Paul, we have our share of disappointments, failures, and conflicts. But, unlike him, sometimes we miss the glory on the other side of the shadow.

It would have been understandable if Mary had focused on her hardships. The angel's brief appearance, the shepherd's short visit, and the wise men's moments on their knees took far less time than the long voyage to Bethlehem in the last stages of her pregnancy. The stress of finding no accommodations in a crowded city, and the resulting trauma of giving birth to her baby in a dark, smelly, unsanitary stable, could have stayed with her for many years.

But, as Paul did, Mary saw beyond whatever disappointments she had to the glory beyond. Today look back and see the glory. Review the year, and make a list of its highlights. Notice how God's hand rests on you as it did on Mary.

Tuck a bit of glory into the treasure chest of your memory.

December 30

Resolution

SCRIPTURE: *Luke 2: 51 - 52*
KEY VERSE: *Jesus grew in wisdom and maturity. He gained favor from God and people.*

> Mary had a little lamb,
> Its fleece was white as snow;
> And everywhere that Mary went
> The lamb was sure to go.

The little lamb was wooly, and it cried baa-baa-baa. But two thousand years ago, another Mary had another little lamb, and his heart was white as snow. Everywhere that she went, he was sure to go.

What follows you wherever you go? Some of us take cheer and some take gloom. We take all the good news we know—or all the bad news. We take the baggage of our past, or we take the new life of the Spirit.

The newborn Lamb of God left the crib and grew in wisdom and in favor with God and men. It is time for us to leave the crib, and do the same.

At the moment of our birth, God dreams that each of us will grow into maturity. Today think about how you are doing.

Of all the things which tag along with you, which would you like to leave behind? What would you like to substitute? Make a resolution which will encourage growth in wisdom, in favor with God, or in favor with man.

Give God the joy of seeing his dreams come true.

December 31

Creative Ideas

SCRIPTURE: *John 8: 12 – 19*
KEY VERSE: *I am the light of the world. Whoever follows me will have a life filled with light and will never live in the dark.*

> Hey, diddle, diddle!
> The cat and the fiddle,
> The cow jumped over the moon;
> The little dog laughed
> To see such sport,
> And the dish ran away with the spoon.

P reposterous? Perhaps a cow hasn't jumped over the moon, but a little dog has orbited the earth. Every time we throw away paper plates and plastic spoons, the dish runs away with the spoon. The cat and the fiddle? Perhaps some circus has solved that one.

Jesus said that everything is possible for the person who believes. You may not want to jump over the moon. But you probably long to jump over some hurdle in your life and go to some distant horizon.

The little dog's flight into space began with some human's faith that it could be done. Only animal trainers who believe in what they are doing can teach cats to fiddle, dolphins to leap through hoops, or elephants to dance.

But preposterous-turned-into-reality means thousands of small steps, and patience to wait for the results. Today begin turning possibilities (or "preposterousabilities") in your own life into reality by making a list of creative ideas to develop your personality, potential, and awareness. Make it a pushing list, encouraging you to reach out in new directions, to take time for the people and the Lord you love, and to discover new dimensions to life.

Whether your list has ten, twenty, or fifty ideas, make it incomplete, a beginning rather than an arrival. Vow to let the power of the gospel light up each day of your life.

Even if you don't want to jump over the moon, begin reaching for it!

Index

397

V

W

Y